IN THE SAME SERIES

THE ACTS OF THE APOSTLES
C. S. C. Williams

In preparation

THE GOSPEL ACCORDING TO ST MATTHEW
Floyd V. Filson, D.D.

THE GOSPEL ACCORDING TO ST MARK
Sherman E. Johnson, Ph.D.

THE GOSPEL ACCORDING TO ST LUKE
A. C. R. Leaney

THE GOSPEL ACCORDING TO ST JOHN
J. N. Sanders

THE FIRST EPISTLE TO THE CORINTHIANS
R. H. Strachan

THE EPISTLE TO THE GALATIANS
Henry Chadwick

THE EPISTLE TO THE HEBREWS
H. W. Montefiore

HARPER'S
NEW TESTAMENT COMMENTARIES

GENERAL EDITOR: HENRY CHADWICK, D.D.

THE EPISTLE TO THE ROMANS

A COMMENTARY ON THE EPISTLE TO THE ROMANS

C. K. BARRETT

HARPER & ROW, PUBLISHERS

New York, Hagerstown, San Francisco, London

A COMMENTARY ON THE EPISTLE TO THE ROMANS

Copyright © 1957 by C. K. Barrett

Printed in the United States of America
All rights in this book are reserved.

This series is published in England under the title
BLACK'S NEW TESTAMENT COMMENTARIES

Library of Congress catalog card number: 57-12722

PREFACE

THE translation upon which this commentary is based is my own, and is intended to serve as part of the commentary; that is, I have used it in order to make clear what I think Paul meant. I have deliberately refrained from consulting other translations, though I do not doubt that my happier phrases will prove to be subconscious recollections; and I have never varied traditional renderings merely for the sake of novelty. The reader will find that in the commentary occasional Greek words appear. If he knows Greek, he will, I hope, be glad to see them; if he does not, he may pass over them without losing the thread of a single sentence. The occasional notes on variants in the Greek text may also be omitted without disturbance of the book as a whole.

There are few commentators (and I am not one of them) who do not build on the work of their predecessors. The commentator on Romans in particular enters into a goodly heritage, and cannot fail to feel regret when space forbids him to fill his pages with grateful—and controversial—footnotes.

For very much learned information I am indebted especially to Hans Lietzmann (see p. vii) and to Otto Michel (see p. vii). Also to be mentioned in this category is the work of W. Sanday and A. C. Headlam (*The Epistle to the Romans*, in the International Critical Commentary, Edinburgh; first edition, 1895; fifth edition, 1902; many subsequent reprints), which, old as it is, is by no means out of date.

Other writers to whom I am indebted are, among commentators, P. Althaus (in *Das Neue Testament Deutsch*, Göttingen, fifth edition, 1946), J. Denney (see p. vii), C. H. Dodd (see p. vii), E. Gaugler (see p. vii), K. E. Kirk (see p. 12), A. Nygren (*Commentary on Romans*, English translation, London, 1952), and A. Schlatter (*Gottes Gerechtigkeit*, Stuttgart, 1935; second edition, 1952); among others, R. Bultmann (especially *Theologie des Neuen Testaments*, Tübingen, 1948–1953), W. D. Davies (*Paul and Rabbinic Judaism*, London, 1948), W. L. Knox (*St. Paul and the Church of Jerusalem*, Cambridge, 1925 ; *St.*

Paul and the Church of the Gentiles, Cambridge, 1939), and A. Schweitzer (*Paul and his Interpreters*, English translation, London, 1912; *The Mysticism of Paul the Apostle*, English translation, London, 1931).

Not a few others could be named, but I must reserve a paragraph for special mention of three: Martin Luther, John Calvin, and Karl Barth. Barth's commentary (see p. 171) I read as an undergraduate. If in those days, and since, I remained and have continued to be a Christian, I owe the fact in large measure to that book, and to those in Cambridge who introduced it to me. Calvin has long been a companion whose patient exegesis is a model of critical and theological thoroughness. In the summer of 1953, in the University Library at Göttingen, I read through Luther's Scholia on Romans (Weimar Edition, Vol. 56, by J. Ficker, 1938) with a sustained enthusiasm and even excitement which I never thought 400 large pages of medieval Latin could evoke. Less sound in detail than Calvin, Luther wrestles at perhaps even greater depth with sin and righteousness, grace and predestination, and rarely fails to reach the heart of the matter, and to take his reader with him. To have sat at the feet of these three interpreters of Paul is one of the greatest of privileges. This book is by no means a transcript of their opinions; but I hope that it too may be used *in verbi divini ministerium*.

Durham.   C. K. BARRETT

ABBREVIATIONS

Bauer, *Wörterbuch*

W. Bauer, *Griechisch-Deutsches Wörterbuch zu den Schriften des Neuen Testaments und der übrigen urchristlichen Literatur* (Berlin, 1952).

B.D.

F. Blass, *Grammatik des neutestamentlichen Griechisch*; eighth edition by A. Debrunner (Göttingen, 1949).

Denney

J. Denney, Commentary on Romans in *The Expositor's Greek Testament*, Vol. II (London, 1900).

Dodd

C. H. Dodd, *The Epistle of Paul to the Romans* (Moffatt New Testament Commentary, London, 1932).

Gaugler

E. Gaugler, *Der Brief an die Römer*, Vol. I (Zürich, 1945); Vol. II (1952).

J.T.S.

The Journal of Theological Studies.

Lagrange

M. J. Lagrange, *Épître aux Romains* (Paris, 1950).

Lietzmann

H. Lietzmann, *An die Römer* (Handbuch zum Neuen Testament); fourth edition (Tübingen, 1933).

Michel

O. Michel, *Der Brief an die Römer* (Kritisch-exegetischer Kommentar über das Neue Testament); tenth edition (Göttingen, 1955).

Moule, *Idiom Book*

C. F. D. Moule, *An Idiom Book of New Testament Greek* (Cambridge, 1953).

Moulton, *Prolegomena*

J. H. Moulton, *A Grammar of New Testament Greek*, Vol. I: Prolegomena (third edition; Edinburgh, 1908).

S.B.

H. L. Strack and P. Billerbeck, *Kommentar zum Neuen Testament aus Talmud und Midrasch* (Munich, 1922–1928).

T.W.N.T.

Theologisches Wörterbuch zum Neuen Testament, edited by G. Kittel (†) and G. Friedrich (Stuttgart, 1933 ff.).

THE EPISTLE TO THE ROMANS

TEXTUAL SIGLA

Greek Manuscripts

P⁴⁶	The Chester Beatty Papyrus of the epistles. Third century.
ℵ	Codex Sinaiticus. Fourth century.
A	Codex Alexandrinus. Fifth century.
B	Codex Vaticanus. Fourth century.
C	Codex Ephraemi Rescriptus. Fifth century.
D	Codex Claromontanus (Graeco-Latin). Sixth century.
G	Codex Boernerianus (Graeco-Latin). Ninth century.
L	Codex Angelicus. Ninth century.
P	Codex Porphirianus. Ninth century.
33	Minuscule. Ninth–tenth century.
1739	Minuscule. Tenth century.
ω	*Codices plerique*—as in A. Souter's *Novum Testamentum Graece*.

Versions

lat	Consensus of the Latin versions.
it	The Old Latin version.
vg	The Latin Vulgate.
pesh	The Peshitto Syriac version.
hcl	The Harclean Syriac version.
sah	The Sahidic Coptic version.

INTRODUCTION

I. Romans in the Framework of Paul's Career

That the Epistle to the Romans was written by the apostle Paul is a proposition which it is unnecessary to discuss because it is not in dispute. That this epistle is the apostle's greatest piece of sustained theological writing is self-evident. That its influence upon the life and thought of the Christian Church has been radical and far-reaching needs no demonstration; it suffices to mention the names of Augustine, Luther, Wesley, and Barth. The document before us can indeed be read simply as a work of apostolic theology, through which the unchanging Gospel of the grace and righteousness of God is proclaimed to each generation; but this proclamation may reach men of the twentieth century with greater clarity and power if they are prepared first to consider and understand the man of the first century who wrote it.

Saul, or Paul, was born at Tarsus (Acts xxi. 39). From his early years we can infer with certainty nothing that throws a clear light upon the background of his thought. Tarsus was a Hellenistic city in which many faiths and philosophies were taught. Of these, Paul as a youth may have heard something; but it is equally possible that, brought up in a strict Jewish home (Phil. iii. 5), he regarded all such doctrines as of the devil, and paid them no attention at all. His education took place not in Tarsus but in Jerusalem. He was 'brought up at the feet of Gamaliel' (Acts xxii. 3). This was Rabban Gamaliel I, one of the most distinguished Rabbinic teachers before the fall of Jerusalem in A.D. 70. Acts v. 34-9 records his intervention on behalf of the apostles, but this narrative does not prove that Gamaliel adopted a favourable attitude to the Church. Paul's own statements indicate clearly enough that he had been brought up as an orthodox Jew. They show, moreover, that he was not content with a merely formal acceptance of the ancestral faith; he outstripped his contemporaries in zeal and in achievement (Gal. i. 14).

His zeal for Judaism led him to persecute the Church, which he no doubt quickly recognized as the one serious danger to Judaism, so like the parent faith, and so unlike. His activity as a persecutor is colourfully described in Acts (vii. 58; viii. 1; ix. 1 f.), and attested in his own epistles (1 Cor. xv. 9; Gal. i. 13; Phil. iii. 6). He was in mid-career as a Jewish persecutor when he became a Christian, arrested (Phil. iii. 12) by the glorified Christ himself, who granted him an exceptional 'resurrection appearance' (1 Cor. xv. 8; Gal. i. 16). From this time onward it was impossible for Paul to doubt that Jesus was alive; Jesus was his Lord, and he was Jesus' slave. The theological consequences of this conviction will be discussed below. The immediate sequel was a visit to Arabia (Gal. i. 17). Three years later Paul visited Jerusalem, where he saw Cephas (Peter), and James the Lord's brother (Gal. i. 18 f.). He was in Jerusalem again fourteen (or seventeen)[1] years later, having spent some at least of the interval in Syria and Cilicia, without making direct contact with Judaea.

Paul's second visit to Jerusalem was the occasion of serious conflict, which touched the substance of his Gospel. The discord was for a time resolved, but broke out again later in Antioch, when agreement between Paul, Peter, and Barnabas was disturbed by 'certain' that 'came from James' (Gal. ii. 12). Of the outcome of this dispute we are not informed.

So far the record of Paul's Christian life has been given on the basis of his own words. There is a parallel narrative in Acts, but it is safer to follow Paul's own account. With Acts xvi, however, we reach a narrative which, though by no means complete, furnishes us with a reasonably trustworthy outline of the middle period of Paul's work as an apostle. It is in this middle period that the writing of Romans must fall.

After traversing Asia Minor Paul crossed the Aegean from Troas to Neapolis and passed through Macedonia to the neighbouring province of Achaea. Here Acts gives a long account (xviii. 1-18) of the founding of a church in Corinth. From Corinth Paul returned to Syria, touching at Ephesus on his way (Acts xviii. 19 ff.). On his next journey he settled for between two and three years in Ephesus (Acts xix. 8, 10, 23;

[1] The interval depends on whether the period mentioned in Gal. ii. 1 is counted from the conversion or the first visit to Jerusalem.

xx. 31). During this period he maintained close relations with the church at Corinth, as his epistles show. Finally, he himself again travelled through Macedonia (2 Cor. ii. 13; Acts xx. 1), and spent three months in 'Greece' (Acts xx. 2 f.)—no doubt for the most part in and near Corinth. Throughout this 'Ephesian' period Paul was busy with the collection he had undertaken for the relief of the Jerusalem, or Judaean, church (1 Cor. xvi. 1-5; 2 Cor. viii, ix; Acts xxiv. 17). When his arrangements were (as may be supposed) complete, he left Greece, travelling to Syria by way of Macedonia (Acts xx. 3), Troas (xx. 6), Miletus (xx. 15), Tyre (xxi. 3), Ptolemais (xxi. 7), and Caesarea (xxi. 8).

It is hardly open to question that Romans was written during this period. When Paul wrote, he had engaged in missionary work between Jerusalem and Illyricum (Rom. xv. 19). He was on the way to, or was about to set out for, Jerusalem (xv. 25). He hoped to visit Rome (i. 13, 15; xv. 22 ff., 28 f.), but before he could realize this hope had to complete the ministry he had undertaken to the poor at Jerusalem, in which the churches of Macedonia and Achaea were taking part (xv. 25 f.). He foresaw the possibility of danger in Judaea (xv. 31). These circumstances taken together can mean only that Paul was writing towards the close of his so-called 'Third Missionary Journey', at the end of his Ephesian period. It is further to be noted that the epistle contains a commendation of Phoebe, a minister of the church at Cenchreae (xvi. 1—Cenchreae was the eastern port of Corinth, about seven miles distant; on the question whether ch. xvi is an original part of Romans see pp. 9-13, 281 f., 286 f.), and conveys greetings from (among others) Timothy, Sosipater, Gaius 'my host', and Erastus the city treasurer (xvi. 21 ff.). These are not unfamiliar names. Paul baptized a Gaius at Corinth (1 Cor. i. 14). He sent 'Timothy and Erastus' into Macedonia while he stayed in Asia (Acts xix. 22; cf. 2 Tim. iv. 20); a visit of Timothy to Corinth was planned in 1 Corinthians (iv. 17; xvi. 10), and Timothy and Sopater (possibly a variant form of the name Sosipater) appear among Paul's travelling companions on his last journey from Ephesus through Macedonia and Greece to Jerusalem (Acts xx. 4). It is thus overwhelmingly probable that Romans was written from Corinth (conceivably from Cenchreae) during the three months before Paul left Greece for Jerusalem. This view finds slight support, which it scarcely needs, in the manifest fact that Romans is the work of a theologian and preacher at the height of his powers, is akin to but represents an advance upon Galatians,[1] and lacks some of the themes developed in the 'Captivity Epistles'.[2]

So far we have endeavoured to place the writing of Romans within the framework of events which can be reconstructed with reasonable certainty out of Acts and the Epistles, but not to assign it to an absolute date. This is a much more difficult matter.

Fortunately it is possible to bring Paul's ministry in Corinth into relation with external history. According to Acts xviii. 12, when Gallio was proconsul of Achaea the Jews made an attack upon Paul, and brought him before the judgement seat. It appears, from a dated inscription set up in Delphi,[3] that Gallio was in office in his province in A.D. 52. Proconsuls in senatorial provinces were appointed for one or two years, and, since it is unlikely that Gallio had taken up his post immediately before the inscription was made, he must have held office for one of the following periods: 50–52; 51–52; 51–53. An overall period of 50–53 is a safe estimate. There is, further, much probability (though no certainty) in the view that the Jews made their attempt early in Gallio's proconsulship—they hoped to be able to win the new magistrate to their side. If this may be assumed, Paul was brought before Gallio in or about July (proconsuls entered upon office in early summer) in A.D. 51, or, a little less probably, in A.D. 50. How long had Paul then been in Corinth? According to Acts xviii. 11, Paul stayed in Corinth a year and six months; according to Acts xviii. 18, he remained, after Gallio had washed his hands of the case, 'a number of days' (ἡμέρας ἱκανάς). It is implied that the bulk of Paul's stay fell before his appearance in Gallio's court; this is not certain, but may be tentatively assumed. It seems probable then that Paul reached Corinth in March 50, and left in September 51 (each

[1] Written probably during the Ephesian period.
[2] Written probably from captivity in Rome.
[3] See F. J. F. Jackson and K. Lake, *Beginnings of Christianity*, v. (1933), pp. 460–4; C. K. Barrett, *The New Testament Background: Selected Documents* (1956), pp. 48 f.

date being very approximate). This would enable him to sail, by one of the last boats of the summer, to Syria (Acts xviii. 21 f.). How long he spent in Antioch (Acts xviii. 23) we do not know; probably he renewed his travels with the return of favourable weather in the spring of the next year—52. His journey through 'the region of Galatia and Phrygia' (Acts xviii. 23) and through the 'upper country' (Acts xix. 1) might well last most of the following summer; he would reach Ephesus (Acts xix. 1) in the autumn. The length of his stay there is given by Acts xix. 8 (three months) and xix. 10 (two years), confirmed by xx. 31; the Pentecost therefore which he was anxious to keep in Jerusalem will have been that of 55, and his three months in Greece (Acts xx. 3) must have come to an end a few weeks earlier.

This chronological scheme could be verified, (a) if Acts xxiv. 27 were unambiguous, (b) if the date when Porcius Festus succeeded Felix could be certainly established. There are good reasons for thinking that Felix was recalled very early in the principate of Nero—perhaps in A.D. 55.[1] On the usual view of Acts xxiv. 27 this will mean that Paul had been arrested in Jerusalem in 53, which is sadly inconsistent with the date arrived at above. It is, however, possible that 'when two years were fulfilled', a clause which has no certain point of reference in the sentence, means not 'when Paul had been under arrest for two years' but 'when Felix had been procurator for two years'. If this view can be accepted, the data fall into place: Paul reached Jerusalem in the year in which Felix was recalled and Festus succeeded him. If not, an earlier alternative must be accepted for the date of Gallio; and it may be possible to place the date of Festus's accession a year or two later.

The chronology of Paul's movements cannot be settled beyond dispute, but on the whole no view meets with fewer difficulties than that which places the 'three months' of Acts xx. 3 in or about January—March 55. We have seen reason to think (pp. 3 f.) that the Epistle to the Romans was written in this interval.

When Paul wrote the Epistle to the Romans he had reached in Corinth the most westerly point of his missionary

[1] For details, see Jackson and Lake, *op. cit.* v. pp. 466 f.

travels;[1] but he was looking a further 600 miles north-west. The Roman church fell outside the scope of his own apostolic labour. Its origin is completely obscure. No early authority claims that it was founded by Peter (though the evidence that he visited Rome is early and seems sound), and it is probable that, if Paul had known that Peter had already, when he wrote, worked in Rome, he would have mentioned the fact in some way.

There was a considerable Jewish colony in first-century Rome.[2] It originated in the large number of Jewish slaves brought to the city by Pompey after his capture of Jerusalem in 63 B.C., and from that time appears steadily to have increased, notwithstanding occasional repressive measures. Of these we may note the expulsion of the Jews under Claudius. This is referred to in Acts xviii. 2 as the reason for the presence in Corinth of Aquila and Priscilla. According to Suetonius (*Claudius*, 25) the emperor acted against the Jews because they were *impulsore Chresto assidue tumultuantes*. The meaning of this clause is much disputed, but it seems quite probable that *Chresto* is an error for *Christo*, and that riots had taken place when Jesus the Messiah had first been proclaimed in the Roman synagogues. Against this view is the profession of the Roman Jews in Acts xxviii. 21 f. that they had no first-hand knowledge of Paul or of the Church. This profession, however, must be treated with some reserve, since Romans itself is evidence that there was a sizeable Christian community in Rome some years before Paul reached the city.

The Jewish colony was organized in synagogues, but these did not form wholly distinct units; for example, there were common cemeteries.[3] It is not impossible that the first Christians in Rome, won to the faith by travellers unknown to us by name and perhaps of no official standing, formed a synagogue community within the general framework of the Jewish groups in the city; but if this was so at the beginning changes had happened before Romans was written, for the epistle presupposes the existence of a community which, though probably not ex-

---

[1] On the map, Beroea lies half a degree further west, but marks an earlier stage in the journey.

[2] See especially G. La Piana, 'Foreign Groups in Rome during the first centuries of the Empire', in *Harvard Theological Review*, xx. (1927), pp. 183-403.

[3] La Piana, *op. cit.* pp. 363-7.

clusively Gentile, contained at least a strong Gentile element; see i. 6 and note. It is important to remember that there were a Gentile mission and Gentile churches independent of Paul's; the Gentile church of Antioch was not of his founding, and 1 and 2 Corinthians attest the independent activity of other missionaries in the Gentile world.

Paul's letter, then, represents not merely his approach to the capital of the Empire, and not merely the first preparatory step to the mission in Spain; it is also Paul's exposition of 'his' Gospel to the Gentile churches which had come into existence independently of his efforts. They did not see eye to eye with him, for example with regard to the future of the Jews, and there is no good reason to think that his views immediately carried the day; but it may well be that, but for this circumstance, we should not have had so full and vigorous an exposition of his theology.

II. ROMANS IN THE FRAMEWORK OF PAUL'S THOUGHT

On the road to Damascus, Paul met with Jesus Christ (above, p. 2). This is the plain meaning of the three narratives in Acts (ix. 4 ff.; xxii. 7-10; xxvi. 14-18), and it is confirmed by Paul's own references to the occasion. Jesus therefore was alive, and had appeared in the character of a supernatural Lord (κύριος). He had not merely survived death as a man, or as a disembodied human spirit; he was a glorious, heavenly being, before whom the beholder could only prostrate himself in adoration and obedience. All this was certain; but it was equally certain that Jesus had lived a human life, and that he had been as truly dead as he was now truly alive. The past of frailty and corruption could be linked with the present of heavenly glory only by an act of divine power. Only God (as Paul the Rabbi well knew) could raise the dead. God therefore must have approved of Jesus; resurrection and exaltation could be understood only as the manifest seal of his approval. It followed that Jesus had all the time been right; he had been the Messiah, and Paul, the persecutor of the Church, had been wrong.

A man with a smaller mind than Paul's might have been content simply to accept this reversal of his opinions on the crucial issue; Paul could not. The basic assumptions of his thought had been proved wrong, and his theology had to be built up again from the foundations. He continued to be a Rabbi[1] in that a man who for thirty years or more has been brought up to a pattern of intellectual activity can scarcely be expected to free his thinking from that pattern; he ceased to be a Rabbi in the presuppositions of his thinking. In two fundamental points in particular his thought was revolutionized by the new conviction that the crucified Jesus had been raised from the dead and become Lord: eschatology, and the law.

(1) It is very unlikely that it was as a Christian that Paul learned the eschatological language which appears in his epistles. It is much more probable that before his conversion he shared the widespread beliefs of Judaism, and looked to the coming of a Messiah (he may have used the term Son of man also), and the establishment of the kingdom of the Messiah, the kingdom of God, and the Age to Come. It is not necessary for us to attempt to distinguish between these terms in Jewish usage. The essential point is that the Messiah, and the Age to Come, belonged to the future. For Paul the Christian, this was no longer true; or rather, it was not the whole truth. It remained true that Jesus would come in glory to judge the secrets of men (Rom. ii. 16), and that the Age to Come was still to come; but it was also true that Jesus had come, and that at least the first-fruits of the future were available to faith (Rom. viii. 23).

The fact that God's ultimate dealings with mankind had thus been manifested in a person gave an objective content to the new faith, and the invasion of the present by the future made possible an immediate awareness of God's power which orthodox Judaism could not accept without blurring the distinction between divine and human. It was a proper reaction to the danger of such a blurring that prevented Judaism from using the sacramental and mystical language of the Hellenistic and oriental cults; in Paul this language enters decisively. It enters, however, not as an element in an eclectic religious philosophy, but as a means of expressing the re-orientation of eschatology caused by the coming of the Messiah.

---

[1] This is emphasized, very convincingly, by W. D. Davies in *Paul and Rabbinic Judaism* (1948); but the discontinuity in Paul's thought is perhaps greater than Dr Davies suggests.

(2) Jesus had been condemned by the law. He had been tried and found guilty of blasphemy (Mark xiv. 64) by the supreme court of his people; moreover, he had died a death which exposed him to the curse declared in the law (Deut. xxi. 23; Gal. iii. 13). Yet God had not cursed him; on the contrary, he had ratified his claims and declared his approval of him by raising him from the dead. On this crucial issue, therefore, the law—or, at least, Israel's understanding of the law—had been wrong. This did not mean that the law was to be rejected out of hand. Jesus himself had reaffirmed its validity as the word of God, and, rightly understood, it bore witness to him. But it must be rightly understood, and not understood in the old way. It could no longer be regarded as the mediator between God and man; this function had been assumed by Jesus Christ.

Paul's theological development consists in the adjustment of old convictions based upon the Old Testament and formulated within Judaism to the new Christian conviction that Jesus is Lord. Many of the decisive steps in this development are represented in the Epistle to the Romans, and will therefore be traced in this commentary. It is better, however, to allow them to arise naturally out of the text, than to attempt to systematize them in an introduction.

III. Literary Problems

In its familiar form the document before us appears as an epistle directed to Rome (i. 7, 15), and ending, after much theological and practical instruction, with greetings from Paul himself, and from his companions, to the Roman church, and in particular to many named persons in that church. But certain facts cast doubt upon both the original form and the original destination of the letter. These are as follows.

(1) There is MS. authority for the omission of the references to Rome in i. 7, 15. See pp. 15, 23. If in these verses the shorter text is accepted there is nothing in the epistle which necessarily connects it with Rome or with any other specific destination; though it may be noted that passages such as i. 6, 8-13; xv. 14, 22 ff., 28 f., as well as ch. xvi, suggest that the epistle was written to a clearly defined group of readers, whose circumstances are not inconsistent with their having been the Roman church.

(2) There are important textual variations in the last three chapters. These concern (a) the Grace, and (b) the Doxology.

(a) In AV the words 'The grace of our Lord Jesus Christ be with you [all]. Amen' occur twice, as xvi. 20 b, and as xvi. 24. This is the reading of the mass of late MSS.—the so-called Byzantine text. But the formula is omitted in xvi. 20 by the Western text (D G it), and at xvi. 24 by the earliest non-Western authorities (P⁴⁶ B ℵ, *et al.*). There is some slight authority for placing the Grace after the Doxology (i.e. after xvi. 27). It will be noted that it is broadly true that only those MSS. have the Grace at xvi. 24 that omit the Doxology (xvi. 25 ff.) or put it in another place (see (b)).

(b) In AV the epistle ends with a Doxology, 'Now unto him that is of power . . . To God only wise, be glory through Jesus Christ for ever. Amen', which occurs as xvi. 25 ff. In this reading AV follows the Latin Vulgate. A variety of different readings exists, which may be summarized in the following list (for Marcion's text see p. 11).

The Doxology appears—

(i) at the end of the epistle (after xvi. 23 (24)) in some of the oldest and best MSS., including B ℵ D vg it pesh, and in Origen;

(ii) after xiv. 23 in ω hcl, and in MSS. known to Origen;

(iii) after xiv. 23 *and* at the end of the epistle in A P 33;

(iv) after xv. 33 in P⁴⁶;

(v) not at all in G (but in this MS. a space is left after xiv. 23).

(3) Several other facts bearing on the transmission of the last three chapters must now be set out.

(a) The vulgate MS. Codex Amiatinus, which contains the text of the epistle in the usual vulgate form, contains also a set of *breves*, or chapter summaries, fifty-one in number. Of these the fiftieth runs:

> On the danger of grieving one's brother by one's food; and that the kingdom of God is not eating and drinking, but righteousness and peace and joy in the Holy Spirit.

Evidently this corresponds to xiv. 13-23. The fifty-first chapter summary runs:

> On the mystery of the Lord, kept in silence before his passion, but revealed after his passion.

This must correspond to xvi. 25 ff. It is clear therefore that the *breves* (though not the text) of Codex Amiatinus bear witness to the existence of a copy of Romans which consisted of only fourteen chapters followed immediately by the Doxology.

(b) Chs. xv, xvi are never quoted by Irenaeus, Tertullian, or Cyprian. Arguments based on silence are always precarious, but it is worth noting (i) that the works of these authors are considerable in extent; (ii) that Tertullian and Cyprian in particular could several times have used material from these chapters with effect; and (iii) that Clement of Alexandria uses the chapters.

(c) Tertullian not merely does not quote chs. xv, xvi; in *adv. Marcionem*, v. 14 he refers to Rom. xiv. 10 in these terms, '*in clausula tribunal Christi comminatur*'. In classical Latin, *in clausula* should mean 'at the end (of a document)'; this would be an odd (though not quite impossible) expression if the verse in question were followed by two and a half more chapters. But in later Latin *clausula* was used for any division of a document (commonly of a legal document), and little can be built on Tertullian's use of the word.

(d) The evidence of Tertullian (in *adv. Marcionem*) suggests that Marcion himself did not use chs. xv, xvi; this receives probable (though not quite certain) confirmation from a passage in Origen's commentary on Romans (on xvi. 25 ff.; unfortunately extant only in Rufinus's Latin translation).

(4) Finally, the contents of ch. xvi call for examination.

(a) Several scholars have maintained that the long list of salutations contained in xvi. 1-23 is a very unlikely constituent of a letter written by Paul to Rome, where he had never been. It is impossible, they think, that he should have known so many Christians in Rome; moreover, some of the names (especially Aquila and Priscilla) would be more appropriate in a letter directed to Ephesus. See pp. 281 f.

(b) xvi. 25 ff. has in part a Marcionite sound. The reference to the 'scriptures of the prophets' is indeed not Marcionite, but it is awkwardly attached to the sentence as a whole, and the conception of a mystery kept secret through the ages but at length made manifest at the command of the eternal God is consistent with Marcionite teaching, and the language in which it is expressed is not characteristically Pauline. It is accordingly possible to regard the Doxology, whose place in the epistle is so variable, as in essence a Marcionite production; at all events, not Pauline. See pp. 286 f.

To deal with the facts which have now been set forth in outline, several hypotheses have been constructed. They may be summarized under three heads.

(1) Some take seriously the readings of G in i. 7, 15, and suppose that the epistle existed in two or more different forms, of which not more than one was directed to Rome. The most recent statement of a view of this kind is that of Dr G. Zuntz, who writes:[1] 'The doxology [xvi. 25 ff., which Dr Zuntz believes to be Marcionite in origin] commended itself to orthodox believers, was adapted for their requirements, and variously added, in the copies used by the orthodox, at one or other of the points at which the Epistle in its varying forms ended; namely at the end of the Roman form, i.e. after ch. xv, or of the (?) Ephesian form, i.e. after xvi, or finally of the Marcionite form, i.e. after xiv'. It will be seen that it is here suggested that ch. xvi was directed not to Rome but to Ephesus, and that the shortest form of the epistle (i-xiv) was made by Marcion, presumably on account of objections he felt to chs. xv, xvi.

(2) One of the neatest attempts to take account of the singular reading of P[46] is that of the late Dr K. E. Kirk.[2] It is most simply set out in the form of a diagram, in which (the bulk of the epistle, i-xiv, being taken for granted) A stands for xv, B for xvi. 1-23, C for xvi. 25 ff. A (that is, i-xiv + xv) represents the lost Pauline original. In one copy, B was added, either as a separate note, or as a message to Ephesus added by Paul

---

[1] *The Text of the Epistles* (1953; Schweich Lectures for 1946), p. 227. See a fuller statement of a similar view (and a full discussion of the evidence) by T. W. Manson, in the *Bulletin of the Rylands Library*, xxxi. (1948), pp. 224-40.

[2] *The Epistle to the Romans* (Clarendon Bible; 1937), pp. 12-22.

himself to the original letter. In another copy the spurious ending C was added to A. Out of the forms A + B and A + C

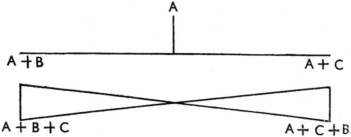

arose the forms A + B + C and A + C + B. A + B is contained in G; A + B + C in ℵ B C D lat pesh; and A + C + B in P[46].

(3) It may well be felt, however, that these two suggestions pay too great deference to the reading of P[46]. In the epistle as a whole this MS. contains a number of very curious readings which it is impossible to take very seriously. Perhaps it is best to ignore its placing of the Doxology, and to revert to the hypothesis of Lietzmann (pp. 130 f.), which may be summarized as follows:

(a) The original text of the epistle was i. 1–xvi. 23.

(b) This was early shortened (perhaps by Marcion) to i. 1–xiv. 23. A conclusion was now wanting, so a liturgical formula (possibly of Marcionite origin) was appended, so giving rise to

(c) the form i. 1–xiv. 23; xvi. 25 ff. Once in circulation the Doxology became popular and was appended to the original text, thus producing

(d) the form i. 1–xvi. 23; xvi. 25 ff. At the same time, form (b) was expanded by the addition of chs. xv, xvi, together with the usual Pauline 'grace'. Thus arose

(e) the form i. 1–xvi. 23; xvi. 24. A similar expansion based on form (c) led to

(f) the form i. 1–xiv. 23; xvi. 25 ff.; xv. 1–xvi. 23; xvi. 24, or even in rare instances to

(g) the form i. 1–xiv. 23; xvi. 25 ff.; xv. 1–xvi. 23; xvi. 25 ff.

It is unlikely that this problem—which in no way affects the substance of the Epistle to the Romans—will ever be satisfactorily cleared up; but it is probable that this solution is not far from the truth.

THE EPISTLE TO THE ROMANS

1. i. 1-7. THE ADDRESS

(1) Paul, slave of Christ Jesus, by divine call an apostle, set apart for the Good News God is now setting forth (2) (Good News which in the past he promised through his prophets, whose word still stands in Holy Writ; (3) Good News about his Son, who in the sphere of the flesh was born of the family of David, (4) in the sphere of the Holy Spirit was appointed Son of God in power after his resurrection from the dead—Jesus Christ our Lord; (5) through whom we received grace and our apostolic commission to win believing obedience on his behalf among all the Gentiles—(6) among whom are you, Jesus Christ's, by divine call): (7) to all who in Rome[1] are God's beloved, by divine call, saints. I wish you grace and peace from God our Father and the Lord Jesus Christ.

Greek letters commonly opened with the formula, A to B, greeting. Paul, and other New Testament writers, follow this custom, but habitually expand the titles of writer and recipients, and give a Christian sense to the greeting. This expansion and modification are rarely carried out at greater length, and never more significantly, than in Romans.

Paul describes himself in the first instance as a **slave of** 1 **Christ Jesus.** This is a common term with him (cf. especially Gal. i. 10; Phil. i. 1), imitated also by other New Testament writers (James i. 1; 2 Pet. i. 1; Jude 1). It is particularly appropriate to an apostle, but can be used of any Christian (cf. vi. 22);

---

[1] The words 'in Rome' are omitted by G; there is also some evidence that they were omitted by Origen. G continues 'in the love of God' (ἐν ἀγάπῃ θεοῦ, instead of ἀγαπητοῖς θεοῦ); some other MSS., which have 'in Rome', have this expression. Cf. the variant at i. 15; and for Paul's usage see 1 Cor. i. 2; 2 Cor. i. 1; Phil. i. 1. It is probable that the variant (here and at i. 15) reflects a desire to show that the epistle is of universal, and not merely local, application. See also Introduction, p. 9.

that is, Paul begins by describing himself as a Christian before he goes on to mention his special status and vocation. The description is more striking in a Greek work, such as this epistle, than in Semitic literature. A Greek did not think of himself as the slave (δοῦλος) of his ruler or king, nor did he think of himself as the slave of his divine king, or god, or speak of his service to the god as slavery. The Semitic king, however, was a slave-owner, and the highest of his ministers could be regarded as his slave (e.g. 1 Sam. viii. 17; 2 Sam. xiv. 22). The king in turn is God's slave (e.g. 2 Sam. vii. 19). Other distinguished members of the theocracy are described in the same terms (e.g. Ps. cv. 26, 42; Amos iii. 7). Thus Paul, as the slave of Christ Jesus, appears as a member—as the context will show, an outstanding and privileged member—of a people of God analogous with the people of God in the Old Testament.

Paul is also, **by divine call** (cf. *v.* 6), **an apostle**. Compare *v.* 5, where Paul refers to his 'apostolic commission', again emphasizing its divine origin. The pre-Christian history of the Greek word 'apostle' (ἀπόστολος) does little or nothing to illustrate its Christian usage. The word itself calls to mind, however, the Hebrew *shaliah*, *shaluah* (from the verb *sh-l-h*, 'to send'), which are commonly used in post-biblical Hebrew of an authorized representative or delegate, legally empowered to act (within prescribed limits) on behalf of his principal. It cannot be regarded as certain that Greek-speaking Jews already in the first century A.D. used the word *apostolos* to represent this technical term, but it is probable that they did so, and that this usage is reflected in Paul's own. At Phil. ii. 25 and 2 Cor. viii. 23 he uses it to describe men acting on behalf of Christian communities. Paul himself, however, is not an apostle 'of a church' (cf. Gal. i. 1), but an apostle of Jesus Christ (1 Cor. i. 1; 2 Cor. i. 1; Col. i. 1; cf. Gal. i. 1), from whom alone his mission and authority are derived. As such an apostle he appeals to men 'on behalf of Christ', 'as though God were intreating by us' (2 Cor. v. 20). The word of God has been entrusted to him, and through his proclamation faith is born (*v.* 5). His privileged status as a special representative of Christ gives him authority (2 Cor. x. 8) but none of the ordinary human accompaniments of authority; his privilege is suffering (1 Cor. iv. 9-13; Col. i. 24), a participation in, and manifestation of, the sufferings of Christ himself. Beyond the suffering lies resurrection (2 Cor. xiii. 4), but this is not the visible aspect of the apostle's ministry.

The apostle is **set apart** for the Gospel. Again the background of Paul's thought is to be found in the Old Testament. The prophets were set apart by God for their work; for example, 'Before thou camest forth out of the womb I sanctified thee; I have appointed thee a prophet unto the nations' (Jer. i. 5). This passage is alluded to in Gal. i. 15, and may be in mind here also, as 'unto the nations' (cf. *v.* 5) suggests. 'Set apart' means much the same as 'sanctified', but may perhaps have further significance. The Greek word is not only similar in meaning to, but also has the same consonants as the Hebrew root *p-r-sh*, which underlies the word Pharisee. Paul had been a Pharisee (Phil. iii. 5), supposing himself to be set apart[1] from other men for the service of God; he now truly was what he had supposed himself to be—separated, not, however, by human exclusiveness but by God's grace and election.

He was set apart **for the Good News;** that is, in order to proclaim it. Here Paul's word (εὐαγγέλιον) has been translated Good News, in order to bring out its meaning. Elsewhere the familiar term Gospel is used; an English technical term is a suit able equivalent for the Greek word, which, in Paul's usage, has also a technical sense. It is the message of salvation he is commissioned to preach, the announcement of the manifestation of God's righteousness (see *vv.* 16 f.). Behind this usage, lies not only the common Greek meaning of the word but also its use in the Old Testament, especially in Isaiah where it (and particularly the cognate verb) points to the coming of God whose saving righteousness will bring deliverance to his people (e.g. Isa. xl. 9; lii. 7). Paul's Gospel is more than this. It is not merely an account of God's saving acts in Christ; the active righteousness of God is revealed in it; it is itself part of the eschatological event through which God brings salvation to men. See belov on *vv.* 16 f.

Paul's words here could be literally rendered, 'Gospel of God'. The genitive can scarcely be objective in view of *v.* 3

---

[1] The origin of the word Pharisee is not certain, but this meaning was probably attached to it.

('about his Son'), and it is best to take it as a genitive of the author: the Gospel is the Good News **God is now setting forth.** Paul's theology is theocentric in that God is the source of salvation and thus of the Gospel, and of the theology that rests upon the Gospel; christocentric in that the historical manifestation of the truth of God lies in the deeds of Jesus Christ.

The Good News God is now setting forth through his
2 apostles is **Good News which in the past he promised through his prophets, whose word still stands in Holy Writ.** The relation between the Old Testament and the New (or rather, the apostolic proclamation upon which the New Testament rests) is one of the major themes of the epistle. Here Paul echoes the common conviction of the primitive Church that the saving acts of Christ were foretold by the prophets. The more difficult problem, of the relation between Law and Gospel, is not raised.

3 The Good News is **about his Son,** in whom all the Old Testament promises were fulfilled (2 Cor. i. 20), and the saving acts were wrought. A brief (perhaps credal) formula expounds the nature of the Son of God in this verse and the next. It consists of two lines in antithetical parallelism. He was

in the sphere of the flesh, born of the family of David;
4 **in the sphere of the Holy Spirit, appointed Son of God.**[1]

The preposition (κατά) here rendered 'in the sphere of' could also be rendered 'according to', and 'according to the flesh' is a common Pauline phrase; in this verse, however, Paul does not mean that on a fleshly (human) judgement Jesus was a descendant of David, but that in the realm denoted by the word flesh (humanity) he was truly a descendant of David. Similarly, 'in the sphere of the Holy Spirit' does not introduce a truer evaluation of Jesus' person, but a second evaluation also true in another (divine) sphere. (For the translation 'Holy Spirit' see below, p. 19.)

That Jesus was of Davidic descent is attested in various parts of the New Testament (e.g. Matt. i. 1; Acts ii. 30; Rev. v. 5), but nowhere else by Paul (but cf. xv. 12). It is a probable view

---

[1] It seems best to stop at this point, allowing 'in power' and 'after his resurrection from the dead' to be Pauline supplements to an earlier formula.

that he mentions the matter here because he is quoting a formula which he did not himself compose; and not impossible that he quotes it in order to commend his orthodoxy to persons who he knew would recognize the formula. Evidently he saw no reason to question the fact; it was part of the conviction that Christ had fulfilled the prophecies of the Old Testament (e.g. 2 Sam. vii. 12; Isa. xi. 1); but for him a more significant statement of the Old Testament background out of which the Christ emerged was that he was 'born under the law' (Gal. iv. 4; cf. Rom. xv. 8, with the note).

Jesus, then, as a man was a descendant of David; but 'in the sphere of the Holy Spirit he was appointed Son of God'. This translation is not universally accepted. For 'in the sphere of' see above. 'The Holy Spirit' is literally 'spirit of holiness', and this has been taken to refer not to the Holy Spirit, but to Jesus' own (human) spirit, marked as it was by the attribute of holiness. It is true that, though Paul frequently refers to the Holy Spirit, he nowhere else uses this descriptive genitive, which is probably of Semitic origin; but this fact is explained if we accept the view that the Christological formula is pre-Pauline. Further, the word here translated 'appointed' is sometimes translated 'defined', or 'declared' (to be). This rendering has the evident advantage that it avoids the charge of adoptionism which can be brought against 'appointed' (see below), but there is little else to be said for it. Hellenistic evidence and New Testament usage both favour 'appointed' (e.g. Acts x. 42; xvii. 31).

We now have before us an antithetical Christological couplet, which we have some reason for regarding as pre-Pauline. It is important to note what it contains.

The very fact of the antithesis is significant. It is implied that there are two things to be said about Christ, not indeed contradictory but complementary to and different from each other. Christ belongs to two spheres or orders of existence, denoted respectively by flesh and Spirit; in these he can be described as Son of David and as Son of God. He was *born* as Son of David, *appointed* Son of God. We have no grounds for taking any other than the most natural view, namely, that the birth preceded the appointment. When the appointment took place is not stated. The Baptism (Mark i. 9 ff, and parallels) may be suggested; or perhaps the further words **after his resurrection from the dead** belonged to the original formula, or, if added by Paul, were a true interpretation. The preposition (ἐξ) is consistent with this, since even if (as is possible) it means not 'after' but 'on the ground of', the resurrection of Christ must still have preceded his appointment. Jesus then was born Son of David and appointed Son of God, most probably, perhaps, at the resurrection (cf. Acts ii. 36). His descent from David means that he was the Messiah, in whom Judaism found its fulfilment (v. 2). When he was born, the Age to Come of Jewish expectation began to dawn; that is, the Gospel consists in the fulfilment of eschatology in Jesus. The fulfilment, however, was not yet complete, for the Messiah who had been exalted to the right hand of the Father was to return in power and glory when all his foes were subjected to him.

If the view suggested above is correct, Paul adds two supplements to the primitive formula. One, 'after his resurrection from the dead', has already been discussed. The other, **in power,** is ambiguous. It may be taken either adverbially (modifying 'appointed'), or adjectivally (qualifying 'Son of God'). If the sentence is taken as it stands, it seems impossible to decide between these alternatives. If, however, 'in power' is a Pauline addition, it is most plausibly understood as adjectival, and as intended to soften the adoptionism of the words quoted. If the passage is taken in this way, Paul means that Christ was, after the resurrection, appointed Son of God *in power*; this would not exclude his having previously been Son of God, though without the manifestation of power which took place in the resurrection. This would be consistent with what Paul says elsewhere of the weakness of Christ in his earthly life and death. God, in the person of his Son, disclosed himself in weakness and humility that men might know him and live by faith only, without the confirmation of sight.

Undoubtedly, the earliest Christology has superficially an adoptionist tinge; but this is not to say that it was 'Adoptionist' in the technical sense. The first attempts at Christological thought were made not in essential but in functional terms.[1] Pre-existence was a possibility that had not been explored (Paul

[1] See G. Dix, *Jew and Greek* (1953), pp. 76-81.

himself was perhaps the first explorer); there was a manifest difference between the obscure private life of Jesus and the public ministry which was inaugurated at his baptism, and an even greater difference between the earthly life and the heavenly glory of **Jesus Christ our Lord** (on the term Lord see further on x. 9). The Son of man had come in weakness and humility; he was to come in glory and power. This was the primitive Christian conviction about Jesus; behind the Chalcedonian orthodoxy of 'two natures' united in Christ's person lies an earlier belief in the two tenses of his activity.[1]

It was Jesus the heavenly Lord who bestowed upon Paul **grace and our apostolic commission.** Here, as in *v*. 1, Paul 5 speaks both as Christian and as apostle; hence, probably, the plural **we received,** since all Christians have received grace (xii. 6). Grace is the undeserved favour of God for sinful men, operative in the eschatological event of Jesus Christ (see further on iii. 24); for the 'apostolic commission' see above on the word apostle.

The aim of Paul's apostleship is here defined as **to win believing obedience.** A literal translation is, 'unto obedience of faith'. It has been suggested that this means 'with a view to securing obedience to the faith', 'the faith' being 'the Christian religion'; but a better explanation is that Paul is using a short-hand expression and means that the object of his apostolic work is that men should (a) become obedient to Christ, and (b) put their faith in him. For the meaning of faith see on *vv.* 16 f., and many other passages; for the close relation of obedience and faith see, for example, vi. 15 ff.

As an apostle, Paul acts **on his** (Christ's) **behalf** (literally, on behalf of his name). The scope of his activity also is laid down; it is **among all the Gentiles.** This was settled in consultation with the Jerusalem apostles; see Gal. ii. 9. The intention, interpretation, and execution of the agreement here described give rise to difficult problems; Paul certainly felt free to preach to Jews, and there was a Gentile mission independent of his—he was at this moment writing to a Gentile church which he had not founded. But the present verse emphasizes the fact that a

---

[1] It is not denied that the doctrine of the two natures is a proper metaphysical interpretation of the primitive eschatological faith.

real division of apostolic work was agreed upon (cf. xi. 13; xv. 16, 18).

6 The next words, **among whom are you,** show that a majority of the Roman Christians were Gentiles. See Introduction, pp. 6 f. Apart from their racial origin, the Roman Christians were **Jesus Christ's, by divine call;** literally, 'called ones of Jesus Christ'. This genitive is not subjective— 'called *by* Jesus Christ'—for in Paul's usage it is God the Father who calls (iv. 17; viii. 30; *et al.*). Contrast 'God's beloved' (*v.* 7). Christians are the property of Jesus Christ. Like Paul himself (*v.* 1), they are his slaves; he is their Lord (*v.* 4). And he and they stand in this relationship not because they have chosen it but because they have been called to it by God himself, just as Paul, against his own inclination and will, was called to be an apostle.

The next verse adds to the description of the recipients of
7 the letter. It is addressed to **all who in Rome are God's beloved, by divine call, saints.** The readers of the letter are in the world—indeed, they are in the very heart of it. At the same time they are not of the world, for they are saints, that is to say, holy persons. The word is one of Paul's most common designations of Christians; in Romans see also viii. 27; xii. 13; xv. 25 f., 31; xvi. 2, 15. That the word is regularly plural (Phil. iv. 21 is only an apparent exception) confirms the fact that the usage looks back to the Old Testament (the holy people, e.g. Ex. xix. 6), as developed in later Judaism (e.g. Dan. vii. 18; Ps. Sol. xvii. 28; 1 Enoch xliii. 4). Christians are the elect, messianic people. Nothing is implied about their moral behaviour, though their separation from the world and for Christ is bound to have moral consequences. They are singled out as the people of God because of the love God has for them. This is the root out of which Christian doctrine and action grow (cf. v. 8).

Paul's **grace** ($\chi\acute{\alpha}\rho\iota\varsigma$) may be a Christianizing of a common Greek salutation ($\chi\alpha\acute{\iota}\rho\epsilon\iota\nu$). He adds, **peace**—which was, and is, a common greeting among Semitic peoples.[1] It is unthinkable, however, that he did not enrich the word with its specific Christian content (see on v. 1).

---

[1] In letters as well as in speech; e.g. *Sanhedrin* 11 *b*: 'To our brothers of upper Galilee . . .: May your peace multiply'.

2. i. 8-15. PAUL AND ROME

The greeting may owe something to other sources. It recalls the priestly blessing of Num. vi. 24 ff. (The Lord . . . be gracious unto thee . . . and give thee peace), and there is a similar combination in 2 Baruch lxxviii. 2 (Thus saith Baruch the son of Neriah to the brethren carried into captivity: Mercy and peace). The Pauline formula may perhaps reflect an early Christian liturgical usage.

Paul has now introduced his letter, and, at the same time, in general terms, himself and his Gospel. He will say a little more about himself (i. 8-15) and then turn to expound the Gospel at length.

2. i. 8-15. PAUL AND ROME

(8) First of all, I give thanks to my God through Jesus Christ for you all, because your faith is spoken of in the whole world. (9) For God (to whom I render spiritual service in proclaiming the Gospel of his Son) is my witness that I make mention of you unceasingly, (10) always in my prayers making the petition that I really may in the end succeed (if that be God's will) in coming to you. (11) For I long to see you, that I may impart to you some gift of the Spirit, for your strengthening, (12)—or rather, what I wish is that we may be mutually encouraged when I am among you by our mutual faith, yours and mine. (13) Indeed, I should not like you, brethren, to be unaware that I have often intended to come to you that I might get some fruit among you too, as I have among the other Gentiles; only up to the present I have been prevented from doing this. (14) To Greeks and barbarians alike, to wise and foolish equally, I am under obligation; (15) that is why I desire to preach the Gospel to you in Rome[1] as well as to the rest.

In the first seven verses of the epistle Paul followed, though he also modified, the conventional form of a Greek letter. In the

---

[1] The words 'in Rome' are omitted by G. See on i. 7, and Introduction, p. 9.

thanksgiving, intercession, and personal news of the present paragraph he continues, as he does elsewhere, to follow the same model.

8   Paul's **First of all** is never followed by a 'secondly'; he is carried away by his train of thought. He can **give thanks** for the Roman Christians, **because your faith is spoken of,** publicly reported, **in the whole world.** 'Your faith' does not mean 'the Christian faith *which* you, in common with all other Christians, hold', for this would be pointless in a thanksgiving; but 'the faith *as* you hold it', that is, the understanding, constancy, and charity with which you hold it. There is doubtless a natural exaggeration in these words (cf. 1 Thess. i. 8), but they cannot be meaningless. The Roman church was not a foundation of yesterday; already it had made its presence felt. This harmonizes readily with the view (see Introduction, p. 6) that the riots *impulsore Chresto* (Suetonius, *Claudius*, 25) were provoked by the proclamation of Jesus as Messiah; less well with Acts xxviii. 21 f., where the Roman Jews appear to have no direct acquaintance with Christianity.

9   Paul not only gives thanks but makes intercession. **God ... is my witness** (an Old Testament form of asseveration) **that I**
10 **make mention of you unceasingly, always in my prayers making the petition. . . .** This sentence may be punctuated differently. It is possible to place the comma after 'prayers'; the sentence might then be rendered, '. . . that I always in my prayers unceasingly make mention of you, making the petition . . .'. But it seems better to separate 'unceasingly' and 'always' which are so nearly synonymous that in one clause they are tautologous. The God whom Paul calls to witness is he **to whom I render spiritual service in proclaiming the Gospel of his Son.** 'Spiritual' would be more literally rendered, 'in' or 'by my spirit'; it is by using his spirit, in the field of activities proper to the spiritual side of his nature, that Paul renders God service. The service is 'in the Gospel', that is, it consists in preaching the Gospel. For 'the Gospel', see on *v.* 1.

   In particular, Paul prays **that I really may in the end succeed (if that be God's will) in coming to you.** Paul wishes to visit Rome, even though it was not a church of his own founding and it was his custom not to build on foundations laid by others (xv. 20). Reasons of a sort for this unusual proceeding are given in *vv.* 11 ff., 15, but the basic reason does not appear till xv. 24: Paul is (or hopes to be) on his way to Spain, and for this new field of missionary activity Rome will prove an indispensable base.

The reason is sound enough; but Paul's plans are sufficiently anomalous to make him embarrassed, and his embarrassment appears in the loose and inaccurate construction of the next verses. He begins straightforwardly enough: **I long to see you, that I may impart to you some gift of the Spirit.** 'Gifts' are dealt with at some length in xii. 6 ff.; see also 1 Cor. xii. Whether it is explicitly stated (as here) or not, they are the result of the activity of the Spirit, and thus a sign of the Church's supernatural life. Since elsewhere Paul lays stress on the variety of such gifts it is hardly profitable here to inquire what precise gift he may have had in mind. 11

After this straightforward beginning the construction changes and it becomes difficult to establish Paul's meaning with certainty. The obscurity and confusion are probably due to Paul's recognition that, though a visit intended **for your strengthening** might have been mentioned appropriately in a letter to Corinth, where he was both apostle (1 Cor. ix. 2) and father (1 Cor. iv. 15), it came less suitably when he was writing as a stranger to an old-established and well-known (*v.* 8) church in the capital of the Empire. 'For your strengthening' needs correction: **or rather, what I wish is** (these last four words are not expressed in the Greek, but if they are not supplied, 'that we may be mutually encouraged' must be made to depend on 'I long', which is very awkward) **that we may be mutually encouraged when I am among you by our mutual faith.** The stress falls on the mutuality of what will take place when Paul visits Rome. He trusts that he will be able to impart a spiritual gift, but he is equally sure that the Romans will have something to bestow on him. The translation 'encouraged' is not certain. The word means sometimes 'comfort', sometimes 'exhort'. The latter sense would be difficult here (though doubtless exhortation or preaching is involved); on the other hand more than consolation seems to be intended, and 12 in modern English 'comfort' is scarcely a strong enough word.

Paul may be a stranger in Rome, and the church there another man's foundation; yet as an apostle he can write that 13 **I have often intended to come to you that I might get some fruit among you.** 'Fruit' is the result of apostolic labour—the winning of new converts, and the building up of the Church; and Paul might expect to find it in Rome, **as I have among the other Gentiles** (cf. *v.* 6). There was no question of his freedom, or of his desire, to preach in Rome.

I should not like you to be unaware is a common Pauline expression (xi. 25; *et al.*); and **brethren** is a word commonly used of fellow-members of both Jewish and heathen religious communities. It was common in early Christian usage too; cf. Mark iii. 35, as well as many passages in the epistles.

The sentence **only up to the present I have been prevented from doing this** has for clarity been taken out of the awkward parenthetical position it occupies in the Greek (between 'to you' and 'that I might get'). Paul does not here (as at 1 Thess. ii. 18) speak of a hindering by Satan; indeed, the use of the passive may (in Semitic fashion) conceal a reference to God —it had not been God's will that Paul should come (cf. Acts xvi. 6 f., and perhaps 1 Cor. xvi. 12). This should probably be understood to mean that urgent tasks (only recently completed— xv. 18 f., 22 f.) had kept him in the East.

Thus both Paul's desire to visit Rome (for its own sake, and as a stage on the journey to Spain), and the fact that he had so far failed to do so, were due to the obligation under which he 14 stood as an apostle. **To Greeks and barbarians alike** (the word Greeks is not to be taken in a strict racial sense; Paul means, Both those who inhabit the city states of the inner Mediterranean world, and those outside that cultivated circle), **to wise and foolish equally, I am under obligation.** The notion of debt is not emphasized (cf. viii. 12; xv. 27; Gal. v. 3); it is a duty Paul owes, and it is this duty which leads him to 15 Rome: **That is why I desire** (an alternative way of rendering the awkward Greek sentence is, 'As far as I am concerned, I am ready') **to preach the Gospel to you in Rome as well as to the rest.**

But what does preaching the Gospel mean? What is the Gospel (cf. *v.* 1)? Paul begins at once to answer these questions, and is not done with them until the epistle is at an end.

3. i. 16, 17. THE GOSPEL

(16) For I am not ashamed of the Gospel, since it is the operation of God's power working towards salvation, effective for everyone who has faith—Jew first, and then the Gentile too. (17) For in it God's righteousness is revealed on the basis of nothing but faith—as it is written, He that is righteous by faith shall live.

These two verses are at once the continuation of *vv.* 8-15, and the beginning of *vv.* 18-32; it seems best to take them as a separate paragraph. Most commentators recognize in them the 'text' of the epistle; it is not wrong to see in them a summary of Paul's theology as a whole.

An obscure provincial, Paul plans to visit the centre of the world; a self-styled apostle, lacking the self-evident authorization of the Twelve, he approaches a church where his authority and even his credentials may well be questioned; yet—**I am not** 16 **ashamed** (cf. Mark viii. 38; 2 Tim. i. 8) **of the Gospel.** This is simply because the Gospel is what it is (cf. *v.* 1).

Paul's argument turns upon **salvation.** The word itself, even when the cognate verb 'to save' is included in the reckoning, is not one of the commonest in Paul, but it is certainly central in his thought. Salvation itself lies in the future (e.g. xiii. 11), and means man's eventual safe passage through human trials and divine judgement to eternal bliss. In particular, salvation means being saved from the wrath of God (v. 9); it is thus a term which belongs within the framework of eschatological thinking. Like all such terms, it suffered a change when it was taken over from the vocabulary of Judaism into that of primitive Christianity. The salvation ready to be revealed at the last time, though it could be complete only at the return of the Messiah in glory, was already, in virtue of his death and resurrection, anticipated

27

in the present. Thus the Gospel itself is **the operation of God's power working toward** salvation; not merely an announcement of the fact that salvation will at some future time take place, but a divine activity or power leading to salvation. Like the word of God in the prophets, the Gospel itself is a power which leads either to life or to death (cf. 1 Cor. i. 23 f.; 2 Cor. ii. 15 f.). It is one element in the eschatological situation in which Paul believed that he and his fellow-Christians stood.

The work of salvation was begun, though not completed, in the ministry, death, and resurrection of Jesus, and from the beginning it was marked by power: in the miracles, in the resurrection, and subsequently in the work of the Holy Spirit. It was in virtue of this power that the Gospel preached by Paul and his apostolic colleagues had its effect among those who heard it, and experienced the 'powers of the age to come' (Heb. vi. 5). This proleptic enjoyment of salvation in the power of the Gospel, which at once announces and anticipates it, is a most important key to Paul's thought, for many of his central theological ideas (for example, the doctrines of justification, and of the Holy Spirit) are built upon it.

It is *God's* power which is at work in the Gospel, not man's; it is at work not because man has chosen that it should be, but because God has acted through Jesus. It follows that the divine power operative in the Gospel is not dependent upon any human activity or condition. It is never without its effect (see above); and that which determines what the effect shall be is not human virtue or wisdom, not works done in obedience to any law, however sacred, but nothing more or less than faith: the Gospel is the operation of God's power acting toward salvation, **effective for everyone who has faith.** What faith is will become gradually clearer as the epistle proceeds; but its primary meaning is already apparent. It is the 'believing obedience' of *v.* 5. He believes who accepts the power of God which is at work in the life, death, and resurrection of Jesus as—the power of God, and therefore submits himself to it, claiming no rights over against his Creator but ready to trust himself wholly to his grace and wisdom. Only when man is prepared to stand still and see the glory of God can he apprehend God's action as salvation.

The Gospel means salvation for *everyone* who has faith, but it was delivered to the **Jew first, and then the Gentile too.** (The word here translated 'Gentile' was in *v.* 14 translated 'Greek'; the meaning is determined by the context, and especially by the contrasting partner, in each case). That the Jews were the first to hear the Gospel is to Paul more than a fact of history; it was due to God's election (see especially chs. ix-xi). It was inconceivable that God's Anointed should appear outside the context of messianic prophecy, where alone there existed a vocabulary suitable for describing him. Further, it was impossible that he should be understood except against the background of law. Only where human achievement in religion had reached its highest point could its absolute negation in the universality of human guilt (iii. 19 f.) and the freedom of God be proclaimed. Grace could be fully grace only where sin abounded (v. 20), and the exceeding sinfulness of sin could be demonstrated only through the law (vii. 13).

No one insisted more strongly than Paul that the Gospel was for the 'Gentile too'; but it is important to see that for him the extension of the Gospel to the Gentiles was the result not of easy-going charity but of theological conviction; nor did it contradict the election of the Jews (see on chs. ix-xi). There is only one God (iii. 29), and therefore only one Gospel.

This short paragraph carries Paul's argument yet further in a second decisive step. Paul is not ashamed of the Gospel, because it is the divinely appointed means to salvation. It is this means because **in it God's righteousness is revealed.** Here for the 17 first time we touch upon the dominating theme of the epistle. As a Jew, instructed in the Old Testament, Paul knows that salvation presupposes righteousness. On God's side, salvation means the operation of his righteousness, which is not simply his property or attribute of being right, or righteous, but also his activity in doing right, and (as we say) seeing right done; thus his righteousness issues in his vindicating—those whom it is proper that he should vindicate. This view of God's righteousness is brought out with special clarity in a number of passages in Isaiah and the Psalms (e.g. Isa. xlv. 21; li. 5; Ps. xxiv. 5; xxxi. 1; xcviii. 2; cxliii. 11), where righteousness appears to be almost a synonym of salvation; God manifests his righteousness by delivering his people.[1]

On man's side, salvation requires that he be found righteous before God; that, when the great assize is held, he secure a favourable verdict. If the verdict is Guilty, punishment, not salvation, must be his fate.

Thus, before salvation can be completed, righteousness must be manifested. God, the righteous judge, must do righteous judgement in his court; and, in this court, man must secure the verdict, Righteous. When defined in this way, salvation seems remote—remote in time, for the last judgement has not yet taken place, and remote as possibility, for there seems no likelihood that man will ever attain any verdict other than Guilty. Paul, however, asserts that the righteousness of God (not salvation, for that remains future) is now being revealed (ἀποκαλύπτεται). The very word he uses (in the present tense) confirms that he is thinking of a preliminary manifestation of that divine righteousness which, in orthodox Jewish thought, could be vindicated only at the last judgement. Paul, the Christian, is convinced that this judgement (and in some measure its consequences) has been anticipated through Jesus Christ, and that in the paradox of grace God has manifested his righteousness by establishing man's. As a Jew, Paul had believed that man's status of righteousness before God was to be achieved by himself, through obedience to the law. As a Christian, he had come to believe that God, gracious as Jesus had shown him to be, justified men freely on the basis not of works done in obedience to the law but of faith. This revision of fundamental conceptions was not the result of the academic manipulation of theological counters; it took place because God had sent his Messiah to suffer humiliation and death and thereby to manifest his righteousness in a way accessible to faith, the only human attitude corresponding to grace on God's part.

God's righteousness, then, is revealed **on the basis of nothing but faith;** literally, from faith unto faith. Several formal parallels to this obscure expression can be adduced; for example,

---

[1] The importance of these passages should not be exaggerated. In them, God vindicates those who deserve to be vindicated; in Paul, he justifies—the ungodly.

Ps. lxxxiv. 7 (They go from strength to strength); 2 Cor. iii. 18 (From glory to glory). These suggest the meaning, ' from one level of faith to a higher', 'to ever greater faith'. This does not, however, suit the present context; in all probability the phrase is rhetorical and means (as the translation suggests), 'faith from start to finish'.[1]

Paul clinches his argument with a reference to the Old Testament: **He that is righteous by faith shall live** (Hab. ii. 4). The Greek contains here an ambiguity which has been retained in the translation. Does 'by faith' modify the adjective 'righteous' or the verb 'shall live'? The position of the phrase is indecisive. It is to be noted that both the Hebrew text and the LXX of Habakkuk supply possessive pronouns with 'faith'. The Hebrew has, 'He that is righteous shall live by his faithfulness', the Greek, '. . . by my faithfulness'. The fact that Paul drops both pronouns may lend some force to the view that he wishes to bring out his own characteristic phrase, 'righteous by faith'. More probably, however, he is again emphasizing the principle of 'faith all the time': man (if righteous at all) is righteous by faith; he also lives by faith.

These two verses contain a rich selection of Paul's characteristic vocabulary: Gospel, power, salvation, faith, Jew and Gentile, righteousness. Something has now been done to bring out the meaning of these basic terms, but the present exposition is not complete, and it will be necessary to return to them again and again, as Paul himself does. See especially on iii. 21-31.

4. i. 18-32. JUDGEMENT AND THE GENTILE

(18) A clear signal of the revealing of God's righteousness is the fact that his wrath is being revealed from heaven against all the ungodliness and unrighteousness of men who, by their unrighteousness, hold the truth imprisoned.

---

[1] Dr. Barth, noting correctly the ambiguity of the Greek word ($\pi\iota\sigma\tau\iota\varsigma$), understands the phrase to mean, 'from (God's) faithfulness to (man's) faith'. This seems quite possible; but to ascribe different meanings to the same word in one phrase is very harsh, and the interpretation given above should probably be preferred.

(19) Justly so, for that which can be known of God is manifest among them, since God himself made it manifest among them. (20) From the creation of the world onwards, the invisible attributes of God are plainly seen since the mind can grasp them in the things that he has made. By his ' invisible attributes ' I mean his eternal power, his very Godhead. (21) These were manifested that men might be without excuse, because, though they knew God, they did not glorify him as God or give thanks to him; instead, they grew vain in their thinking, and their senseless heart was darkened. (22) Even as they made themselves out to be wise they were turned into fools, (23) and exchanged the glory of the incorruptible God for the mere shadowy image of corruptible man—or indeed of birds, animals, or snakes. (24) So God handed them over, as punishment, by the lusts of their own hearts, to an unclean life, that by their own activities their bodies might be dishonoured. (25) This was the fate of men who exchanged the truth of God for a lie, and worshipped and served the creation rather than the Creator—Blessed be he for ever. Amen.

(26) So God handed them over to dishonourable passions. For example, the women among them exchanged the natural kind of intercourse for an unnatural. (27) In the same way, the men forsook natural intercourse with a female partner and were consumed in their lust for one another. Men wrought obscenity with men, and received the due reward of their folly in their own persons.

(28) And as they did not see fit to take cognizance of God, God handed them over to an unfit mind, to do unseemly things, (29) to be replete with every kind of unrighteousness, wickedness, covetousness, malice; full of envy, murder, strife, deceit, evil constructions. They became gossipping whisperers, (30) God-hated slanderers, insolent, proud, boastful persons, good at inventing new forms of evil, disobedient to parents, (31) senseless, faithless, loveless, pitiless. (32) They all are men who knew God's righteous ordinance, that those who practise such

things as these are worthy of death; yet they do them, and (for I would include these also) they approve of those who practise them.

The first and most difficult problem to be solved in this paragraph is the question of its place in the argument of the epistle. It is often said that, after stating briefly, in *vv.* 16 f., the substance of the Gospel, Paul begins at this point a long digression which he continues until he resumes, in iii. 21, the theme of the saving righteousness of God. The digression deals (it is said) with the state of mankind apart from the Gospel; it is therefore by no means irrelevant to a presentation of the Gospel, but it is not directly connected with *v.* 17. This popular exegesis cannot be maintained.

Two points determine the exegesis of the opening verses of the paragraph. The first is the particle (*γάρ*, generally translated *for*, *because*) with which it is introduced. It is true that this particle is sometimes weakened so as to become no more than a note of transition, but it is well, if at all possible, to give it its proper force (as in the present translation). The second point is the fact that with the new subject (wrath) Paul uses the same verb, in the same tense, as with the subject (righteousness) in *v.* 17. Paul does not say that the wrath of God *was* revealed in the old time before the promulgation of the Gospel, or that it will be revealed at the last day. He says that God's **wrath is 18 being revealed from heaven** now; and this is exactly what he has said of God's righteousness. We are therefore encouraged to see a close positive relation between *vv.* 17 and 18; and this is confirmed by detailed exegesis.

It has been noted that in only one other place does Paul add to the word 'wrath' the genitive 'of God' (Col. iii. 6; cf. Eph. v. 6), and that he never uses the verb 'to be wrathful' with God as subject; and deduced that Paul thought of the divine wrath in impersonal terms, as an almost automatic force which resists evil. It is doubtful whether this view can stand. When Paul speaks of wrath, it is in general quite clear from the context that the wrath is God's; so, for example, iii. 5; ix. 22. Wrath is God's personal (though never malicious or, in a bad sense, emotional) reaction against sin.

Properly, wrath belongs to the last day (ii. 5), but the idea of its anticipation in divine judgements is common. Here, however, it is a unique anticipation which is in mind. If the *for* ($\gamma\acute{\alpha}\rho$) which introduces *v.* 18 is a real *for*, the assertion of *v.* 17 must be understood to be demonstrated or supported by the manifestation of wrath which is described in the following verses. This is quite suitable to the context, for the latter part of the paragraph depicts an observable situation capable of forming the basis of an argument. Wrath, like salvation and righteousness, is an eschatological term. Righteousness (so Paul as a Jew would undoubtedly believe) would be manifested at the last judgement in terms of salvation and wrath. But (as Paul the Christian now believed) righteousness had been manifested *to faith* in the event of Jesus Christ, and in consequence salvation and wrath also were being anticipated in history (though each was still to be consummated in the future). It follows logically (assuming Paul's premises) that if the revelation of wrath can be demonstrated (as Paul believes), the revelation of righteousness is demonstrated too.

Paul's argument is developed in a clear and consistent way. The Gospel rests upon a manifestation of righteousness; to those who believe, it proves to be the power of God unto salvation (cf. 1 Cor. i. 18); to those who do not believe, but are disobedient and rebellious, it means God's wrath (cf. 2 Cor. ii. 16). The revelation of wrath therefore is **a clear signal of the revealing of God's righteousness.**

Wrath is revealed **from heaven** (that is, from God himself) **against all the ungodliness and unrighteousness of men who, by their unrighteousness, hold the truth imprisoned;** that is, the truth about God as Creator, Judge, and Redeemer, is concealed by the fact that they are what they are. The words 'hold imprisoned' translate the same word ($\kappa\alpha\tau\acute{\epsilon}\chi\epsilon\iota\nu$) as is used in vii. 6 ('held fast'). The word has, however, another meaning, that of holding firmly doctrines or traditions (as at 1 Cor. xi. 2). If this meaning of the word is adopted, the ungodly and unrighteous men are blamed for their hypocrisy; they hold the truth in a state of ungodliness, their orthodox belief is accompanied by unrighteous life. But hypocrisy is not a sin attacked by Paul in this paragraph, and the other translation is to be preferred.

At this point a serious objection might be made. 'This manifestation of divine wrath would be credible, and just, if the abandoned Gentile world consisted of men who had wilfully rejected the Gospel. But this is not so. The vast majority have never heard of the Gospel.' The fact that Paul proceeds to meet precisely this objection confirms that our interpretation of his thought is on the right lines. The words **justly so** are inserted 19 in the translation as a necessary connecting link since it is evident that Paul intends in *v.* 19 to justify what he has said.

Men are without excuse, **for that which can be known of God is manifest among them, since God himself made it manifest to them.** It is not Paul's intention in this and the following verses to establish a natural theology; nor does he create one unintentionally. He is concerned with the moral principles of God's judgement, and in order to vindicate these he makes use of terminology which he draws mainly from the field of Hellenistic Judaism. What it is that can be 'known of God' will appear in the next verse. It is manifest 'among them'; an equally possible translation would be 'in them'—that is, in their minds and consciences. But the context shows that the men in question did not in fact possess this knowledge in themselves; it was available in their midst, in creation, where God himself had made it manifest, but it was not *in them*.

The next verse justifies the statement that God had manifested in creation what could be known about him.

From the creation of the world is here taken in a temporal 20 sense, partly because the word for creation ($\kappa\tau\iota\sigma\iota\varsigma$) refers properly to the act or process of creation and partly because instrumentality is sufficiently suggested in the words **in** (or, by) **the things that he has made.** As long as there has been a created universe, **the invisible attributes of God are plainly seen.** These invisible attributes are those which are mentioned in this verse: **his eternal power, his very Godhead.** That is, what is clearly seen is that God is God and not man. Observation of created life is sufficient to show that creation does not provide the key to its own existence. Paul does not teach that there exist rational means of proving from creation that God exists. A mechanistic or fortuitous account of the universe never occurs to him. Of course, men set in God's world should have perceived that they were his creatures and that their Creator stood infinitely above them. In fact, those with whom Paul is here concerned, and whose sins he castigates in this chapter, did not (for the most part) deny the existence of deity; but they did fail (*v.* 21) to give God due honour and praise.

These truths—where they are perceived at all—are perceived by the mind, **since the mind can grasp them** in the things that he has made. The contrast between perception by the eye and perception by the mind was common (e.g. Plato, *Republic*, VI, 507 b); Paul means simply that the being of God is inwardly perceived. His line of argument so far can be paralleled without difficulty; it appears in the Stoic literature, and, more significantly perhaps, in that of Hellenistic Judaism (e.g. Wisdom xiii. 5).

21   God manifested his power, and the fact that he was God, man's Creator and Lord, **that men might be without excuse.** 'That' ($\epsilon\dot{\iota}s\ \tau\dot{o}\ \epsilon\dot{\iota}\nu\alpha\iota$) indicates, not result merely but purpose. This (as was pointed out above) is the important result Paul seeks to establish in these verses. God may rightly visit men with wrath because, though they have not had the advantage of hearing the Gospel, they have rejected that rudimentary knowledge of God which was open to them. The inexcusability of man is similarly emphasized in Wisdom xiii. 8 f., but Paul's accusation is far more searching, because it penetrates further into the meaning of idolatry.

The root of the matter is that **though they knew God, they did not glorify him as God or give thanks to him.** Paul assumes that the raw materials of the knowledge of God exist among men. An awareness of this kind is in itself no great matter —it is God's knowledge of man that is really significant (1 Cor. viii. 1-3; Gal. iv. 9; cf. 1 Cor. xiii. 9, 12). As God's creature, man was bound to render glory and thanksgiving to his Creator; this means not merely to acknowledge his existence, and to employ the words and rites of religion, but to recognize his lordship and live in grateful obedience—in fact (in the Pauline sense) to believe, to have faith This men failed to do; instead they rebelled against God, and their fault lay not in lack of knowledge but in their rebellion. Man was unwilling to recognize a Lord; he chose to be Lord himself, and to glorify himself.[1] This is the universal state of mankind, and it follows that God's wrath is justly visited upon men because the race as a whole is in revolt against him.

In contemporary pagan society this revolt is manifested in idolatry. A vicious circle operates: denying the knowledge of God they have, men plunge further and further into unbelief. The result is that they are ignorant of God, and of themselves cannot know him; yet their ignorance is culpable ignorance, for it is rooted in rebellion. Their idolatrous minds and practices are themselves a punishment from God. When they failed to honour God, **they grew vain in their thinking, and their senseless heart was darkened** (for the language, cf. Ps. xciv. 11; Wisdom xi. 15). Once man had fallen from his true relation with God, he was no longer capable of truly rational thought about him.

'Heart' is one of Paul's most important psychological terms, and has a wide range of use. It is not necessarily good (i. 24; ii. 5), nor is it necessarily evil (ii. 15; v. 5; vi. 17); it is the organ of thought (x. 6), but also of feeling (ix. 2). It is essentially inward, hidden (ii. 29; viii. 27).

At this point Paul resumes the main thread of his argument. The manifest decadence of the pagan world is an indication to him that in this last age of history God's wrath is already at work. He has shown that this is no more than a just punishment of what is, ultimately, not unfortunate ignorance but culpable rebellion, in which man has sought to dethrone his Creator, and to render to himself the glory and praise which were due to God. The immediate result of this rebellion was a state of corruption in which men were no longer capable of distinguishing between themselves and God, and accordingly fell into idolatry, behind which, in all its forms, lies in the last resort the idolization of the self. All this was, in a sense, a natural process; but it was accelerated and illuminated in the last age.

Even as they made themselves out to be wise they were 22 **turned into fools;** in their 'wisdom' they thought it possible to escape their obligations to God. But God is not mocked. Men thought to attain a higher place than that appointed them by

[1] This account of the root of sin is fundamentally the same as that given in ch. v; see p. 111.

God, by constructing new gods of which they, the manufacturers, were undoubtedly the masters; but instead of rising above their place they fell below it, for they were now worshippers 23 not of God but of idols. They **exchanged the glory of the incorruptible God for the mere shadowy image of corruptible man—or indeed of birds, animals, and snakes.** Paul's language owes something to Ps. cvi. 20, but he has adapted his quotation to a Hellenistic setting. The allusion probably accounts for the obscure expression 'the mere shadowy image of . . .', which is literally 'the likeness of the image of . . .'. 'Likeness' ($\delta\mu o\acute{\iota}\omega\mu a$) is the word of the Psalm in Greek; 'image' ($\epsilon\grave{\iota}\kappa\acute{\omega}\nu$) suggests the idolatrous object Paul has in mind. Perhaps he uses the two words but means no more than either would have signified separately; perhaps (as the translation suggests) the reduplication emphasizes the inferior, shadowy character of that which is substituted for God.

Idolatry is not the end of the story. It was a commonplace of Jewish propaganda that false worship led to moral depravity (e.g. Wisdom xiv. 12), and that idolatry was punished by God with a punishment made to fit the crime (e.g. Wisdom xi. 15 f.). Paul uses these beliefs, but deepens them in the using. On the one hand, he understands idolatry acutely enough to perceive that the idol-hating Jew himself is not free from it (ch. ii); on the other, he has a far more terrible sense of the punishment of idolatry— the man who worships beasts is not (as in Wisdom xi) devoured by them, but becomes like them.

The process by which idolatry becomes moral evil is neither 24 automatic nor impersonal: **God handed them over, as punishment, by the lusts of their own hearts, to an unclean life.** The words 'God handed them over' stand three times in this paragraph (*vv.* 24, 26, 28), repeated with horrifying emphasis. God's judgement has already broken forth; only he has consigned sinners not to hell but to sin—if indeed these be alternatives. 'Lusts', though in non-Biblical Greek the word ($\epsilon\pi\iota\theta\upsilon\mu\acute{\iota}a\iota$) is neutral, must here refer to sexual (or homosexual) passions (for the word see further on vii. 7), and the clause which follows—**that by their own activities their bodies might be dishonoured**—is epexegetic. By dishonouring God, men in the end dishonour their own bodies.

Paul sums up. **This was the fate of men who exchanged** 25
the truth of God for a lie (some understand this to mean
'substituted a lie—that is, an idol—for the true God'),
**and worshipped and served the creation rather than
the Creator—Blessed be he for ever. Amen.** He adds a
brief doxology in Jewish form; compare the very common
'The Holy One (blessed be he!) . . .' of the Rabbinic
writings.

Paul has now conducted his argument to its close, and made
his point. In what follows, he adds nothing strictly new till *v.* 32,
but contributes a number of practical illustrations of the ways
in which idolators fall into sin.

So God handed them over to dishonourable passions. 26
**For example, the women among them exchanged the
natural kind of intercourse for an unnatural. In the same** 27
**way, the men forsook the natural intercourse with a
female partner and were consumed in their lust for one
another. Men wrought obscenity** (the word ($\dot{\alpha}\sigma\chi\eta\mu o\sigma\acute{v}\nu\eta$)
does not have this meaning elsewhere in Paul; but it is normal,
and required by the context) **with men, and received the
due reward of their folly** (or, error) **in their own persons.**
No feature of pagan society filled the Jew with greater loathing
than the toleration, or rather admiration, of homosexual practices. Paul is entirely at one here with his compatriots; but his
disgust is more than instinctive. In the obscene pleasures to
which he refers is to be seen precisely that perversion of the
created order which may be expected when men put the creation
in place of the Creator. That idolatry has such consequences is
to Paul a plain mark of God's wrath.

And as they did not see fit to take cognizance of God, 28
God handed them over to an unfit mind. 'See fit . . . unfit'
is an attempt to represent a word-play in the original. By rejecting God men show that their own mind ($\nu o\hat{v}s$) is, or is meet to
be, rejected. The substance of the thought has already been
noted above; here, however, it may be observed that for Paul
(and here he differs from his Hellenistic contemporaries) the
mind is not a higher, divine, element in man, or even necessarily good. It is capable of, but it is thereby implied that it
needs, renewal (xii. 2). In Romans, the mind appears sometimes

to be related to the conscience; see on vii. 23, 25; xiv. 5; and, for conscience, on ii. 15.

As in *v.* 24, an epexegetical clause follows. To have an unfit mind means in practice **to do unseemly things** (τὰ μὴ καθήκοντα). Paul here borrows—and negatives—a Stoic term for *duty, that which befits* a man. Thus Epictetus (II, xvii. 31) describes an inquirer who wishes to know 'what is my duty (καθῆκον) to the gods, what to my parents, what to my brothers, what to my country, what to strangers'. Paul, however, was not a Stoic, and does not think of the duty arising out of a man's place in society, but of that imposed by his place in creation. He and the Stoics agree, on the whole, in their account of unseemly things, but for Paul they are unseemly not because they are anti-social but because they are indicative of rebellion against God.

He proceeds with a list of vices, which has parallels in, and may be based upon, Hellenistic and Hellenistic-Jewish lists. Similar lists appear in the New Testament at xiii. 13; 1 Cor. v. 10 f.; vi. 9 f.; 2 Cor. xii. 20 f.; Gal. v. 19 ff; Eph. iv. 31; v. 3 ff.; Col. iii. 5, 8; 1 Tim. i. 9 f.; 2 Tim. iii. 2-5; see also 1 Clem. xxxv. 5. Only a few of the details call for consideration here.

29 **Covetousness** (and cognate words) is fairly common in Paul; see especially Col. iii. 5, where the word is given an important theological development which does not appear in Romans.

Full of . . . evil constructions. Paul's word (κακοήθεια) is defined by Aristotle (*Rhetoric*, II. xiii. 3) as 'taking everything for the worse'.

30 **God-hated slanderers.** The word (θεοστυγεῖς) translated 'God-hated' is ambiguous, and might also be taken as active ('God-hating'). The Vulgate takes it as passive (*Deo odibilis*), and there is much to be said for this rendering; on the other hand, the passage as a whole deals with human activities. Moreover, in 1 Clem. xxxv. 5, where the cognate abstract noun is used, the context (see xxxv. 6) suggests that the word is active. The best suggestion (followed in the translation) is that of Pallis (*To the Romans*, 1933) who takes the word as an adjective qualifying the preceding Greek word.

Good at inventing new forms of evil seems a curious expression, but in fact has several parallels, of which the most familiar is probably Vergil's, in *Aeneid*, ii. 164: 'Ulysses, crime-contriver' (*scelerum inuentor*).

The paragraph comes to a close with a verse which reiterates the main point. Sinners are not excusably ignorant but guilty and responsible. **They all are men who knew God's right-** 32 **eous ordinance.** This is certainly the correct translation, though the word (δικαίωμα) for 'righteous ordinance' occurs elsewhere with somewhat different meanings (ii. 26; v. 16, 18; viii. 4; for this meaning, see Luke i. 6). The content of the ordinance follows at once: **that those who practise such things as these are worthy of death** (cf. Gen. ii. 17).

The next words raise a problem, which is in part removed in the translation: **Yet they do them, and (for I would include these also) they approve of those who practise them.** A more literal rendering would run: They not only do them, but also approve of those who practise them. The words 'not only . . . but also' suggest an increase in the offence; but to approve of those who sin can scarcely be regarded as worse than sinning (notwithstanding the old suggestion that mere doing may be excused if it is passionate and therefore unpremeditated, whereas approval implies the deliberate choice of evil). The difficulty is brought out by comparison with 1 Clem. xxxv. 6, which runs: Those who practise these things are hateful to God; and not only those who practise them, but also those who approve of them. There is no difficulty in Clement's words, and in the textual tradition of Romans there are traces of attempts to make Paul's equally straightforward. There can, however, be no doubt that he wrote the sentence in the difficult form, and the difficulty can be solved only by looking forward to ii. 1 ff. In his next paragraph Paul proceeds to deal with those who do not approve the sinful actions just described. Before doing so he deals with those who do approve. His 'not only . . . but also' would thus mean: 'I am not speaking only of those who do these things, but also of those who approve—you are all in the same condemnation. And', he continues in ch. ii, 'you who disapprove, who judge—so too are you.' See further on ii. 1.

5. ii. 1-11. JUDGEMENT AND THE CRITIC

(1) That means, my good man, that, whoever you are, whenever you act as judge you are without excuse, for in judging someone else you condemn yourself, since you who judge practise the same conduct as he. (2) Now[1] we know that 'God's judgement on those who practise such things is fair'; (3) but, knowing this, do you think, my man, that you, who judge those who practise such things as these and do them yourself, will escape God's judgement? (4) Or is it that you despise the wealth of his kindness, his forbearance and long-suffering, ignoring the fact that God's kindness is intended to lead you to repentance? (5) Yes, with your hardness, your unrepentant heart, you are storing up for yourself wrath which will break forth in the day of wrath, the day when God's just judgement is revealed. (6) As Scripture says, he will render to every man according to his works. (7) To those who with patient endurance look beyond their own well-doing to the glory, honour, and incorruption God alone can give, he will render eternal life. (8) To those who are out for quick and selfish profit on their own account, and disobey the truth and obey unrighteousness, he will render wrath and anger. (9) Tribulation and anguish will fall upon every human soul that works that which is evil—Jew first and Gentile too; (10) glory, honour, and peace will be for everyone who works that which is good—Jew first and Gentile too; (11) for God shows no favouritism.

Paul has argued that the visible degradation of pagan life proves that the wrath of God (one aspect of his righteousness) is now being poured out upon those who have rejected him. But there exist those who join in Paul's condemnation of moral wickedness: can it be that these escape condemnation and are in no need of the Gospel? It is with this question that Paul now

---

[1] ℵ C lat and some other authorities read, 'For we know'. This reading, though well attested, is surely wrong. Paul is not here supporting the statement of *v*. 1, but introducing a new thought.

deals. It is not till *v.* 17 that he turns specifically to the problem of the Jews; here, as *vv.* 9 ff., 12-16, show, his thought applies to both Gentiles and Jews. He addresses his readers directly, using the second person singular, and an occasional vocative (**My good man,** *v.* 1). These features are characteristic of the 1 so-called diatribe style, affected by philosophical teachers and preachers of the time. It often becomes easier to follow Paul's arguments if the reader imagines the apostle face to face with a heckler, who makes interjections and receives replies which sometimes are withering and brusque. It is by no means impossible that some of the arguments in Romans first took shape in this way, in the course of debates in synagogue or market place.

At the beginning of the paragraph the connexion of thought is difficult. The first sentence begins with a particle (διό) which normally means 'therefore'. Sometimes, it is true, it is no more than a conjunctive particle, but it is best not to assume that it is without argumentative force unless attempts to explain it otherwise fail. When the repetition of 'without excuse' (cf. i. 20), and the material noted below on *v.* 4, are borne in mind, the simplest solution is to regard i. 32 b as a parenthesis. The particle then connects with i. 32 a: Men know God's verdict on such sinners as are described in i. 29 ff.; *therefore* the man who judges proves himself to be without excuse, for he sins (see below), and in the act of judging proves that he knows what is right. This is the major connexion; but it seems probable that within it there is also a contrast between those who approve (i. 32 b), and those who judge.

Paul's own words now become clear. **That means that, whoever you are** (Jew or pagan moral philosopher), **whenever you act as judge you are without excuse, for in judging someone else you condemn yourself, since you who judge practise the same conduct as he.** The last clause is fundamental to the argument. The judge is without excuse *if he does wrong*, because *ex hypothesi* he knows the law—he of all men cannot plead ignorance. In fact, says Paul, he does the same things as the man he judges. This cannot mean that the critic also practises homosexual perversions and the like. The moral purity of the Jews was their legitimate boast, and moral philosophers such as Epictetus and Marcus Aurelius may have been prigs but were certainly not hypocrites. Paul's point is that in the very act of judging (ἐν ᾧ κρίνεις) the judge is involved in the same conduct as the man he condemns. Behind all the the sins of i. 29 ff. lies the sin of idolatry, which reveals man's ambition to put himself in the place of God and so to be his own Lord. But this is precisely what the judge does, when he assumes the right to condemn his fellow-creatures. All alike fall under God's judgement, and before him all are without excuse.

2   At this point the objector speaks. **Now we know** introduces his complaint: cf. iii. 19; vii. 14. It seems to be a Jew who speaks —it is perhaps not wrong to say, the Jew in Paul himself. **'God's judgement on those who practise such things is fair'**—that is, there is no favouritism (v. 11) in it. Paul agrees; he has just argued that God may justly visit Gentile sinners

3 with wrath. But there is a qualification to come. **But, knowing this, do you think, my man, that you, who judge those who practise such things as these and do them yourself, will escape God's judgement?** The second 'you' is emphatic: Do you suppose that *you* of all men will escape? The objector doubtless did suppose this, and not without reason, for the visible handing over to reprobate mind and behaviour (i. 24, 26, 28) which was the token of God's wrath upon Gentile sinners, did not apply to him. He was rather the object of God's kindness. But this was a privilege he had misinterpreted. He is now to be enlightened.

4   **Is it that you despise the wealth of his kindness** (χρηστό-της), **his forbearance** (cf. iii. 25; ix. 22) **and long-suffering** (μακροθυμία)? The full force of this accusation will be felt if we set beside it words from Wisdom (which Paul evidently knew). At the end of Wisdom xiv stands a list of pagan vices, similar to that which Paul has given in i. 29 ff. The author continues (xv. 1-4): But thou, our God, art gracious (χρηστός) and true, long-suffering (μακρόθυμος), and in mercy ordering all things. For even if we sin, we are thine, knowing thy dominion; but we shall not sin, knowing that we are accounted thine: for to know thee is perfect righteousness, yea, to know thy dominion is the root of immortality. For neither did any evil device of man lead us astray, nor yet the painters' fruitless labour, a form stained with various colours.

This passage describes the critic Paul has in mind. He is (he thinks) superior to the idolater; even if he does sin he avoids the really fundamental sin of idolatry, and he belongs to the people of God, and is thereby assured of salvation. But God shows no such favouritism as is assumed here; judgement looks to deeds, not privilege. The Jew boasts of God's goodness; in fact he despises it, **ignoring the fact that God's kindness is intended to lead you to repentance.** The fact that judgement has not yet begun to be executed upon him (as upon the Gentiles) has led him not to humble gratitude but to boasting (*v.* 17); he has abused God's grace. He will, however, make no profit out of his attitude. **With your hardness, your unre-** 5 **pentant heart**—these correspond exactly to the despising of God's mercy (*v.* 4)—**you are storing up for yourself wrath which will break forth in the day of wrath, the day when God's just judgement is revealed.**

Of course, the Jew was looking forward to a day of wrath (Zeph. i. 15); but for him also that day will be darkness and not light (cf. Amos v. 18). It will be a day when righteous judgement is revealed, and the wrathful sentence of i. 18 is confirmed.

It is the present which is sadly misunderstood by the Jew. (1) It is marked by God's forbearance and mercy, which the Jew takes as a privilege which he possesses in his own right, whereas they ought to bring him to his knees in penitence and gratitude. (2) He supposes that by his cherishing of the law he is storing up for himself merit with God; in fact it is wrath which he is storing up. (3) Paul subtly inverts the common belief that the wicked received their few rewards in this life in order to have unmixed punishment in the next, and the good received their few punishments in this life in order to have unmixed reward in the next. In his view, the virtuous Jews (and other critics of the wicked) are now being spared only that (if they do not repent) they may receive their full share of wrath hereafter.

When the judgement is held, national privilege, and an attitude of moral superiority, will be irrelevant: **As Scripture says, he** 6 **will render to every man according to his works.** Paul does not himself make the reference to Scripture, but there can be little doubt that he intends it to be understood; see Ps. lxii. 12; Prov. xxiv. 12; Jer. xvii. 10; in the New Testament compare

Matt. xvi. 27; 2 Cor. v. 10; 2 Tim. iv. 14; 1 Pet. i. 17; Rev. ii. 23;
xx. 12; xxii. 12. His own Bible tells the Jew that he can appeal
only to what he himself has done, not to what others have left
undone. This emphasis persists throughout the chapter; see *vv.*
7, 9, 10, 13, etc. Not hearing the law, being the proud and
privileged possessor of it, but doing it is what matters.

This emphasis upon works is intelligible in the present context; but is it compatible with Paul's theology of grace and faith?
The answer to this serious and important question must inevitably begin, 'It depends on what you mean by works'. The
next two verses, which form a balanced couplet, point to Paul's
meaning, and demand detailed consideration.

7   Paul deals first with the reward of **eternal life.** This is the
opposite of corruption (Gal. vi. 8), and describes not the blessed-
ness of the Christian life in this world but the greater blessed-
ness of life beyond the final judgement. It will be bestowed on
**those who with patient endurance look beyond their own
well-doing to the glory, honour, and incorruption God
alone can give.**

'Patient endurance' (ὑπομονή) occurs frequently in Paul's
writings. It is closely related to hope; see especially viii. 24 f.;
1 Thess. i. 3; cf. 1 Cor. xiii. 7. It suggests a readiness to look
beyond the present moment, to see the full meaning of the
present, and, in particular, of the things men do in the present,
not in themselves but in the future, that is (for one who looks
upon the future in the biblical manner), in God. Paul's words
are very awkwardly co-ordinated—literally the phrase runs 'in
patient endurance of (a) good work'—but the meaning appears
to be that suggested in the translation. This is confirmed both
by the words that follow, and by the parallel sentence in the
next verse. Those who view their own activity with patient endurance attest thereby that they are seeking what is not to be
found in any human being and doing. Glory and incorruption
(to a less extent honour) are matters which are exclusively in
God's gift; they are eschatological terms. For glory, see viii. 18,
21; ix. 23; 1 Cor. xv. 43 (where *dis*honour suggests that honour
may be regarded as a synonym of glory), and of course the
common phrase, 'glory of *God*'; for incorruption, see 1 Cor. xv.
42, 50, 53 f. The reward of eternal life, then, is promised to

those who do not regard their good works as an end in themselves, but see them as marks not of human achievement but of hope in God. Their trust is not in their good works, but in God, the only source of glory, honour, and incorruption.

The second member in Paul's couplet deals with the recompense of **wrath and anger.** (In Greek, these words are not in 8 the accusative but in the nominative; Paul has evidently forgotten the construction of the two previous verses, and writes as if he were beginning a new sentence. In the translation the construction has been made uniform throughout *vv.* 6-8.) 'Wrath and anger' need no long comment; they describe God's attitude on the day of wrath to those whom he does not reward with eternal life. But who are these persons? **Those who are out for quick and selfish profit on their own account, and disobey the truth and obey unrighteousness.**

In *v.* 7, the vital word, on which the meaning of the sentence turns, was 'patient endurance'. In *v.* 8 also there is a single Greek word (ἐριθεία) which is vital to the thought, but many English words are needed to express it—'those who are out for quick and selfish profit on their own account'. The rendering of RV ('them that are factious') assumes the derivation of ἐριθεία from ἔρις (strife). This etymology is false.[1] The word is in fact derived from ἔριθος, a hireling; ἐριθεύειν, to act as a hireling, to work for pay, to behave as, show the spirit of, a hireling. ἐριθεία should therefore mean the activity, or characteristics, or mind, of a hireling. This meaning is suitable to all the Pauline passages where the word is employed (2 Cor. xii. 20; Gal. v. 20; Phil. i. 17; ii. 3). In the first two, the word occurs in lists along with ἔρις, and if the familiar translation 'faction' is employed, Paul is made to repeat himself. Compare also James iii. 14, 16; Ignatius, *Philad.* viii. 2. The word is rare outside the New Testament, and little help can be obtained from non-biblical usage. It seems very probable that Paul intends by means of this word to describe the motives (the Greek preposition ἐξ suggests that their actions arise *out of* the quality just described)

---

[1] It is, of course, possible that Paul (consciously or unconsciously) accepted the false etymology and understood the word accordingly. But the correct meaning of the word is much more suitable to the context than the false, and there is therefore no reason why it should not be accepted.

of those who look on their works as achievements of their own, complete in themselves, by means of which they may acquire rights. This makes them as disobedient to the truth (of God's sovereign lordship) and as prone to unrighteousness (rebellion against their Creator) as the men of i. 18, upon whom God's wrath is with evident justice poured out. They too will be the objects of wrath and anger.

In a second balanced couplet Paul repeats the thought of the 9 last, with one significant addition. **Tribulation and anguish will fall upon every human soul that works that which is** 10 **evil—Jew first and Gentile too; glory, honour, and peace will be for everyone who works that which is good—Jew first and Gentile too.** Tribulation and anguish are the result of wrath and anger (*v.* 8); to glory and honour (*v.* 7) is added peace (see on v. 1).

The analysis of works presupposed by *vv.* 7 f. has the important consequence of dissolving the barrier between Jew and Gentile. The former no longer possesses the exclusive privilege of performing good works done in obedience to the revealed law. The 'good' which God will reward does not consist in 'works of law', but in patient seeking, in looking beyond human activity to its divine complement; the 'bad' which he punishes may include good deeds, 'works of law', done in a servile spirit with a view to profit. Both for good and ill the Jew retains a certain priority (cf. i. 16)—not necessarily an enviable priority; but inevitably must be added—and the Gentile too. 11 This inclusion is ultimately grounded upon the fact that **God shows no favouritism.** His election of the Jews (cf. chs. ix-xi), and the undoubted advantage which they possess (iii. 1 f.), do not mean that they, or any other self-righteous, self-appointed judges of mankind, enjoy an exclusive right to his favour.

6. ii. 12-16. CONSCIENCE

(12) Those who have sinned outside the sphere of the law shall also perish outside the sphere of the law; those who have sinned within the sphere of the law shall be judged

by means of the law—(13) for it is not those who listen to
the law who are righteous with God; no, it is those who
do the law who shall be justified. (14) For when Gentiles
(who have not the law) do by nature the things which the
law requires, then, since they have not the law, they are a
law for themselves. (15) They show the effect of the law
written in their hearts; their conscience bears witness
with the law, and their inward thoughts in mutual debate
accuse or else excuse them, (16) in the day in which,
according to my Gospel, God judges the secret things of
men through Jesus Christ.

In the preceding paragraph Paul has reached the conclusion
that Jew and Gentile are equal before God. To this statement
there is one evident objection. The difference between Jew and
Gentile is not simply a matter of race, but of religion, or rather,
of revelation. God through Moses gave the law to Israel; this
was an advantage the Gentiles never had. The objection, however, is not insuperable. In i. 19 ff. Paul showed that the Gentile
was guilty of a responsible act of rebellion against the Creator;
lack of a special revelation did not excuse him. In the same way,
lack of a revealed law is now seen not to open a way of escape
from judgement. The fact is first laid down in general terms:
Those who have sinned outside the sphere of the law 12
shall also perish outside the sphere of the law. The law of
Moses is the plainest statement (outside the Christian revelation)
of the claim of God upon his creatures, but the claim is independent of the statement of it, and failure to acknowledge
the claim can never be anything other than culpable.

So far a Jewish reader would have applauded Paul. But he
proceeds, **Those who have sinned within the sphere of the
law shall be judged by means of the law.** The law is not a
talisman calculated to preserve those who possess it. It is an
instrument of judgement, and sin is not less sin, but more, when
it is wrought within the sphere of the law (cf. vii. 13). **For it is** 13
not those who listen to the law (for example, Sabbath by
Sabbath, in synagogue) **who are righteous with God; no, it is
those who do the law** (by obeying it) **who shall be justified.**
For the contrast between hearing and doing compare James i. 22.

It is also common in Rabbinic teaching (e.g. *Aboth*, iii. 10: He whose works exceed his wisdom, his wisdom endures; but he whose wisdom exceeds his works, his wisdom does not endure), and Paul must have been familiar with it. Elsewhere he argues that the essence of the law is (as the law itself declares) a matter of doing; see x. 5, and especially Gal. iii. 10 ff. What the law commands is good (cf. vii. 12; Gal. iii. 21); if only men would not merely listen to it but do it, they would be righteous.

It is important to pause for a moment upon the word *righteous*. We have already considered the meaning of God's righteousness (above, pp. 29 f.; further, p. 73), and pointed out (p. 30) that, in Jewish thought, before salvation could be enjoyed the righteousness of man must also be established. This means that man, arraigned in God's court, must secure from his judge a favourable verdict. The vital question, therefore, which determines man's eternal fate, is how he can achieve this state of 'rightness' with God. The state itself is not a moral quality but a relation—a relation of gracious favour, and peace—between God and man, but it could, hypothetically at least, be achieved by a perfect performance of what the law required, but certainly not by mere acquaintance with the contents of the law. The present passage refers only to the sentence, whether of condemnation or acquittal, pronounced at the last judgement; that is, it does not deal with the specifically Christian conception of justification which rests upon the anticipation of the eschatological righteousness of God in the saving event of Jesus Christ. On this much more must be said later (see pp. 75 f., 81 f.). But it is relevant here to note the parallel between the two clauses of *v.* 13:

> Not those who listen . . . are righteous;
> Those who do . . . shall be justified.

This suggests that 'to be justified' means 'to be (or to be made) righteous'. This is not the common interpretation of Paul's usage, and the point must be discussed in detail later; here the reader may be reminded that 'righteous' describes a relation not a quality, and that accordingly 'to make righteous' does not mean 'to make virtuous', but 'to grant a verdict of acquittal'.

Paul returns to his opening assertion, which, as it stands, is open to objection. How can judgement take place 'outside the sphere of the law'? Paul himself suggests that apart from the law sin (at least in the sense of positive transgression) cannot exist (v. 13; vii. 7, 9, *et al.*). The fact is that the Gentile is not really outside the sphere of law, though he is of course outside the sphere of the law of Moses. **For when Gentiles (who have not** 14 **the law) do by nature the things which the law requires, they are a law for themselves;** hence the possibility of sin and of judgement.

It is implied by the construction that Gentiles sometimes do the things which the law requires (literally, the things of the law). What are these? Clearly not the detailed precepts of the Mosaic code: in *vv.* 26 f. Paul says that the 'uncircumcision' (which in the nature of the case does not observe the ritual law) may keep the righteous requirements of the law, and fulfil it. Again, Paul never distinguishes between 'ritual law' and 'moral law'; and in any case to suggest that the Gentiles kept the moral law would make nonsense of Paul's thought as a whole, since in the next chapter he conducts a detailed argument to prove that all men without exception, Jews and Greeks, are 'under sin' (iii. 9; cf. iii. 19, 23; xi. 32; Gal. iii. 22). What the law requires is ultimately neither ceremonial nor moral conformity (though wilful non-conformity would be sin) but believing obedience, or obedient faith (cf. i. 5). This (when the matter is viewed from the human side) is the only tolerable basis of relationship between man and his Creator, and, just as the Gentile finds (or ought to find) the creature-Creator relationship written in the natural universe (i. 19 ff.) so also he finds (or ought to find) it written in his heart.

When man recognizes and accepts this relationship he may be said to do what the law requires 'by nature' (φύσει). This word arises out of the notion of growth (φύειν, to grow), but comes to mean *the way* things grow, hence what they have (in virtue of their own proper being) become, their nature. Thus there is a nature (φύσις) of an individual (which gives him his individuality), of a genus (in which the several individuals comprising it share), and finally of the cosmos. This inward nature of things Aristotle distinguished from law (νόμος), law being for him convention;[1] but the Stoics taught that true law was rooted in nature.[2] Now the Jews had come to believe that their law was the ground and means of creation,[3] so that the Hellenistic synagogue was able to adopt the Stoic doctrine of 'natural law', with the further proposition that *their* (revealed) law was the supreme expression of natural law (cf. *v.* 20). This notion appears most clearly in Philo,[4] and was evidently of great propaganda value. It can scarcely be doubted that this Stoic-Jewish use of nature was in Paul's mind, though he makes of it something different from what Philo made of it.[5]

There is, then, something, Paul argues, in the very pattern of created existence which should, and sometimes does, lead the Gentiles to an attitude of humble, grateful, dependent creatureliness. When this takes place they are a law for themselves. In saying this Paul draws again upon the language of Hellenistic Judaism. Philo, for example, speaks of the patriarchs (who since they lived before Moses could not know the law in its written form) as themselves 'laws endowed with life and reason' (*Abraham*, 5). Paul does not go as far as this (see the next verse), but far enough to justify what he had said in *vv.* 9 ff.; the Gentile comes into judgement with the Jew, even though the Jew comes first.

The relation between man, nature, and the law requires further elucidation. The Gentiles who do the things required by
15 the law **show the effect of the law written in their hearts**—not the law itself, for this would imply the fulfilment of Jer. xxxi. 33. In the phrase 'the effect of the law' (τὸ ἔργον τοῦ

[1] E.g. *Nicomachean Ethics*, 1133 a 30: Money is 'what it is not naturally (φύσει) but by custom or law (νόμῳ)'.
[2] E.g. Cicero, *Laws*, I. vi. 8: 'Law is the highest reason, planted in nature, which commands those things which are to be done, and prohibits their opposites'.
[3] E.g. *Aboth*, iii. 15: '. . . it was made known to them that to them was given the precious instrument [the law] by which the world was created'.
[4] E.g. *Creation of the World*, 3: 'The world (κόσμος) is in harmony with the law (νόμος), and the law with the world, and . . . the man who observes the law is constituted thereby a loyal citizen of the world (κοσμοπολίτης), regulating his days by the purpose and will of nature (φύσις), in accordance with which the entire world itself also is administered'.
[5] It has been suggested that Paul here alludes to the precepts given to Noah (Gen. ix. 1-7), and believed to be binding upon Gentiles. But there is no evidence whatever in support of this. Paul is not interested in Noah, but goes back from Moses to creation.

νόμου) the genitive is probably subjective. The law has, as it were, left its stamp upon their minds; this stamp is **their conscience.** Once more, Paul draws on Stoic terminology. By the Stoics, and Philo, the conscience is often described as an accuser, or convictor; in Romans it is a witness (so here, also ix. 1; cf. 2 Cor. i. 12). This is in accord with the etymology of the word. It implies man's ability to detach himself from himself and to view his character and actions independently. He is thus able to act as a witness for or against himself. His conscience is not so much the bar at which his conduct is tried, as a major witness, who can be called on either side as the case may be. This role of the conscience appears in the following words: their conscience **bears witness with the law, and their inward thoughts in mutual debate accuse or else excuse them.** This clause is sometimes taken differently, and is said to mean that there are three witnesses: (1) the Gentiles themselves, (2) their consciences, and (3) their inward thoughts. But it is better to take it as suggested here. All that Paul says is that the conscience bears witness with (συμμαρτυρεῖ)—he does not say with what. It suits his argument if we think of the conscience bearing witness with the divine law whose imprint it is; the clause 'their inward thoughts   excuse them' then describes the operation of conscience. The thoughts enter into debate (this is an attempt to render the obscure Greek μεταξὺ ἀλλήλων); some are for acquittal, some for conviction.

The connexion of the next verse with the context is obscure. Many expositors think that it must be taken with *v.* 13, *vv.* 14 f. being regarded either as a parenthesis or as having been misplaced. This view has much to commend it. To say, 'Not hearers but doers of the law shall be justified in the day when God judges . . .' makes excellent sense, whereas the alternative (connecting *v.* 16 with *v.* 15) seems to imply that the Gentile conscience comes into operation only at judgement day. But the objection is not serious. Whatever the conscience may do inwardly in men's experience, what matters ultimately is the witness borne by it **in the day in which . . . God judges.**   16

Two problems remain in this verse. In full it runs, In the day in which, **according to my Gospel,** God judges **the secret things of men through Jesus Christ.** How can judgement be part of the Gospel? And what does Paul mean by *my* Gospel (cf. xvi. 25)? The connexion between Gospel and judgement is closer than is sometimes recognized; see on i. 16. 'My Gospel' is not that God will judge the world, since all Christians and all Jews believed this; nor is it (as Lagrange suggests) that God will judge the world through Jesus Christ, since all Christians believed this. It is unlikely too that 'my Gospel' is that the heathen also come within the jurisdiction of the Messiah; it is doubtful whether this conviction was peculiar to Paul. The answer to both questions appears to lie in the emphasis laid upon the 'secret things'. God's judgement does not rest upon the observable behaviour of either Gentile or Jew (cf. *v.* 29), but upon the secret things of the heart, the faith which a man has to himself before God (xiv. 22). This is judgement, but it is also good news for the sinner, to whom it opens the prospect of justification by faith.

7. ii. 17-29. JUDGEMENT AND THE JEW

(17) But if you bear the name 'Jew', and put your trust in the law, and make your boast in God, (18) and know his will, and (instructed by the law) are able to judge what is significant and good; (19) and if you are confident that you are a guide of the blind, a light for those who are in darkness, (20) an instructor of fools, a teacher of babes, provided with the embodiment of knowledge and truth in the law—(21) well then, you who teach your neighbour, do you not teach yourself? you who preach that men ought not to steal, do you steal? (22) you who say that men ought not to commit adultery, do you commit adultery? you who regard an idol as an abomination, do you commit sacrilege? (23) You, who make your boast in the law, by your transgression of the law dishonour God. (24) For (as Scripture says) 'On your account the name of God is blasphemed among the Gentiles'.

(25) This is what I mean. Your circumcision is profitable to you—if you practise the law. But if you are a

transgressor of the law, your circumcision is turned into uncircumcision. (26) If then (to take the opposite point of view) an uncircumcised man keeps the righteous requirements of the law, will not his uncircumcision be counted as circumcision? (27) Yes, and the man by race uncircumcised who fulfils the law will judge you, who, for all your observance of the letter, and your circumcision, are a transgressor of the law. (28) For not the outward Jew is a Jew, nor is outward fleshly circumcision circumcision; (29) but the secret Jew is a Jew, and circumcision of the heart, in spirit not letter, is circumcision. He is a Jew, whose due comes not from men but from God.

All men stand under the judgement of God: the licentious, and the timid who would be licentious if they dared; no less, the moral critics who look with disfavour upon the grossness of their fellow-men. These critics preach virtue, some from the philosopher's platform, some from the pulpit of the synagogue. In *vv.* 1-11 Paul addressed both groups; now he turns to the supreme critic of his fellows, the self-righteous Jew. We should probably not be wrong in the guess that the most notorious example of the class was the unconverted Paul. The paragraph as a whole may properly be headed 'Judgement and the Jew', but towards the end Paul further clarifies the position by introducing the Gentiles again.

But introduces a formal counterpart to *v.* 12. **If you bear the** 17 **name 'Jew'**—perhaps a contrast is intended with the true Jew, who is a Jew secretly (*v.* 29)—**and put your trust in the law,** literally, rest upon the law. The Jew relies upon the law to provide him with a secure standing before God. If further you **make your boast in God . . .** confident that because of his promises to the fathers of the race you are certain of salvation. These are the grounds of confidence which enable the Jew to face the world, sure that he is in a position to pass sentence on it. He is wrong at every point. As a Jew, he is the supremely vulnerable man. He cannot rest upon the law, because the law accuses him; he cannot glory in God (though there is of course a sense in which this is proper; cf. Jer. ix. 24; 1 Cor. i. 31), because

God is his Judge. The next clauses are hardly more than corollaries of what has been said.

18 If you **know his will** (literally, *the* will; cf. perhaps I Cor. xvi. 12), **and (instructed by the law) are able to judge what is significant and good** (an alternative translation is, 'try, have experience of, things that differ', that is, 'be acquainted with, and know the difference between, good and

19 evil'; but this is less probable); **and if you are confident that you are a guide of the blind, a light for those who are in**

20 **darkness** (cf. Isa. xlii. 6; xlix. 6; Matt. xv. 14; xxiii. 16, 24), **an instructor of fools, a teacher of babes, provided with the embodiment of knowledge and truth in the law—**. The sentence breaks off. Paul has (characteristically) forgotten how it began, and starts again.

The Jew is persuaded that in the (book of the) law he has truth in visible form. Paul does not disagree with him; he himself says little less in vii. 12, 14.

Paul does not disagree; but, with an abrupt break in the con-

21 struction, faces his compatriot with a fresh challenge. **Well, then, you who teach your neighbour, do you not teach yourself?** Since you know the truth, do you not mean to apply it? **You who preach** (κηρύσσειν, the technical term for Christian proclamation, perhaps borrowed from Jewish usage) **that men ought not to steal, do you steal?** The question to be faced here and in the next verse is whether Paul means that the Jew commits theft, adultery, and sacrilege in a literal sense. It is certainly possible to adduce instances of all three, but such instances are beside the point. Paul's argument is lost if he is compelled to rely on comparatively unusual events, and it is simply not true that the average Jewish missionary acted in this way. It was the purity of Jewish ethics (and of Jewish ethical practice as well as Jewish ethical theory) which (together with Jewish monotheism) made the deepest impression on the Gentile world. Paul's point here is the same as in *v.* 1. The fact that the actual crimes were occasionally committed adds of course some vividness to the argument, and the criminals in some sense involved the nation in their guilt; but the nation was inwardly guilty already. When theft, adultery, and sacrilege are strictly and radically understood, there is no man who is not guilty of all

three. Compare Matt. v. 21-48, and the Old Testament passages quoted below.

For theft, compare Mal. iii. 8 f. Israel as a whole has robbed God of the honour due to him; even their boasting in God (*v.* 17) is a subtle arrogance which gives to man what is due to God.

You who say that men ought not to commit adultery, 22 **do you commit adultery?** For Old Testament parallels see Hos. i-iii *passim*; Jer. iii. 8. Israel as the bride of God can hardly escape the charge of adultery.

You who regard an idol as an abomination (this attitude is written all over Jewish literature), **do you commit sacrilege?**[1] (RV: Dost thou rob temples?—but the word is conclusively proved by inscriptions and papyri to have a wider meaning.) The Jew regards an idol with horror because it claims a devotion to which only the true God is entitled; but when he exalts himself as judge and lord over his fellow-creatures he renders this devotion to—himself!

The construction changes, and this may well be taken to mean that the next sentence is not a question (though grammatically there is no reason why it should not be one) but a statement summing up the position that has now been reached. **You, who** 23 **make your boast in the law** (cf. *v.* 17), **by your transgression of the law dishonour God.** This is not merely Paul's opinion. It is the verdict of Scripture itself. **For (as Scripture** 24 **says) on your account the name of God is blasphemed among the Gentiles** (from Isa. lii. 5, quoted after the LXX rather than the Hebrew; cf. Ezek. xxxvi. 20). The greater the privilege, the greater the abuse; the revolt of the people of God is the most subtle, and the most grievous, of all.

Up to this point, Paul has dealt with the Jewish privilege of the law in general terms. Now a particular commandment is invoked—in response, we may guess, to a Jewish objector, who interrupts Paul's argument: 'You say that the Jew has no advantage over the Gentile; but we have what he has not—circumcision'. Paul replies, **Your circumcision is profitable** 25 **to you—if you practise the law.** This sentence throws light

[1] It is interesting to note that theft, adultery, and sacrilege often stand side by side in lists of vices and sins; so, e.g., Philo, *On the Confusion of Languages*, 163.

upon what Paul means by practising, or doing, the law (cf. *vv.* 14 f.). The Jew would reply to Paul that the contrast he implies, between circumcision and 'practising the law', is unreal; circumcision is part of the law, and you cannot 'practise the law' without being circumcised. But for Paul, 'doing the things which the law requires' does not mean carrying out the detailed precepts written in the Pentateuch, but fulfilling that relation with God to which the law points; and this proves in the last resort to be a relation not of legal obedience but of faith (iii. 31; x. 6 ff.). This revolutionary conviction leads to the striking conclusions stated in the remainder of the paragraph. Thus **if you are a transgressor of the law, your circumcision is turned into uncircumcision.** The Jew who boasts of his circumcision as a visible badge of his superiority, as a certain passport to salvation, thereby abandons his proper relation with God and automatically his circumcision is annulled; that is, it no longer is circumcision in the only true sense (*v.* 29). Outwardly he obeys the law, by being circumcised; inwardly he transgresses it, by failing to recognize that to which his own circumcision points, namely, the fact that he belongs completely to God and has no ground of boasting in himself.

26   To illuminate the matter further, it is possible **to take the opposite point of view,** and consider the man who does recognize and adopt the relation with God implied by the law, even though he stands outside the visible legal framework of Jewish life. **If an uncircumcised man keeps the righteous requirements of the law, will not his uncircumcision be counted as circumcision?** 'Righteous requirements' here translates the plural of the word ($\delta\iota\kappa\alpha\acute{\iota}\omega\mu\alpha$) translated at i. 32 'righteous ordinance'. The sense is, 'that which the law requires if a man is to be righteous with God'; and though one answer to this question is, a complete performance of everything written in the law (x. 5; cf. Gal. iii. 12), the new answer to which the eschatological activity of God in Jesus Christ points is—faith. If an uncircumcised Gentile has this faith (and the 'when' of the parallel in *v.* 14 suggests that the possibility is not merely hypothetical), outward circumcision becomes irrelevant; God treats him as if he were circumcised, counting him as fully a member of his people as the born Jew. 'Will ... be counted' is

significant. The passive conceals (in Semitic manner) a reference to God, and the verb 'to count', or 'to reckon' is one that appears at key-points in the epistle (see especially iv. 3). No mere fiction, but a creative act of God is meant. God, who commanded circumcision, is free to dispense with it.

Paul is not appealing for tolerance of the man who, in his uncircumcision, stands outside the religious framework of the holy people. The Jew must seek, not grant, tolerance. **The man by race** (literally, by nature; see on *v.* 14) **uncircumcised who fulfils the law** (see above on *vv.* 14, 26; Paul nowhere else uses this verb ($\tau\epsilon\lambda\epsilon\hat{\imath}\nu$) of the law; perhaps the best interpretation is 'give full effect to'—2 Cor. xii. 9; Gal. v. 16; also Rom. x. 4; James ii. 8) **will judge you** (for this use of 'judge' cf. Matt. xii. 41 f.), **who, for all your observance of the letter, and your circumcision** (cf. iv. 11, 13), **are a transgressor of the law.** Again, Paul makes clear beyond all doubt what he means by keeping, and by transgressing, the law. It is possible to neglect so weighty a command as circumcision—and fulfil the law; it is possible to observe the letter of the law, including circumcision —and transgress the law. This is not Rabbinic Judaism, or any other orthodox kind of Judaism. Paul's new Christian conviction, that Jesus, whom the law had cast out, crucified, and cursed, was the risen Lord in heaven, led him to a revaluation of religion, and in particular of the law, the basis of his own national religion, far more radical than is often perceived. He not merely had a new faith, and a new theology; in the light of these he came to the conclusion that the old faith—the Old Testament and Judaism—meant something different from what he had thought. It was not a closed system, complete in itself, requiring only strict and unimaginative obedience; for those who had eyes to see it pointed forward to Christ, and the Gospel which was the power of God unto salvation—for everyone who has faith.

Words like 'Jew' and 'circumcision' retain great significance, but they require new definitions, which Paul supplies, negatively and positively, in *vv.* 28 f. The Greek of these verses is elliptical, but the meaning is not in serious doubt. In the translation the simplest grammatical supplements are added. **Not the outward Jew is a Jew** (that is, a *real* Jew, under the new definition), **nor is outward fleshly circumcision circumcision** (that is,

29 *true* circumcision, under the new definition); **but the secret Jew is a Jew, and circumcision of the heart, in spirit not letter, is circumcision.** By the 'outward Jew' Paul does not mean simply the circumcised Jew; if he did he would merely repeat himself in the next clause. The 'outward Jew' is the Jew marked by 'works of the law', who externalizes his religion and esteems his membership of the people of God as a visible privilege which he can parade before the world. He also, of course, as Paul goes on to say, regards his circumcision as a kind of visible badge or passport.

In fact, being a Jew, being circumcised, is a matter of which the truth is known only to God, who looks on the heart. By the 'secret Jew' Paul does not mean a good, modest Jew, who does not boast of his virtues or national status. The decision upon men's modesty, as upon their other virtues and their sins, is God's; the 'secret Jew', who is the true Jew, is the man who is declared to be so by God (see further below).

'Circumcision of the heart' is an Old Testament expression; cf. Deut. x. 16, where it means (as here) man's humble response to God's gracious love and election; and Jer. iv. 4, where it means repentance.

For the contrast between spirit and letter compare vii. 6; 2 Cor. iii. 6 ff. 'Letter' was probably suggested in this verse by its occurrence in *v.* 27. In the other passages referred to, 'spirit' means the Holy Spirit, and the possibility that it does so here also cannot be excluded;[1] probably, however, the meaning is more general—'in a spiritual way'.

Paul concludes: **He is a Jew, whose due** (literally, praise) **comes not from men but from God.** There is a play upon words here; in Hebrew, 'Jew' is *yᵉhudi*, 'praise', *hodayah* (there are other cognate words, including a verbal form *yᵉhodeh*). The translation attempts to bring out this play. But though Paul uses a rhetorical trick his meaning is serious and profound, and points forward to the long discussion of God's elective purpose in chs. ix-xi. It is God, not man, who decides and knows what being a Jew means. All is of God's election, not of man's achievement; and so far as there exist visible traces of his purpose they are to

---

[1] Cf. Odes of Solomon, xi. 1 f.: 'My heart was circumcised. . . . For the Most High circumcised me by his Holy Spirit'.

be found not in human rites (even in rites commanded by God himself) but in humility before God, and in the absence of boasting—that is, in *not* judging (from an eminence of supposed superiority).

8. iii. 1-8. THE ADVANTAGE OF THE JEW

(1) **What then does the Jew possess which others have not? What profit is there in circumcision? (2) Much in every way. In the first place, they were entrusted with the oracles of God. (3) And what of that? If some have proved unbelieving, will their unbelief make void the faithfulness of God? (4) Of course not. Rather, let God be found true, though that should mean that every man (to use Scriptural language) be found a liar. Again as Scripture says, 'That thou mayest be proved right when thou speakest, and be victorious when thou enterest into judgement'.**

(5) **But if (as appears) our unrighteousness demonstrates God's righteousness, what shall we say? Is God, who inflicts his wrath, unjust? (Forgive these human arguments.) (6) Of course not; otherwise, how is God to judge the world? (7) Yes, but[1] if by my falsehood the truth of God increased and thereby increased his glory too, why am I actually judged to be a sinner? (8) And why should we not do evil that good may come of it? (That is what some of our detractors actually allege that we say; they will get what they deserve).**

The style of this paragraph is again that of the diatribe. This may be mere literary form, but it is more probable that behind the written matter there lie real debates, though it is possible that to some extent it was Paul's own mind that formulated the objections which are so eagerly brushed aside.

The argument of ch. ii seems (to the objector) to lead to the conclusion that the Jew has no advantage over the Gentile; there

---

[1] Instead of 'Yes, but' (δέ), 'for' (γάρ) is strongly supported (by B D G ω); but it gives precisely the wrong connexion between *vv*. 6 and 7.

is no good in being a Jew, and no profit (cf. ii. 25) in observing
1 the ordinances of Judaism. **What then** (in view of ch. ii) **does
the Jew possess which others have not? What profit is there
in circumcision?** If negative answers were returned to these
questions the result would be offensive not only (as is often
supposed) to Jewish national sentiment but to theology. If the
Old Testament is to be believed God did choose the Jews out of
all mankind and did bestow special privileges upon them. To
reduce them therefore to the level of other nations is either to
accuse the Old Testament of falsehood, or to accuse God of failing to carry out his plans. It is this theological objection to his
thesis that Paul is bound to meet.

2   What then is the advantage of the Jew? Paul answers, **Much
in every way.** Just as the objection is not prompted by
nationalist sentiment, so Paul's answer is not the victory of
patriotism over logic. Paul consistently maintains a real advantage for the Jew, though it is a terrible one. He is first in
election, first in judgement; instructed out of the law, judged by
means of the law. He stands, as it were, nearer to the scene on
which the divine purpose is worked out—a dangerous, but real,
privilege (cf. i. 16; ii. 9 f., 12, 18 ff., 25).

'Much in every way' is a large claim. Paul sets out as if to
support it by means of a list—**In the first place . . .**; but his
first point is never followed by a second. This is not because he
can think of only one 'advantage'—in ix. 4 f. he mentions more;
but because his thought is deflected, and he never follows out
to its conclusion the argument here begun.

The first, and all-inclusive advantage, is that the Jews **were
entrusted with the oracles of God.** In a Jewish context
'oracles' can hardly mean anything other than Scripture, and
it was to the Jews that the divine speech recorded in Scripture
was given. The parallel in ix. 4 suggests that the *whole* Old
Testament is meant. It is therefore not legitimate to restrict the
'oracles' to the law (or the ten commandments), or to the
prophecies of the Old Testament (as if the argument were, The
Jew gets no good out of the law, but he has after all the messianic
promises). To possess the law is itself an advantage. Israel
knows the mind of God (cf. ii. 18), and cannot deny the total
moral claim which he makes upon his creatures (see *vv.* 10-18).

And what of that? Paul continues in the brusque personal 3
style of the diatribe. The advantage is one which nothing can
destroy, since it depends not upon man but upon God. **If some
have proved unbelieving, will their unbelief make void
the faithfulness of God? Of course not.** 'The faithfulness of 4
God' (τὴν πίστιν τοῦ θεοῦ) could, in other contexts, mean 'faith
in God'. Here the genitive must be possessive, and the noun
must refer to the quality of faithfulness (to one's promise, or to
one's character). God has given his word, and whatever men
may do or not do, he will keep it. This is supported from
Scripture itself.

**Let God be found true, though that should mean that
every man (to use Scriptural language) be found a liar.**
Only the concluding words are drawn from Ps. cxvi. 11. The
truth, or faithfulness, of God is to be believed, even though
maintaining it (in the teeth of human unfaithfulness) leads to
the conclusion that all men are liars.

**Again as Scripture says, 'That thou mayest be proved
right when thou speakest, and be victorious when thou
enterest into judgement'.** Paul quotes Ps. li. 4, agreeing
word for word with the LXX. The Old Testament affirms that
God will always be found in the right over against men. Their
untruth and unfaithfulness will serve only to set off his faithfulness. Paul, following the Psalmist, pictures a scene in court,
where God and men plead against each other; when this happens, God is sure to leave the court in the right.[1]

The Jew then has an advantage which he can never lose, since
it rests not upon his merit but upon God's faithfulness to his
declared word. In saying this, however, Paul has laid himself
open to a new objection, brought out and answered in diatribe
style.

The objector (we may suppose) speaks: **But if (as appears)** 5
**our unrighteousness demonstrates God's righteousness,
what shall we say?** The connexion of thought is best brought
out by recalling the part of Ps. li. 4 that Paul does not quote in
v. 4. It runs: Against thee, thee only, have I sinned, and done
that which is evil in thy sight, in order that thou mayest . . .

---

[1] Literally, justified. Evidently this means not 'counted right', but
actually right, the victorious litigant. See pp. 74 ff.

(the LXX underlines the sense of purpose). Man's sin contributes to the glory of God. God might well be grateful to sinful man for bringing out more clearly than would otherwise be possible his righteousness and truth. The question may even be raised, **Is God, who inflicts his wrath, unjust?**[1] This sentence in Greek is so worded as to expect the answer No. Logically, a sentence expecting the answer Yes would have been better. Paul's objector is speaking: If my unrighteousness demonstrates God's righteousness, is not God (on your showing) unjust when he punishes me? Paul alters the expression probably out of reverence. He cannot bring himself to put on paper even the grammatical implication that God is unjust. Such alterations occur in the Rabbinic writings. Paul adds a further apology for carrying human arguments (even though they are not his own) too far: **Forgive these human arguments** (cf. 1 Cor. ix. 8; Gal. iii. 15; also Rom. vi. 19).

The real objection to Paul's case is that it impugns the moral government of the universe. It leaves God with no room to vindicate virtue and punish sin. Paul meets it with a direct

6 negative. **Of course not; otherwise** (for the Greek construction cf. xi. 6), **how is God to judge the world?** There are at least three ways of taking this rhetorical question. (1) If God is unrighteous how is he to judge . . .? (2) If God is not to use his wrath how is he to judge . . .? (3) If God does not punish Jews (as well as Gentiles) how is he to judge the *world*? Of these, (1) is certainly the most likely. We know for a fact that God is the judge of the whole earth, and we can be confident that the judge of the whole earth will do right.

The objector is not yet overcome. He cannot let go the im-

7 plications of *v.* 4. **Yes, but if by my falsehood the truth of God increased and thereby increased his glory, why am I actually** (if the order of words in Greek is strictly followed, ' I too . . .'; but this is certainly not the point) **judged to be a sinner?** The point is unchanged. The objector does not himself wish to draw blasphemous conclusions, but only to point out the dilemma in which Paul appears to be placed by his own

---

[1] The sentence would be neater and more apt if instead of ὁ ἐπιφέρων, 'who inflicts', we could read simply ἐπιφέρων, 'when he inflicts'; but the textual tradition is unanimously in favour of ὁ ἐπιφέρων.

uncompromising reference of all things to God. It is easier to bring such complaints against a profound view of the mysterious divine government of the universe than to answer them; this time Paul makes no fresh attempt to answer (see, however, the last clause of *v.* 8).

But what if the practical conclusion from these disputes is drawn? Paul turns to deal (with an embarrassment reflected in his Greek construction—it is straightened out in the translation) with an accusation which had been brought against himself. **Why 8 should we not do evil that good may come of it?** Why not increase God's goodness by contributing as generously as possible to the stock of human sin? **That is what some of our detractors actually allege that we say; they will get what they deserve.** Evidently Paul had to face the charge that he taught antinomianism, and worse. We need not doubt that some of his contemporaries thought, quite sincerely, that this was what he meant. And it may be that some members of his own churches so far misinterpreted him as to believe and teach that moral evil did not matter (cf. I Cor. v. 1-6, especially *v.* 2).

Again, Paul's answer is a simple and vigorous negative. People who will say that will say anything, and they deserve their punishment. The real answer to the question will be given in ch. vi (for the question itself see especially vi. 1, 15). It cannot be given here, because it rests upon truths of the doctrine of justification by faith which have not yet been established. Paul invokes again, as in *v.* 6, the moral government of the universe.

9. iii. 9-20. ALL HAVE SINNED

(9) What then does this amount to? That we Jews do after all stand on a higher plane than the Gentiles? By no means.[1] For we have already brought against both Jews and Greeks the common charge that they are all under

[1] Instead of the text translated above, the Western Text (D G) reads: 'What then do we Jews possess that others have not?' This seems to be an attempt to alleviate the difficulty of a very obscure passage; see the commentary.

the dominion of sin. (10) And this, moreover, is the verdict of Scripture. Hear these words of Scripture: 'There is no righteous man, not even one; (11) there is none with understanding, none that seeks after God. (12) They have all fallen away, all become worthless. There is none that practises kindness; no, there is not even one. (13) Their throat is an open grave, they practise deceit with their tongues, the poison of asps is under their lips. (14) Their mouth is full of cursing and bitterness. (15) Their feet are swift to shed blood, (16) affliction and wretchedness mark their path; (17) the way of peace they have not known. (18) There is no fear of God before their eyes.'

(19) Now we know that all the things the law says, it says to those who fall within its scope, to the intent that every mouth may be shut, and the whole world be brought to trial before God. (20) For (as Scripture itself says), 'By works of law shall no flesh be justified before him'. For in fact it is through the law that the recognition of sin comes.

The opening sentence of this paragraph is notoriously obscure, and it is impossible to feel confident that any one translation represents what Paul intends.

9 Looking back over his argument, Paul asks: **What then does this amount to?** Here we take Paul's first two words (τί οὖν) as a separate interjection. They could be taken with the main verb which follows. The principal reason for not taking them so is that if Paul had constructed his opening question in this way he would have answered it differently (οὐδὲν πάντως—'nothing at all', instead of οὐ πάντως—'by no means'). In the variant reading mentioned in the footnote, the first two words must be taken with the (different) main verb.

The main verb (προεχόμεθα) which follows the interjection can be taken in no fewer than three ways; the answer (οὐ πάντως) to the question which it asks can be taken in two ways. Our first task must be to set out the various grammatical possibilities, and then consider which of them represents what Paul wishes to say in the present context.

(1) The verb. Its form is that of the middle or the passive voice (these are identical in the present tense in Greek). (i) The

verb may be taken as having the force of a genuine middle. In this case it means, 'to offer as excuse, as self-defence'. The objection to taking it in this way is that, in this sense, it should have a direct object—one offers *something* as a defence, or excuse. An object might be found in the 'what' with which the verse opens; reason has already been given for taking this 'what' as an independent interjection, but it must be allowed that some possibility remains of taking the sentence in this way. (ii) The verb may be taken as middle with active meaning. It is so taken in the Vulgate (*praecellimus eos*). The meaning, on this view, is, 'Are we better off than they? Have we any advantage over them?' The objection to it is evident. Why, if Paul means this, did he not write the verb in the active voice ($\pi\rho o\acute{\epsilon}\chi o\mu\epsilon\nu$)?[1] (iii) The verb may be taken as passive. If it is so taken, the meaning is simply the opposite of that given in (ii): Are we excelled? There seems to be no *grammatical* objection to this.

(2) The answer. Literally rendered, Paul's words are, 'Not altogether' (cf. 1 Cor. v. 10); but there is no question that they were sometimes loosely used as if they stood in the reverse order, that is, they can mean 'Altogether not' (cf. *Diognetus*, ix. 1; Epictetus, *Enchiridion*, i. 5). Only the context can determine the meaning here.

The various grammatical possibilities are now before us. Which is most suitable to the context and to the line of thought which Paul is here pursuing? There is force in the suggestion[2] that the subject of the disputed verb must be the same as that of the verb which follows, 'We have brought the charge' ($\pi\rho o\eta\tau\iota\alpha\sigma\acute{\alpha}\mu\epsilon\theta\alpha$), that is, the 'we' must refer to Paul himself. On this view, Paul says, ironically, 'What do you think I am doing? Defending (1. i above) the Jews and their privileges? No; I have already charged both Jews and Gentiles . . .'. An objection to this way of taking the verb, however, has already been pointed out, and it is by no means unlike Paul to change subjects in the middle of a verse.

If this suggestion is rejected it seems certain that the subject of

---

[1] The Western reading mentioned in the footnote to the translation takes the sentence in this way, but removes its difficulties and ambiguity. It is no doubt a secondary reading, but bears witness to an ancient interpretation.
[2] W. Bauer, *Wörterbuch*, col. 1285.

the verb must be 'We Jews'.[1] This is supported by the fact that the charge against *Jews and Greeks* is represented as the ground of the statement that precedes it. The issue is not yet, however, closed. It will be well to set out the various possibilities.

(i) Are we Jews indulging in self-defence? Obviously not, for we have charged both Jews and Greeks. . . .

(ii a) Well, then, since there is advantage in being a Jew (*vv.* 1 f.), do we Jews excel? Not at all, for we have charged both Jews and Greeks. . . .

(ii b) . . . do we Jews excel? Only in a limited degree, for we have charged both Jews and Greeks. . . .

(iii) The question, Have Jews an advantage over Gentiles? having now been treated, we turn to the converse, Have Gentiles an advantage over Jews, who stand under the law? Not at all, for we have charged both Jews and Gentiles. . . .

Of these suggestions, (i) is not preferable to that which was rejected above. (iii) introduces a thought which seems to be alien to the context. (ii) remains, and it is in the form (ii a) that it harmonizes best with Paul's thought, which on this theme is fundamentally paradoxical. He has laid it down that the Jew has an advantage which not even his own unbelief and disobedience can take from him. Yet what does this amount to? **That we Jews do after all stand on a higher plane than the Gentiles? By no means. For we have already brought against both Jews and Greeks** (i.e. Gentiles; cf. i. 16) **the common charge that they are all under the dominion of sin.** The Jew has an advantage, and he has not an advantage. It is a serious injustice to Paul if we suppose him to have known that theological consistency could allow only the denial of all advantage to the Jew, but to have permitted a sentimental patriotism to lead him from time to time into nationalist parrot-cries which he knew in his heart and mind to be false. The advantage of the Jew is real, but it is an advantage which is (or may at any moment become) at the same time a disadvantage. It

---

[1] The suggestion that it should be 'We Christians' is attractive. Whether of Jewish or Gentile origin, even Christians are still open to the charge of sin, and can claim no superiority over their fellow-men. But if this were intended there would probably have been an emphatic 'we' (ἡμεῖς), or some other clear pointer.

consists in knowing (out of Scripture) that before God all talk of 'advantages' is folly and sin.

Paul has already (i. 18 - ii. 29) brought his charge against Jews and Greeks; but he would not have it regarded as merely an intellectual analysis of the moral life of the first century. Far more important than any such analysis is the fact that **this is the verdict of Scripture.** This is the point of the long cento which follows in *vv.* 10-18. Paul may have put the quotations together himself; it is not impossible that he drew them from an already existing florilegium. They require little comment.

Hear these words of Scripture: 'There is no righteous man, not even one; there is none with understanding, none that seeks after God. They have all fallen away, all become worthless. There is none that practises kindness; no, there is not even one.' The source of the quotation is either Ps. xiv. 1 ff. or Ps. liii. 1 ff. These passages are almost identical. The main point of interest is that Paul has introduced the word *righteous*, which is in neither the Hebrew nor the LXX Greek of either Psalm. It represents, of course, an essential element in Paul's thought. The ultimately significant question is whether man secures a favourable or unfavourable verdict in God's court.

Their throat is an open grave, they practise deceit with their tongues. From Ps. v. 9.

The poison of asps is under their lips. From Ps. cxl. 3.

Their mouth is full of cursing and bitterness. From Ps. x. 7.

Their feet are swift to shed blood, affliction and wretchedness mark their path (literally, paths); **the way of peace they have not known.** From Isa. lix. 7 f.; cf. Prov. i. 16.

There is no fear of God before their eyes. From Ps. xxxvi. 1.

Paul's Old Testament catena is at an end. What is its effect? **We know that all things the law says, it says** (or *speaks*—a different verb from the last, but Paul seems to intend no difference in meaning and the variation does not make pleasing English) **to those who fall within its scope, to the intent that every mouth may be shut, and the whole world brought to trial before God.**

Paul can on occasion (cf. 1 Cor. xiv. 21) use the word law (as the Rabbis used the word *torah*) to cover the whole of the Old Testament, the Prophets and the Writings as well as the Pentateuch. 'All the things the law says' may therefore refer to the composite quotation of *vv.* 10-18, regarded as summarizing the content of the Old Testament. But 'those who fall within its scope (literally, 'those who are in the law') must mean, 'Those who are subject to the law of Moses', that is, Jews. This might determine the earlier use of the word law. There are two possibilities. (i) The Old Testament proves that the Jews, and *a fortiori* all other men, are guilty before God. (ii) The guilt of the Jews is now proved (from the Prophets and Writings), and further we know that the law condemns them too. The latter alternative is very strained, and does not account for the '*every* mouth' and 'the *whole* world' which follow. The former is therefore to be preferred. The change which it implies in Paul's use of *law* is not a serious objection; in fact, it could in each place be translated without serious inaccuracy, 'the Old Testament religion'—which is a ministry of condemnation (2 Cor. iii. 9).

The whole world (this is proved *a fortiori*, as indicated above) is brought to trial before God. In normal Greek usage, the noun coupled with 'brought to trial' should be not the judge but the person wronged; but it can hardly be doubted that here God, though wronged, is primarily the judge. Cf. 'without excuse' in i. 20; ii. 1. No man can answer the charge.

There is no escape from this situation of silent guilt before 20 the God the Judge. **For (as Scripture itself says), 'By works of law shall no flesh be justified before him'. For in fact it is through the law that** (not righteousness but) **the recognition of sin comes.** Paul invokes Scripture once more, and quotes Ps. cxliii. 2; but introduces two significant modifications into the text he quotes. (i) He adds 'by works of law'. He cannot deny the possibility of justification altogether (indeed the Psalmist did not wish to do so), since that is the theme of his epistle, and he must therefore define the scope of the negative expressed in the Psalm. 'Works of law' are not good works simply, but works done in obedience to the law and *regarded as*, in themselves, a means of justification. (ii) Paul substitutes 'no flesh' for 'no man living'. No substantial change is made, but

70

the fact that Paul, in writing of the total failure of mankind, should choose, no doubt unthinkingly, the word 'flesh' is significant for his doctrine of the flesh; see pp. 137, 146, 148, 155-8, 162.

Paul had himself believed that righteousness (that is, a correct relation with God) was to be had on legal terms; his profounder Christian insight is that the law points out the meaning and horror of sin; see on vii. 7.

Paul began at i. 18 to describe the manifestation of God's righteousness in wrath which accompanies the manifestation of righteousness in salvation. He first depicts the operation of wrath upon the wilful sinner, then turns aside to consider the case of those who 'approve' and those who 'judge'. Of these 'judges' the supreme representative is the Jew, who takes his stand upon the law, and from that secure eminence deals out instruction to and passes sentence upon mankind. Is he really secure? Is the man of religion in a position to censure the man of the world? Are his privileges as comfortable as they appear?

Paul speaks of judgement. It is of the essence of his message that the time is come for judgement to begin at the house of God. The Jew becomes not the moral tutor but the scapegoat of humanity. His death warrant is, as it were, written into his own birth certificate. The law, the religion of the Old Testament in which he glories, accuses him, in order that the whole world may be found guilty. The Old Testament, though, when it is rightly understood, it offers justification, yet declares justification to be a universal impossibility. The law, that is the practice of religion, brings to light not righteousness but sin. As long, therefore, as God's righteousness is manifested and understood in terms of the law it must spell wrath. The only hope for man is that God should find some other means, beyond law and religion, of manifesting his righteousness.

10. iii. 21-31. THE RIGHTEOUSNESS OF GOD

(21) But now in fact God's righteousness has been manifested apart from the law, attested indeed by the law and

the prophets, (22) yet God's righteousness manifested through faith in Jesus Christ, and directed to all who have faith. All, for there is no distinction. (23) All have sinned, all lack the glory of God. (24) But they are justified, as a free gift, by God's grace, through the act of redemption which he performed in Christ Jesus. (25) This Christ Jesus God publicly set forth in his bloody sacrificial death as his means of dealing with sin, received through faith. He did this in order to show forth and vindicate his righteousness, because in his forbearance he had passed over, without punishment or remission, the sins men had committed in days gone by. (26) He did it, I say, to show forth and vindicate his righteousness in this present time, so that he might both be righteous himself, and justify the man who relies on faith in Jesus.

(27) If this is what the manifestation of righteousness, and justification, mean, where is boasting?[1] It is excluded. By what kind of law? A law based on works? No, by a law based on faith. (28) (For[2] we reckon that it is by faith, to the exclusion of works of law, that a man is justified). (29) Or does God belong to the Jews only? Is he not the God of the Gentiles also? Of course he is, (30) if indeed God is one, and will justify the circumcision by faith and the uncircumcision through faith.

(31) Do we then, by this insistence upon faith, do away with the law? Certainly not; on the contrary, we establish the law.

21   At this critical stage (see on vv. 19 f.) we find one of the great turning points of the epistle: **But now in fact.** Paul's words in Greek (νυνὶ δέ) could refer to a temporal contrast ('But at the present . . .') or to a logical contrast ('But as it is . . .'); in fact they refer to both. The contrast is not purely temporal because the manifestation of wrath (i. 18) is an eschatological event

---

[1] G lat have 'Where then is your boasting?' This points to the meaning of the better attested text, which does not contain the pronoun. Paul is addressing the Jew.

[2] 'For we reckon' is in ℵ A D G lat; B C ω have 'We reckon therefore'. The former reading gives the right connexion between vv. 27 and 28; the latter is the ground of the former, not vice versa.

taking place in the present; yet there is a temporal contrast, since the law belongs to God's dealings with Israel in old time, and Christians live no longer under the law but under grace (vi. 15).

The new, good news is that now, in the present age, **God's righteousness has been manifested apart from the law.** Compare i. 16 f., and for 'God's righteousness' see on those verses. What Paul means by the term appears best from the accounts of the acts of God given in this paragraph. It has two aspects, represented by the two clauses of *v.* 26 (on which see the notes), 'that he might be righteous himself' and 'that he might justify'. That is, it includes a *justitia passiva*—the quality of being right, or righteous, and a *justitia activa*—the activity of doing right, of delivering, of setting things and persons right. Both aspects of righteousness are revealed in the Gospel, and in the eschatological events to which it bears witness.

In i. 17 Paul said, God's righteousness is (being) revealed (ἀποκαλύπτεται, present tense). Here he says, God's righteousness has been manifested (πεφανέρωται, perfect tense). There is little difference. The present tense emphasizes the continuation of the process in the proclamation of the Gospel, the perfect the fact that the process has a beginning.

This manifestation of righteousness takes place apart from the law; not because the righteousness of God could not be manifested through the law, but because the righteousness which, when manifested through the law, could only lead to wrath (cf. iv. 15), has now been manifested in a different way so as to lead to justification.

Though God's righteousness is thus manifested apart from the law, it is nevertheless **attested by the law and the prophets,** that is, by the Old Testament as a whole. Not only do the prophecies point forward to the saving acts which have now taken place, the law itself (if only men would understand it rightly) points in the same direction. That is to say, though God's righteousness in the saving sense which it has in the Gospel is attested by the Old Testament, it is only to be understood as **God's righteousness manifested through faith in** 22 **Jesus Christ, and directed to all who have faith.** Here one element in the new, non-legal, basis of righteousness appears, namely, faith. The second is not mentioned till *v.* 24. For the meaning of faith see on i. 17. It can hardly be better defined than as the opposite of man's self-confident or self-despairing attempt to establish a proper relationship between himself and God by legal (that is, by moral or religious) means. Instead of concentrating his hope upon himself he directs it towards God, and in particular towards a creative act of God's grace (see below in the rest of this paragraph, and the discussion of Abraham's faith in ch. iv). 'Faith in Jesus Christ' is trust in him as the creative means of reconciliation provided by God. There thus exists a close inner relationship between saving righteousness and faith; only those who have faith are restored to a true relationship with God, since faith (over against works of law) is the only visible expression of that relationship. The manifestation of righteousness then is directed to all who have faith—**All, for there is no distinction,** that is, between Jew and Gentile. Paul looks back to the argument which culminates in *vv.* 19 f. There is a difference between Jew and Gentile (Ex. viii. 23), but in respect of sin each stands guilty before God.

23 **All have sinned, all lack the glory of God.** It is half correct to describe this as a reference to the eschatological glory for which man hopes (v. 2; viii. 18, 30); for man as sinner, and unbelieving, can expect no glory from God. But the present tense (*lack*) is used, and presumably means that man now lacks what he might now have had, that is, the glory with which Adam was created and which he (and all mankind with him) lost through sin. The glorious state of Adam in the Garden of Eden is a common conception in the Rabbinic literature, and in the apocalypses. Of course, the future glory may be regarded as the restoration of the lost, original, glory.

We see, then, men, revealed through the unique and ambiguous privilege of Israel as sinners, guilty before God, deprived of glory both as possession and as hope. In the next verse Paul states succinctly what he believes has happened to them. This is the heart of his Gospel.

24 **They are justified, as a free gift, by God's grace, through the act of redemption which he performed in Christ Jesus.**

No word is more characteristic of Paul's vocabulary than 'to justify' (δικαιοῦν; for other notes see on pp. 63, 87 ff., 107 f).

Before the word itself is discussed it is important to recall (see above, pp. 29 f.) that God's righteousness (δικαιοσύνη) is an eschatological quantity. It is manifested in the 'present time' only by an anticipation of the 'last time'. It implies the verdict of the last judgement, and the verb 'to justify' means an anticipation of this verdict.

Greek verbs of the class to which 'to justify' belongs (verbs in -όω) have normally a factitive, or causative, meaning. Analogy suggests therefore that from 'righteous' (δίκαιος) should be derived a verb 'to make righteous' (δικαιόω). It is, however, very generally recognized that, in Paul's usage, 'to justify' cannot mean 'to make righteous' in an ethical sense—'to make virtuous'. To mention no other consideration, the epistles depict countless Christians who, though justified, are certainly not perfectly good. Accordingly, it is often pointed out that when the Greek verbal suffix in question (-όω) is attached to adjectives denoting moral qualities the meaning is sometimes not 'to make . . .' but 'to count . . .', or 'to treat as . . .'. From this observation is drawn the most popular modern interpretation of the Pauline verb 'to justify' and the Pauline doctrine of justification. The verb means 'to count, or treat as, righteous'. Justification means that God treats sinful men as if they were of complete and unstained virtue.

Two radical objections may be brought against this interpretation. (i) On the linguistic side, it ignores the fact that behind Paul's Greek verb there lies a Hebrew verb, to which the Greek of the LXX points. This Hebrew verb (*hitzdiq*) is in the Hiph'il form, which is regularly causative in meaning; it cannot possibly be weakened so far as to mean 'to treat as righteous'. (ii) Doctrinally, it may be said that this account of justification must lead either to Pelagianism (since faith itself will be treated as a righteous work, or at least as righteousness in germ), or to the kind of legal fiction which men feel instinctively is not legitimate even for God, if he be a moral being. Not even he may pretend that black is white.

It is far better, and more in harmony with Paul's teaching as a whole, to suppose that 'to justify' (δικαιοῦν) does mean 'to make righteous', but at the same time to recognize that 'righteous' does not mean 'virtuous', but 'right', 'clear', 'acquitted' in God's court. Justification then means no legal fiction but an act of forgiveness on God's part, described in terms of the proceedings of a law court. Far from being a legal fiction, this is a creative act in the field of divine-human relations.

This creative act Paul will very shortly describe, but for the moment he emphasizes that God justifies men *as a free gift, by his grace*. The first phrase is an essential element in Paul's thought; since men are undoubtedly sinners they cannot be justified, or acquitted, on the grounds of any merit of their own. It also points to the meaning of the second. 'Grace' ($\chi\acute{\alpha}\rho\iota\varsigma$) is undoubtedly the free, gracious favour of God, the love he bestows on men while they are still sinners (v. 8); but characteristically in Paul it conveys the sense of action. Here, for example, it stands in the dative case as the instrument of God's act of justification. It operates (as Paul goes on to say) through the redemption wrought in Christ Jesus; it is thus pre-eminently, though not exclusively, an eschatological term, referring to a unique gracious activity (cf. v. 2, 15; vi. 1).

So far, then, we see God moved by love to perform an act of grace by means of which it becomes possible for him to manifest his righteousness in justification. Justification (like the 'handing over' of i. 24, 26, 28) is a verdict anticipated from the last day. It is the verdict which faith, and only faith, can hear. Outside faith, as outside grace, men can hear (out of the law) only the verdict of guilty, and the sentence of condemnation.

It has already been pointed out that even God can declare this unexpected verdict only through a creative act of his own—in Paul's words, through the act of redemption which he performed in Christ Jesus. 'Act of redemption' ($\dot{\alpha}\pi o\lambda\acute{v}\tau\rho\omega\sigma\iota\varsigma$) is, like righteousness, salvation, and wrath, an eschatological term; see viii. 23 (and cf. Eph. iv. 30; Luke xxi. 28). At Eph. i. 7 (cf. Col. i. 14) redemption is 'through the blood' of Christ; here also connexion with the death of Jesus is at hand (see *v.* 25). The word can mean simply 'deliverance', 'liberation'; the act, that is, by which God finally sets men free from bondage to evil powers and to corruption; but the connexion with blood and death suggests that it has not completely lost its original sense of 'ransoming', emancipation by the payment of a price; compare Mark x. 45; 1 Pet. i. 18 f.

Paul still has to explain how the death of Jesus was an act of redemption, capable of rectifying the relations between God and man. He says: **This Christ Jesus God publicly** 25 **set forth in his bloody sacrificial death as his means of dealing with sin, received through faith.** There is scarcely a word in this statement that could not give rise to long discussion.

'Publicly set forth' may mean more than at first appears. Paul uses his verb in the middle voice ($\pi\rho o\acute{\epsilon}\theta\epsilon\tau o$; $\pi\rho o$- in composition often signifies 'publicly'). Now it appears[1] that the same verb in the active voice sometimes means 'to offer sacrifice', or 'to offer as sacrifice' (with a direct object). Does Paul mean that God set forth Christ *as a sacrifice*? We cannot be certain that the middle has this meaning; but if it has, it only makes explicit what is implied in the reference to 'his bloody sacrificial death' (literally, his blood).

The death of Christ, thus understood, or rather, Christ thus dying, became God's 'means of dealing with sin'. This cumbersome phrase translates a single Greek word ($\dot{\iota}\lambda\alpha\sigma\tau\acute{\eta}\rho\iota o\nu$). This is derived from a verb ($\dot{\iota}\lambda\acute{\alpha}\sigma\kappa\epsilon\sigma\theta\alpha\iota$; cf. the compound $\dot{\epsilon}\xi\iota\lambda\acute{\alpha}\sigma\kappa\epsilon\sigma\theta\alpha\iota$) of which the normal meaning is 'to propitiate', 'to appease'. This verb is employed in the LXX, where, however, it commonly translates a Hebrew verb (*kipper*), whose original meaning is 'to cover over' or 'to wipe off'; hence 'to conceal' or 'to cleanse'. It is sometimes used with sin (or some such word) as its object; its meaning then naturally becomes, 'to expiate'. The common Greek meaning 'to propitiate' becomes practically impossible when, as sometimes happens, God is the subject of the verb. God cannot be said to propitiate man, still less his sin; he cleanses, and forgives, man, and expiates (wipes out) his sin. Derivatives of the form before us here (in $-\tau\acute{\eta}\rho\iota o\varsigma$) generally refer to the means by which, or the place where, an action is carried out. The word itself may be regarded as an adjective in the accusative masculine, agreeing with Christ Jesus ($\ddot{o}\nu$), or as an accusative neuter, the neuter of the adjective being used as a substantive. Christ crucified was set forth as an 'expiatory person' or as an 'expiatory agency'. We can hardly doubt (since Paul says that God set forth Christ in this capacity) that

[1] W. Bauer, *Wörterbuch, s.v.*

expiation rather than propitiation is in his mind; though it would be wrong to neglect the fact that expiation has, as it were, the effect of propitiation: the sin that might justly have excited God's wrath is expiated (at God's will), and therefore no longer does so.

Christ's death, then, has reconciling power. To say this was not to make a complete innovation in Judaism. For some time, innocent death, and especially the death of martyrs, had been considered to have atoning effect (e.g. 4 Macc. xvii. 20 ff.). It is possible that at this point a reference should be made to the Suffering Servant of Isa. liii; but Paul's language does not require it, and it is doubtful whether this passage had any great effect on his thought. See on iv. 25; viii. 32.

It is, however, possible that another Old Testament symbol is in Paul's mind. The word he employs is used, sometimes alone, sometimes as an adjective qualifying a noun meaning 'cover', to denote the lid of the Ark of the Covenant.[1] This cover was sprinkled with blood by the High Priest on the Day of Atonement; it was here that the gracious God appeared, in thick darkness, once more reconciled with his people. There is much to be said for the traditional view that Paul represented Christ as the true 'mercy-seat'. What else to a Jew represented at once the place and the means of atonement?[2] But we can go with certainty no further than the translation: God set forth Christ as the means of dealing with sin. Other allusions may be no more than overtones.

'Through faith' is not to be connected with 'in his blood'. It is through faith that the act of redemption becomes effective, because faith is the human counterpart of the divine act. See pp. 28, 73 f.

Paul has now asserted the closest possible connexion between the 'act of redemption' necessary if God is to justify sinners, and the death of Jesus; but he has not yet fully answered the question why the death of Christ should be necessary if God is to manifest his righteousness (before the due time) through the

[1] The Hebrew is *kapporeth*, from the same root as *kipper*.
[2] Cf. 1 Cor. v. 7, where Paul makes a similar passing allusion to the Passover. Professor T. W. Manson (*J.T.S.* xlvi (1945), pp. 1-10) brings out other points of comparison and contrast between this passage and the ceremonies of the Day of Atonement.

Gospel. Why should God set forth Christ crucified as the means of dealing with sin?

He did this in order to show forth and vindicate his righteousness, because in his forbearance he had passed over, without punishment or remission, the sins men had committed in days gone by.

'Show forth and vindicate' represents one Greek word (ἔνδειξις) which possesses precisely the same ambiguity as the English 'demonstrate'. It means both a simple showing forth, and also a proof, effected by showing forth. God reveals his righteousness, and thereby proves that it exists, and that it really is righteousness. This is done through the Cross. But why should it be done at all?

We meet here a major problem of exegesis, to which two quite different solutions have been propounded. The problem turns upon the meaning of two Greek words, rendered in RV 'because of the passing over' (διὰ τὴν πάρεσιν). (i) It is sometimes held that the noun has the meaning 'forgiveness' (that is, it is a synonym of the similarly formed ἄφεσις). If this view of the noun is taken, the preposition must mean 'with a view to'. Paul's meaning thus becomes: Christ died and thereby demonstrated God's righteousness in order to secure forgiveness. (ii) The alternative is to suppose that the noun means not 'forgiveness', the full remission of sins, but a mere 'passing over', or ignoring of sins—pretermission. If this view of the noun is accepted, the preposition may have its more usual meaning, 'because of', 'on account of'. Paul's meaning now becomes: Christ died and thereby manifested God's righteousness because in the past God had merely overlooked men's sins.

(ii) is undoubtedly the preferable alternative, for several reasons. That there is a real difference between the two Greek nouns mentioned above (πάρεσις and ἄφεσις) seems certain,[1] and it is hard to see why, if Paul simply means 'forgiveness', he does not use the ordinary word. Further, (ii) provides better links between this point in the argument and those which precede and follow. The question is why God manifested his righteousness in an act of redemption in Christ crucified. The answer is: In the past he had overlooked men's sins, and decisive

[1] See J. M. Creed, *J.T.S.* xli (1940), pp. 28 ff.

action was necessary if his righteousness was to be vindicated. Paul goes on to speak of 'his forbearance'; cf. ii. 4; ix. 22. The meaning is that for purposes of his own God has held his hand when he might have punished (cf. also Acts xiv. 16; xvii. 30).

Paul now repeats himself[1] in order to bring out more completely the connexion between the death of Christ and righteousness.

26 **He did it, I say, to show forth and vindicate his righteousness in this present time, so that he might both be righteous himself, and justify the man who relies on faith in Jesus.**

The first fresh point here is the explicit reference to 'the present time'. This contrasts in the first instance with the time of God's forbearance, that is, with the past. But the present time is also contrasted with the eschatological future. The manifestation of righteousness proper to the last judgement has been brought forward. The second fresh point is the clear statement of the goal intended in the demonstration of God's righteousness. It was intended to show that God (a) was righteous in himself, and (b) justified the man who relied on faith. Purpose (a) is achieved because the crucifixion shows to the full God's abhorrence of sin and his righteous judgement upon it, and at the same time indicates beyond doubt that his apparent disregard of sin in the past was due not to negligence but to mercy which patiently offered to sinners opportunity for repentance (ii. 4). Purpose (b) is achieved, because, though the crucifixion is an unparalleled demonstration of God's love (v. 8), it can be apprehended as such a demonstration only by faith which, viewing it in the light of the resurrection, sees in it God's act of redemption. Thus (cf. p. 73) the Cross vindicates both the *justitia passiva* and the *justitia activa* of God. The Cross anticipates the results of the last judgement: the Judge of all the earth is seen to do right, and, since he chooses to bear himself, in the person of his Son, the affliction antecedent to the Age to Come, he is able righteously to justify those who believe.

---

[1] Not so, according to some exegetes, who take the new reference to the demonstration of God's righteousness with his forbearance; he forbore to punish with a view to the future manifestation of his righteousness in Christ.

The present verse (26) brings us to the close of one of the most crucial and concentrated arguments in the whole epistle, and it will be well to look back over it. It has two aspects, each of which is essential to the whole.

Paul's argument is in part an anthropology. We have already traced his analysis of the human situation. The basic ill of mankind, expressed alike in sheer moral evil, in ethical criticism, and in the practice of religion, is the idolatry of self. Man, designed as God's creature to glorify his Creator, chooses rather to glorify himself, and in the end debases himself, because in so doing he contradicts his own essential nature. Obediently or disobediently, he lives 'under the law'. He may deliberately throw off the yoke, or, alternatively, suppose that by doing what he conceives to be 'right' he can secure his own position by establishing 'rights' over against God; in either case he is exercising a will-to-power (which may be described in general terms as a 'will-to-power over his environment' or in religious terms as a 'will-to-power over God') which can only be harmful because it denies the fundamental insecurity of man's position. The cure of this ill is faith, which may (up to a point) be described in terms of the old maxim, 'Know thyself'. Man's primary responsibility is to recognize his own place in the universe, and to respond to his Creator in grateful and obedient creatureliness. The man who so responds is in harmony with the universe of which he is himself a created constituent; he is what he was meant to be and is therefore at peace. He no longer uses his religion as a means to establish his rights over against God, but perceives through it that he stands under God's judgement, and instead of thinking to control God's judgement through his own activity, accepts it and submits to it, and is thereby at peace with God.

But 'Know thyself' is not the Gospel. It is impossible for man as he is to know himself, for man as he is is not 'himself', that is, he is not the person he was intended in God's purpose to be. This true self he cannot *be* but can only *become*, precisely in the moment of self-recognition, or faith. It follows that faith cannot be regarded as one more religious, or psychological, possibility, among, or additional to, all the other possibilities of human existence. Faith is a divine act. At this point we see how Paul is driven, not by the fact that he lived in the remote world of the first century but by the inward necessity of his own argument, to add to his anthropological analysis the conception (which may perhaps be described as mythical) of an act of redemption. Only in consequence of a divine invasion of the closed system of human affairs is it possible for men to believe and to be reconciled to God. In other words, 'they are justified . . . through the act of redemption which God performed in Christ Jesus'.

The climax of his argument passed, Paul turns again to his 27 Jewish hearer. **If this is what the manifestation of right-eousness, and justification, mean** (this long protasis represents the one word 'then' (οὖν), which looks back upon the whole argument), **where is boasting?** Boasting is the attitude of the natural man, who seeks to establish his position independently of God, and the only alternative to it (outside faith) is despair. Paul's answer is clear. **It is excluded.** Boasting and faith are mutually exclusive. As long as a man boasts in his own deeds, it is impossible for him to trust in God's act of redemption. He can be justified, that is, rightly related to God, only when he ceases to boast, and believes.

How does boasting come to be excluded? **By what kind of law?** Paul's answer to this question is twofold, and the two parts are separated by v. 28, which in modern book-production could best be placed in a footnote. V. 29 is the continuation of v. 27 (though v. 28 gives the ground for v. 27 b). The parenthesis may 28 be dealt with first; it sums up the argument of i. 15 – iii. 26: **We reckon that it is by faith, to the exclusion of works of law, that a man is justified.** What is to be noted here is that Paul sums up his Gospel of the redeeming activity of God as justification (not because 'justification' is itself a complete account of all that God does for men but because it is the *conditio sine qua non* of salvation), and emphasizes that justification comes only by faith. The 'only' (which Origen,[1] not Luther, was the first to bring to the interpretation of this verse) is fully warranted by Paul's own 'to the exclusion of works of law'. If anything other than faith could be the means of justification, then works done in obedience to the law, which was set forth by

[1] *Commentary on the Epistle to the Romans*, iii. 9 (Migne, *Patrologia Graeca*, xiv. 952 D), according to Rufinus's translation.

God himself, and is holy, righteous, good, and spiritual (vii. 12, 14), could justify. If these are excluded, everything is excluded, and faith alone remains. With this fact in mind we return to Paul's question.

By what kind of law is boasting excluded? **By a law based on works? No, by a law based on faith.** Many modern commentators and translators suppose that in this passage the word 'law' (νόμος) should be rendered 'principle'. There is no question that this is a proper meaning of the Greek word, or that it yields good sense. On what principle (Paul asks) is boasting excluded? On the principle of faith, not the principle of works. This rendering is attractive, but cannot be maintained in the face of two weighty objections. (i) The meaning 'principle' is too philosophical for Paul, especially in a passage such as the present. (ii) It is improbable that Paul would change his usage of the word between *v.* 27 and *v.* 28; and we cannot suppose that in *v.* 28 he means, 'to the exclusion of works of principle'. It must, however, be admitted that, since he sets over against each other two 'laws', a law based on works and a law based on faith, he cannot mean simply the Jewish law. The fact (and it will be important to remember it in the discussion of later passages; see especially on vii. 7-25) is that here and elsewhere for Paul law (νόμος) means something like 'religious system', often, of course, though not always, the religious system of Judaism. If, he argues here, religion is a matter of works, boasting is in order, since religious works, moral or ceremonial, may undoubtedly be done and therefore may be boasted of; but if religion has been transformed into a religion of faith, then by definition there are no religious works, and accordingly no ground for boasting.

Paul proceeds to the second part of his answer. **Or does God** 29 **belong to the Jews only** (that they should boast about him)? **Is he not the God of the Gentiles also?** The Old Testament itself laid down that boasting before God was intolerable; men might glory *in* God but not *before* him (e.g. Jer. ix. 23 f.). The Old Testament had also laid it down that a special relation existed between God and Israel (e.g. Ex. xix. 5 f.). But the Old Testament was misunderstood if passages such as these were taken to mean that God was a private possession of the Jews on

which they might pride themselves over against the Gentiles.
30 **Of course he is** the God of the Gentiles also, **if indeed God is
one,** as the Old Testament itself declares (e.g. Deut. vi. 4).

No Jew would have denied that God is one, and that he is
Lord over the Gentiles as well as the Jews. Paul's addition to
this common faith follows. Jew and Gentile are equal before
God, and neither is in a position to boast, because God **will
justify the circumcision by faith and the uncircumcision
through faith.** 'By faith' and 'through faith' are not to be
distinguished. The change of preposition is only a rhetorical
device (cf. iv. 11; v. 10; 1 Cor. xii. 8; 2 Cor. iii. 11), and it is the
foundation of Paul's argument that for circumcised and uncircumcised alike there is but one way to justification, the way of
faith alone.

It is comparatively easy thus to set aside the natural human
desire, which becomes visible in Judaism but is felt universally,
to have a ground of boasting; but the exclusion of works of law
(*v.* 28) raises a far more serious problem than this (cf. on *v.* 1).
31 **Do we then, by this insistence upon faith, do away with
the law?** The objection would be grave enough if 'the law'
meant simply the Old Testament (cf. *v.* 19), for the Old Testament is the 'oracles of God' (*v.* 2), and if it were proved wrong
God's word would be shown to be untrue. But it is probable
that 'law' (as in *vv.* 27 f.) means both more and less than this.
It is not simply the written record of God's revelation of himself to man, but the whole system of religious thought and
practice based upon this revelation—in a word, the religion of
Judaism. Does the Gospel thus cut away the ground from under
its own feet? **Certainly not; on the contrary, we establish
the law.** Here again, 'the law' is not simply the Old Testament, which Paul believes to be fulfilled in the saving events of
the New Testament, and especially in the person of Jesus
Christ himself (2 Cor. i. 20). The full meaning of religion is to
be found and understood in the Gospel, to which the law *as law*
also points.

'The law' is not simply the Old Testament; but the Old
Testament is the visible expression of it, and it is to the Old
Testament that Paul now turns to support his emphatic asser-
tion that faith does not do away with the law.

11. iv. 1-12. ABRAHAM JUSTIFIED BY FAITH

(1) What then shall we say that Abraham (on human terms, our ancestor) has found?[1] **(2) For if Abraham was justified on the ground of works, then after all he has something to boast of. But in fact before God he has no such ground of boasting. (3) For what does the passage of Scripture say? 'Abraham had faith in God, and that was counted to him as righteousness.' (4) Now to a man who does works, his pay is not 'counted' as a matter of grace, but as a due; (5) but to a man who does no works, but has faith in him who 'justifies the ungodly', his faith is counted as righteousness. (6) It is in this way that David speaks of the blessing of the man to whom God 'counts' righteousness apart from works: (7) 'Blessed are they whose iniquities have been forgiven and whose sins have been covered over; (8) blessed is the man whose[2] sin the Lord will not count'. (9) Is this blessing then valid for the circumcision only? or for the uncircumcision too? For the latter also, for we can say, 'His faith was counted to Abraham as righteousness'. (10) In what state was he then when it was counted? In a state of circumcision, or of uncircumcision? Not in a state of circumcision, but in a state of uncircumcision. (11) And he received the sign of circumcision as a seal of the righteousness which came from faith, the faith he had while still uncircumcised. This was in order that he might be the 'father' of all**

---

[1] The word (εὑρηκέναι) translated 'has found' is placed in this position by one group of MSS. (א A D G), in a different place by another group (ω: 'What then shall we say that Abraham our ancestor has found on human terms?'); and is omitted altogether by a third (B 1739: 'What then shall we say of Abraham (on human terms, our ancestor)?'). It is tempting to suggest that the short text is original and that the word which is inserted in different places came into the text from the margin. But Lietzmann is probably right in the view that the text as translated here is original; the reading of ω is an error which produced a senseless text, emended by the omission of the offending word.

[2] 'Whose sin the Lord will not count'; so B א D G, a strong combination of Western and Alexandrian authorities. Alternatively, but less probably, 'To whom (ᾧ for οὗ) the Lord will not count sin' (A C ω). The latter reading is probably due to assimilation.

who, in a state of uncircumcision, have faith, that righteousness may be counted to them, (12) and the 'father' of the circumcision—of those, that is, who do not rely on circumcision only but also follow[1] in the footsteps of the faith our father Abraham had while still uncircumcised.

The last verse of ch. iii has been represented above as the transition from Paul's discussion of justification by faith through God's act of redemption in Christ to the present chapter. Paul vigorously denies that his preaching of faith does away with the law; rather, it establishes the law. It is, however, important to understand what he means by this. If he means that he now proposes to re-establish legal means to justification he is contradicting himself, and must be dismissed as a writer who does not understand the words he uses. But the 'law' he establishes is not a religion of legalism, but the religion of the Old Testament *properly understood*.

In any discussion of the Old Testament and its religion, Abraham must be allowed to be a central figure. He was the father of the race (Isa. li. 1 f.), and perfectly righteous (e.g. *Kiddushin*, iv. 14: We find that Abraham our father had performed the whole law before it was given, for it is written, Because that Abraham obeyed my voice and kept my charge, my commandments, my statutes, and my laws (Gen. xxvi. 5)). In particular, he was the type of absolute trust in God (e.g. *Aboth*, v. 3: With ten temptations was Abraham our father tempted, and he stood steadfast in them all). The Hellenistic synagogue pursued the same theme in its own way by representing Abraham as the fulfilment of all the (Greek) virtues (Philo, *Abraham*, 52 ff.; Josephus, *Antiquities*, i. 256).

The present paragraph opens in the style of the diatribe (see p. 43), and we may suppose that the figure of Abraham is invoked by a Jewish objector. Paul takes up the challenge. **What then shall we say that Abraham (on human terms, our ancestor) has found?** Paul is bound to allow that *on human*

---

[1] This sense, or any other, can only be obtained by omitting one Greek word (the τοῖς before στοιχοῦσιν). There is no question that this is the right course.

terms Abraham is the ancestor of the Jewish race; he will have more to say on the question of the descendants of Abraham below (*vv.* 11 f.; ix. 6-13; cf. Gal. iii. 7; iv. 21-31).

The objector is allowed to speak first: You say that men are justified by faith only, and that therefore no boasting is possible; yet **if Abraham was justified on the ground of works, then** 2 **after all he has something to boast of.** It is clear that Paul must prove the contrary of this, and from Scripture, but he begins by merely stating his case. **But in fact before God he** (Abraham) **has no such ground of boasting.**

There are two ways of translating this last sentence, and connecting it with that which follows. One is that which is adopted here; the 'for' (γάρ) with which *v.* 3 begins is then a genuinely argumentative particle: Abraham has no ground of boasting before God, *for* Scripture says. . . . The alternative translation would run: Yes, Abraham would then have some ground for boasting, but on the human level only; not before God. This translation evacuates the particle (γάρ) of argumentative force, and we should have to continue, But what in fact does the Bible say? This does not seem a probable connexion, and is also open to the objection that it introduces a distinction (boasting before God, and before men) which does not seem to be in Paul's mind. It is therefore better to maintain the rendering given here. Paul is arguing, and his argument, here at least, is not so disconnected as is sometimes thought.

Abraham then (whatever the Jew may think) cannot boast before God. **For what does the passage of Scripture** 3 (relevant to the matter) **say? 'Abraham had faith in God, and that was counted to him as righteousness'.** The reference is to Gen. xv. 6 (Paul follows the LXX in using the passive ('was counted') rather than the active ('he counted it'— RV)). The force of Paul's 'for' has already been discussed; he is using his quotation as the basis of his proof that not even Abraham was in a position to boast before God. But for this purpose he finds it necessary to establish his own interpretation of the passage, for according to current Jewish interpretation the 'faith' spoken of in it was not faith in Paul's sense but a meritorious work (e.g. 1 Macc. ii. 51 f.: . . . the deeds of the fathers. . . . Was not Abraham found faithful in temptation, and it was reckoned unto him for righteousness? See S.B. iii. 199 ff.; J. B. Lightfoot, *Galatians*, pp. 158-64).

Paul's first step is to fasten upon the verb 'to count'. Evidently, if faith is 'counted' as righteousness it is not itself identical with, but distinguishable from, righteousness. The argument which follows is somewhat hurried, and to some extent confused, but it is possible to make the necessary logical supplements without great difficulty. Paul introduces the word 'pay', or 'reward' ($\mu\iota\sigma\theta\acute{o}s$), to make his point clear, drawing it probably from the LXX of Gen. xv. 1: Thy reward ($\mu\iota\sigma\theta\acute{o}s$) shall be exceedingly great (RV: I am thy shield, and thy exceed-

4 ing great reward; but see RV mg). He begins: **To a man who does works, his pay is not 'counted' as a matter of grace, but** is paid **as a due.** The contrast between 'as a matter of grace' and 'as a due' is instructive. 'Works' and 'due' belong together as correlatives; 'faith' and 'grace' similarly correspond, and it is to this pair that 'counting' belongs. It follows that since Abraham had righteousness *counted* to him, he cannot have done works, but must have been the recipient of grace. This is indeed the next stage in the argument, but Paul does not stay to state it. Instead of saying, 'But to him who does no works but has faith the reward (pay) is counted as a matter of grace', he

5 takes the next step in his stride: **But to a man who does no works, but has faith in him who 'justifies the ungodly', his faith is counted as righteousness.** This verse presupposes the conclusion already arrived at: faith and works are opposites, and Abraham is to be found among those who do not perform works with a view to justification but put their trust in God himself. This faith is counted as righteousness; that is, God justifies the man who has it, pronouncing over him a favourable verdict.

In this verse, the three words 'justifies the ungodly' are a very striking allusion to the Old Testament. They describe God as doing what the Old Testament forbids. Thus:

Ex. xxiii. 7: I will not justify the wicked (LXX: Thou shalt not justify the ungodly).

Prov. xvii. 15: He that justifieth the wicked, and he that condemneth the righteous, both of them alike are an abomination unto the Lord. Cf. xxiv. 24.

Isa. v. 23: Woe unto them . . . which justify the wicked for a reward, and take away the righteousness of the righteous from him.

The force of these passages is clear. They indicate (i) that 'to justify' is a forensic term, which does not mean 'to make (ethically) righteous' but 'to acquit'; and (ii) that Paul is describing a divine act absolutely paradoxical in its mercy and grace. Compare v. 8.

Paul has now reached the second step in the argument by which he establishes his own interpretation of Gen. xv. 6. It consists in the application of a Rabbinical exegetical principle known technically as *g^ezerah shawa'*.[1] According to this principle (the second of Hillel's *Middoth*), when the same word occurs in two biblical passages, each can be used to illuminate the other. The word in Gen. xv. 6 that most requires elucidation is 'counted'; Paul proceeds to quote another passage in which the same word occurs.

It is in this way that David speaks of the blessing of the 6
man to whom God 'counts' righteousness apart from
works: 'Blessed are they whose iniquities have been for- 7
given and whose sins have been covered over; blessed is 8
the man whose sin the Lord will not count'. The quotation is from Ps. xxxii. 1 f., given in exact agreement with the LXX.

The conclusion to be deduced from this *g^ezerah shawa'* is that the 'counting of righteousness' is equivalent to the 'not-counting of sin'. It becomes clearer and clearer that justification, or the counting of righteousness, is neither the just evaluation of human merit (such as the Jew supposes Abraham to have had), nor the imparting of virtue, but forgiveness or acquittal. The man is justified, whose iniquities have been forgiven and whose sins have been covered over. The last verb recalls the description of Christ crucified as God's means of dealing with sin (see on iii. 25).

So far Paul has used, first, general methods, and, secondly, a *g^ezerah shawa'* to interpret Gen. xv. 6. He now sees an oppor-

[1] For an account of this exegetical principle, see my *The New Testament Background: Selected Documents* (1956), p. 146. For its application to Rom. iv, see J. Jeremias in *Studia Paulina in honorem J. de Zwaan* (1953; edited by J. N. Sevenster and W. C. van Unnik), pp. 149 ff.

tunity of carrying his argument yet further by applying his *gᵉzerah shawa'*, as it were, in reverse; Gen. xv. 6 can be used to illuminate Ps. xxxii. 1 f.

9 **Is this blessing** (the blessing of forgiveness of which David speaks) **then valid for the circumcision only? or for the uncircumcision too?** There is nothing in the Psalm to enable us to answer this question. Indeed, since David was a Jew we might suppose that he was writing of a peculiarly Jewish privilege. But application of the *gᵉzerah shawa'* provides a different answer. **For the latter also** (these words are not in the text but are clearly presupposed), **for we can say, 'His faith was counted to Abraham as righteousness'.** The quotation is not, as is sometimes thought, a mere parenthesis, but an essential step in the argument. The word 'counted' takes us from Ps. xxxii to Gen. xv, and the question that could not be answered in regard to the Psalm admits of an easy solution in the other

10 passage. **In what state was he then when it was counted? In a state of circumcision, or of uncircumcision? Not in a state of circumcision, but in a state of uncircumcision.** This is a simple statement of fact; the circumcision of Abraham does not take place till Gen. xvii. In terms of religion (though not, of course, of race) he was a Gentile when God counted his faith as righteousness.

V. 11a is a parenthesis to which we must return presently. The argument continues in *v.* 11b.

11 **This was in order that he might be the 'father' of all who, in a state of uncircumcision, have faith, that right-**
12 **eousness may be counted to them, and the 'father' of the circumcision—of those, that is, who do not rely on circumcision only but also follow in the footsteps of the faith our father Abraham had while still uncircumcised.** Here the word 'father' is taken from the promise made to Abraham which is quoted fully in *v.* 17.

That Abraham is the father of the Jewish people is of course a commonplace (*v.* 1). He was also regarded by the Rabbis as the first proselyte, and thus as the father of proselytes (e.g. *Mᵉkhilta* Ex. xxii. 20 (101a): Abraham called himself a proselyte (*ger*), for it is written, I am a stranger (*ger*) and a sojourner with you (Gen. xxiii. 4)). Paul's words thus bear a superficial similarity to those of the Rabbis; but the substance is completely different. (i) Abraham is not the father of Jews first, and then, in a derivative way, the father of Gentile proselytes also. He is first of all the father of believing Gentiles. (ii) He is their father not on the ground of their circumcision but on the ground of their faith. Not outward incorporation into the visible ranks of Israel 'after the flesh' by means of an ancient ceremony, but the trustful and obedient acceptance of God's word admits them to the family of God's people. (iii) In like manner, the privilege of descent from Abraham is accorded to Jews not in virtue of their birth and circumcision but in virtue of their faith (cf. ix. 6-13). They must 'join the ranks' (the words translated 'follow in the footsteps' suggest the metaphor of soldiers walking in file) of faith; and faith is (as the example of Abraham shows) independent of circumcision.

The story of Abraham shows, therefore, not what the Jewish objector (see pp. 86 f.) thinks, but that for Jew and Gentile alike there is but one way to justification, the way of faith alone. This result, however, raises acutely the question to which Paul has already given his answer in the parenthesis of *v.* 11 a. If Abraham was already justified by faith, and if circumcision in itself cannot justify, why was Abraham circumcised? This question derives its force (cf. on iii. 1) from the fact that Abraham's circumcision was performed in obedience to a divine command (Gen. xvii. 10-14, 23-7). It must therefore have had some good meaning.

Paul's answer is that Abraham **received the sign of circumcision as a seal of the righteousness which came from faith, the faith he had while still uncircumcised.**

'Sign of circumcision' means simply a 'sign consisting in circumcision'. That circumcision was such a sign appears immediately from the biblical text (Gen. xvii. 11), and was universally recognized. It was the badge of Judaism (e.g. Jubilees xv. 26: . . . nor is there any sign on him [the uncircumcised man] that he is the Lord's).

This sign Abraham received as a *seal*. The question raised here is whether 'sign' and 'seal' are synonyms, or 'seal' adds a further thought not contained in 'sign'. It is sometimes stated that the Jews regarded circumcision as more than a sign, a seal which actually conveyed divine grace. This is, however, more easily stated than proved. Perhaps the strongest evidence in support of it is found in the Christian writer Barnabas, who puts into the mouth of a Jewish objector the words (ix. 6), 'The people have been circumcised as a seal'. The Jewish evidence itself is too late to prove that the Jews spoke of circumcision as a seal in New Testament times. It is a reasonable conjecture (though hardly more) that the Jews did so speak; then dropped 'seal' as a description of circumcision when the Christians began to use it for baptism (see J. B. Lightfoot, *Apostolic Fathers*, I. ii. 226); and finally revived their old custom when Church and Synagogue had separated. But in any case there is no need to suppose that 'seal' here means more than it does elsewhere in Paul's writings, namely, confirmation. Thus, for example, he writes at 1 Cor. ix. 2, The seal of mine apostleship are ye in the Lord—that is, the very fact that you are Christians confirms by an evident token the fact that I am an apostle. In a similar way, Abraham's circumcision did not confer righteousness upon him, and was not a token that he was obliged henceforth to keep the law in order to be justified, but confirmed by a visible sign the fact that he had already been justified by faith. Thus, like the whole paragraph, this parenthesis inverts the argument of Paul's Jewish objector. Abraham's circumcision, rightly understood, confirms not the doctrine of justification by works of law, but that of justification by faith.

12. iv. 13-25. FAITH AND PROMISE

(13) For the promise that he should be heir of the world was not granted to Abraham or to his seed in the context of law but in the context of faith-righteousness; (14) for if those who rely on the law are heirs, then faith has been emptied of its meaning and the promise has been brought to nothing. (15) For the law produces wrath; and[1] where

---

[1] Instead of 'and' (or 'but'—the Greek is δέ), the Western text and other authorities (D G ω lat pesh) have 'for' (γάρ). This variant may be correct; if not, it is correct interpretation, if, as is probable, the sense is that the law produces wrath by producing transgression.

there is no law, neither is there transgression. (16) Therefore God's plan was made to rest upon faith in order that it might be a matter of grace, so that the promise might be secure for all the seed—not only to that part of the seed which is able to rely on the law, but also to that which relies on the faith of Abraham, who is the father of us *all* (17) (as it is written, 'I have appointed thee as father of many Gentiles'), before God, in whom he believed, God, who quickens the dead and calls into being the things which do not exist. (18) This Abraham believed, hoping against hope, so as to become the 'father of many Gentiles' (according to the Scripture word, 'So shall thy seed be'). (19) He considered[1] without weakening in his faith that his own body was as good as dead (since he was about a hundred years old), and also the dead state of Sarah's womb. (20) Looking rather to God's promise he did not waver in unbelief, but gave God the glory, (21) was fully convinced that what God had promised he had the power also to do, and grew strong in faith. (22) That is why 'it was counted to him for righteousness'. (23) Now it was not on his account only that it was written, 'It was counted to him', (24) but on ours also. Our faith is to be counted to us, who believe in him who raised up from the dead Jesus our Lord, (25) who was delivered up because of the sins we had committed, and raised up because of the justification that was to be granted to us.

The paragraph falls into three parts. The first is *vv.* 13-18: it provides a further argument for the view (already set forth in *vv.* 1-12) that God's relations with Abraham were not on a basis of law. They were based on promise, and the correlates of promise are grace and faith. In *vv.* 17 f., at the end of the first part, Paul begins to deal with the question what faith (and in

---

[1] 'He considered': the Western text (D G ω it) contains a negative, 'he did not consider'. Though opposite to each other, both readings give good sense. 'He considered ... and yet did not lose faith', or, 'He was so strong in faith that he did not even consider ...' The latter is perhaps a little more obvious, and does not give as pointed a contrast with *v.* 20 as does the former, which may therefore be preferred. Perhaps also the Western reviser recalled that according to Gen. xxv. 1 ff. Abraham was still to marry Keturah and to have by her six quite non-miraculous children!

particular Abraham's faith) is. He continues this question, and its answer, up to *v.* 22. The remaining part, *vv.* 23 ff., applies to Christians what has hitherto been said about Abraham.

Abraham received a promise. Paul never quotes it exactly or in full, but it is important to have in mind (as Paul doubtless had) the whole of Gen. xxii. 17 f.:

> In blessing I will bless thee, and in multiplying I will multiply thy seed as the stars of the heaven, and as the sand which is upon the sea shore; and thy seed shall possess the gate of his enemies; and in thy seed shall all the nations of the earth be blessed.

Was this promise, like the 'counting' of righteousness (Gen. xv. 6), a matter of faith only, or was it perhaps dependent upon Abraham's observance of the law? Paul can no longer use the argument of *v.* 10, because in Gen. xxii Abraham has already been circumcised. Moreover, the promise follows and is dependent upon an act (the offering of Isaac) which, though Paul might regard it as a signal instance of faith (as in Heb. xi. 17 ff.), was regularly viewed in Judaism as a supremely meritorious work. Perhaps then the promise is a reward for a good work done in obedience to law.

13 The answer is a direct negative. **The promise that he should be heir of the world was not granted to Abraham or to his seed in the context of law but in the context of faith-righteousness.** 'Heir of the world' is probably drawn from Gen. xxii. 18 ('all the nations') and xxii. 17, where in the LXX 'shall possess' becomes 'shall inherit'. Paul uses it to summarize the content of the promise. 'In the context of' translates a Greek word ($\delta\iota\acute{a}$) which means most simply 'through'. It is often used, however, to denote 'attendant circumstances' (e.g. at ii. 27), and the question here is whether the promise falls within the domain of law, or within that of the righteousness of faith.

Having given his answer Paul justifies it by carefully defining

14 his terms. **For if those who rely on the law are heirs, then faith has been emptied of its meaning and the promise has been brought to nothing.** The main point here can be put in the form of counter-questions: What do you mean by a promise?

and, What do you mean by faith? It is fundamentally the same as that of *vv.* 4 f. A promise is not a contract of payment to be made for work done. That would be not a promise but a legal or commercial agreement. A promise falls within the sphere of gift, that is, of grace (cf. iii. 24). Again, if a man has made a contract with his employer he knows that his employer as well as himself is legally bound by the contract. He does not *believe* that he will receive his pay; he *knows* that (provided he keeps his side of the contract) he will receive it. If then it should be true that the way to be an heir (in the terms of the promise) is to keep the law, we can only conclude that the terms 'faith' and 'promise' have lost their meaning.

A second argument is added parenthetically in *v.* 15. It interrupts the connexion between *vv.* 14 and 16, but may be taken here. Its opening word 'for' looks back to *v.* 13; it is a further ground for the dogmatic pronouncement of that verse.

For the law produces not promise but **wrath; and where** 15 **there is no law, neither is there transgression.**

Paul seems here to be anticipating material which he brings out more fully in v. 12 ff.; vii. 7-13—see the notes on these passages. The purpose of the law was to show how exceedingly sinful sin was by actually producing and increasing transgression, which of course is naturally and rightly visited with God's wrath—a very different matter from his promise. Law, though good in itself (vii. 12, 14) is so closely bound up with sin and wrath that it is unthinkable that it should be the basis of the promise.

Paul now returns to the main line of his argument and his thought becomes clearer, though the new sentence is grammatically imperfect.

Therefore looks back to *v.* 14, with which *v.* 16 is closely 16 connected. Paul insists that promise, faith, and grace belong inseparably together.

God's plan was made to rest upon faith on man's side **in order that** on God's **it might be a matter of grace.** A literal translation of this part of the verse would run, 'Therefore of faith, in order that by grace'. The supplements made in the translation are justified by the context. Instead of 'God's plan' it would be possible to supply 'the promise', but Paul's thought is broadening here, and the wider term is to be preferred. If, on man's side, the plan rested on, for example, works of law, God would be obliged to pay the reward under constraint, not freely; only when we recognize that it rests upon faith alone, can God's freedom in grace be maintained; only so can God truly be God.

Paul continues: all this was done, **so that the promise might be secure for all the seed—not only to that part of the seed which is able to rely on the law, but also to that which relies on the faith of Abraham.** It is clear that if the promise had been based upon law only those who had the advantage of possessing the law could hope to inherit the promise. But (as Paul will presently show from Scripture) the promise was intended for Gentiles as well as Jews; hence it was necessary that it should not be based on law. Only on the basis of faith and grace could the promise be secure for all who were destined to inherit.

The argument is closed by the proof that Abraham **is the**
17 **father of us all (as it is written, 'I have appointed thee as father of many Gentiles').** Abraham is the father of *all*—of believing Jews and Gentile Christians; see on *v.* 11. This is proved by Gen. xvii. 5, where the LXX renders the word 'nations' by the word which to Paul regularly means 'Gentiles' (ἔθνη). Abraham is thus proved by Scripture itself to be the father of non-Jews.

Paul's argument is now essentially complete. It is proved that the promise (like justification) rests upon faith because (a) only grace and faith are congruous with promise; (b) only on the basis of grace and faith can Gentiles be admitted (as Scripture demands that they should) as fellow-heirs with Jews; and (c) the law (the only serious alternative to grace and faith) is known to produce not promise but wrath. The apostle ties up a loose end by showing that Abraham himself holds his position as father of the 'heirs' not in his own right, but by faith.

Abraham is the father of Jewish and Gentile Christians not in virtue of any human relationship with them but **before God, in whom he believed, God, who quickens the dead and calls into being the things which do not exist.** In this verse and the following Paul has in mind the story of the birth (and perhaps also of the intended sacrifice; cf. Heb. xi. 19, and see below, p. 99) of Isaac, the child of promise. This theme is developed further in *vv*. 19 ff. The God to whom Abraham's faith was directed quickens the dead. Further, he calls into being things which do not exist (this is the only translation of Paul's words that makes sense, and the linguistic difficulty is not insuperable; see Lietzmann, and cf. Barnabas vi. 13); he is the Creator, and faith means reliance upon his creative power. The man who believes has his attention turned away from himself and fixed upon God as the only source of life. It was such faith as this that made Abraham the father of believers, according to the promise.

This Abraham believed, hoping against hope, so as to 18 **become the 'father of many Gentiles' (according to the Scripture word, 'So shall thy seed be').** Paul alludes again to Gen. xvii. 5, and, in the last five words, to Gen. xv. 5.

'Hoping against hope' is a neat rhetorical phrase, which may be compared with 'on the basis of nothing but faith' (i. 17). Literally it runs, 'Against (or, beyond) hope, in hope'. The two 'hope's' are different; it is when human hope is exhausted that God-given hope (cf. viii. 24 f.) comes into effect; in the midst of human death and non-existence it looks to God, who quickens and creates.

In completing his argument about the promise Paul has already, in *vv*. 17 f., begun to discuss the meaning of faith. He carries the discussion further in *vv*. 19 ff., first emphasizing the scene of human death in which faith is exercised. Abraham **considered** (see note (2) on p. 93) **without weakening in his** 19 **faith that his own body was as good as dead (since he was about a hundred years old), and also the dead state of Sarah's womb** (Sarah was ten years younger than her husband —Gen. xvii. 17). The procreation of new life in these circumstances was impossible. But the promise had been given, and this, not human weakness, was the decisive consideration. **Looking rather to God's promise he did not waver in un-** 20 **belief, but gave God the glory, was fully convinced that** 21 **what God had promised he had the power also to do, and grew strong in faith.**

'Not wavering' and 'being fully convinced' appear to correspond; but in fact the translation of the latter is not certain. The word ($\pi\lambda\eta\rho o\phi o\rho\epsilon\hat{\iota}\nu$) when used, as here, in the passive, can mean 'to be full of', and is used with moral attributes (e.g. love, at 1 Clement liv. 1). An analogous use ('to be full of *the idea of doing* something') points to the meaning here: Abraham was full (of confidence) that God . . . Compare xiv. 5 and the note.[1]

By his unwavering confidence that God could and would fulfil his promise, Abraham gave glory to God; that is, he did precisely what the unbelievers of i. 21 did not do. He recognized God as God; the Creator, as such altogether different from creation, powerful where men are weak, living where they are dead. Only faith can so give glory to God; to perform 'works of law' with a view to establishing a claim upon him, or to throw off all sense of obligation to him, is to dishonour God.

When Paul adds that Abraham grew strong in faith he does not mean that on account of his faith Abraham became a strong man, a forceful 'personality'. It was in his faith that he was strong, unlike those (mentioned in chs. xiv, xv, where see the notes) who were 'weak in faith'. These were scrupulous persons, whose faith was still mingled with legalistic righteousness. Faith (in Paul's sense) grows stronger as it is unmixed with confidence in any thing or any one other than God himself.

Paul concludes his argument about Abraham by quoting again the passage from Gen. xv. 6 with which he opened the dis-
22 cussion. **That is why** (because Abraham's faith was what it was, the complete submission to God which is the human reflection of a right relationship with him) **'it was counted to him for righteousness'**.

Paul's discussion of Abraham is nowhere a purely historical investigation, for Abraham believed, and was justified, not as a private individual but as the father of believers. At this point, however, Paul begins to apply in express terms what he has deduced about faith from the story of Abraham to Christian
23 believers in his own age. **Now it was not on** Abraham's **account only that it was written, 'It was counted to him'** (these key words are intended to bring to mind the whole Old

[1] See the admirable discussion in W. Bauer, *Wörterbuch, s.v.*

Testament basis of the argument), **but on ours also.** The 24
principle of justification by faith cannot apply to one man only;
if true at all, it must be universally true. **Our faith is to be
counted** (this futuristic expression looks forward with confidence to God's vindication at the last judgement of those whom
he has chosen) **to us, who believe in him who raised up
from the dead Jesus our Lord.** Our justification is the same
as Abraham's, for it is rooted in the free and gracious will of
God, who counts faith as righteousness. Our faith is the same as
Abraham's, for it is in the same God, whose properties are unchanged—he is the God who brings life out of death. But for
Christians this power of the living God can no longer be
described in terms of the unexpected birth of Isaac from aged
parents. That which the Old Testament foreshadowed has
become manifest in the death and resurrection of Jesus, in which
God raised up his own Son not from a dead womb but from the
grave.

The parallelism between Isaac and Jesus would be even
closer if it could be maintained that Paul had in mind the
'binding of Isaac', which from time to time plays an interesting
part in Rabbinic theology. It is just possible that this theme is
in mind in *v.* 25; rather more likely that it appears in viii. 32.
But Paul makes no serious use of it; like the 'Noachian precepts'
(see on ii. 14 f.) it is material he might have been expected to
use, but in fact leaves out of account. His concern is with Jesus
himself, rather than with analogies to him and his experiences;[1]
he means to insist that the God in whom Christians believe is
indeed the God of Abraham, now made known by an even
clearer, and universally valid and effective, demonstration of his
life-giving and creative power than was vouchsafed to Abraham.

Having mentioned Jesus and the resurrection Paul winds up
the chapter by using what appears to be a Christological
formula, though its history before its use by Paul must remain a
matter of speculation. Jesus Christ **was delivered up because** 25
**of the sins we had committed, and raised up because of
the justification that was to be granted to us.**

In 'delivered up' some see an allusion to Isa. liii. 12 (LXX):

---

[1] The parallel and contrast with Adam in v. 12-21 stands on a different
footing; see the notes.

His soul was delivered up unto death. This is not impossible, but compare 2 Cor. iv. 11, where the same verb is used in the first person plural present.

The word (διά) which here is twice translated 'because of' may have retrospective or prospective reference. Here it is taken to be retrospective in the first occurrence, prospective in the second. If this change of reference seems too harsh, the word may at its first occurrence also be taken as prospective—'he was delivered up with a view to dealing with our (future) sins'. It is very unlikely that Paul meant anything so artificial as, 'He died on account of the sins which we had committed, and was raised on account of our justification (which by dying he had already accomplished)'. On the whole, it seems best to translate as here, and to recognize in the doubled 'because of' an attempt at rhetorical antithesis in a credal formula.

The same rhetorical motive accounts for the apparent separation of the death and resurrection of Christ. Paul does not mean to ascribe one consequence to the death, another to the resurrection. The two events jointly were responsible for both consequences.

13. v. 1-11. JUSTIFICATION AND SALVATION

(1) Since then we have been justified on the basis of faith we have[1] peace with God through our Lord Jesus Christ. (2) It is moreover through him that we have gained our access to this grace in which we now stand, and, looking to the future, exult in our hope of the glory of God. (3) Further, we even exult in our afflictions, because we know that affliction produces endurance, (4) and endurance tried character, and tried character hope; (5) and our hope is not one that can put us to shame, for God's love for us has already been poured out in our hearts through the Holy Spirit who was given to us. (6) For

---

[1] The great majority of MSS. have not 'we have' but 'let us have'. This variant has such an important bearing on the sense of the passage that it must be discussed in the Commentary proper.

while we were still[1] powerless, at the due moment Christ died for us ungodly men. (7) For scarcely will anyone die for a righteous man / for on behalf of a good man someone might even dare to die, (8) but God proves his love for us by the fact that while we were still sinners Christ died for us. (9) Since then we have now been justified at the cost of his blood, much more shall we be saved through him from God's wrath; (10) for if when we were enemies we were reconciled to God through the death of his Son, much more, now that we have been reconciled, shall we be saved by his life. (11) And not only have we this hope: we even exult in God through our Lord Jesus Christ, through whom we have here and now received reconciliation.

For three and a half chapters Paul has dealt with righteousness, judgement, and justification. He can now presuppose justification, the result of God's gracious act of redemption in Jesus Christ, and proceed to consider some of its consequences. He presupposes it not as a human experience on which men may build, but as an act of God, a stage in God's dealings with his people.

Since then we have been justified on the basis of faith 1 **we have peace with God through our Lord Jesus Christ.** The first consequence of justification is peace with God. Indeed, to say that we have peace with God is hardly more than to say that we have been justified, since justification puts an end to the legal strife between Judge and accused. No more than justification

---

[1] There is much textual confusion in this verse and only the most important variants can be mentioned here. The text preferred is awkward because it contains the word 'still' (ἔτι) twice. The second occurrence is wanting in many late MSS., but is undoubtedly genuine (it is contained in ℵ A B C D G 33 lat). There is more doubt about the beginning of the verse. 'For still' (ἔτι γάρ) is read by the majority of MSS. (ℵ A C D ω 33 Marcion); the main alternatives are 'For to what end' (εἰς τί γάρ), a rhetorical question (G lat); and 'if indeed' (εἴ γε), connecting with the previous verse ('The love of God has been poured out . . . if indeed . . .; this is read by B sah). It seems, however, likely that these alternatives are attempts to avoid the repeated 'still'; but this reading is not so difficult as to be impossible. Paul wishes to emphasize that Christ died for us while we were still weak; to do so he places the word first in the sentence, and then uses it again in the normal place, perhaps forgetting that he had uttered it (he was dictating; cf. xvi. 22).

is 'peace' an experience; it is an objective status or condition, a relation which exists between God and those whom he justifies. Of course, the objective state is reflected in the *feeling* of peace and security which man enjoys when he knows that he is reconciled to God, and peace in biblical and Jewish usage is a comprehensive description of the blessings of salvation (e.g. Isa. xlviii. 18; 2 Thess. iii. 16).

So far it has been assumed that Paul wrote and intended the indicative, 'we have peace'. But (see note (1) on p. 100) there is strong evidence for the view that he wrote 'let us have peace'. The difference between the two words ($\check{\epsilon}\chi o\mu\epsilon\nu$, we have; $\check{\epsilon}\chi\omega\mu\epsilon\nu$, let us have) is slight, and was not noticed in pronunciation in the Hellenistic age. It follows from this that great stress should not be laid upon the strong numerical superiority of the reading 'let us have'.

It may be said at once that, if 'let us have peace' implies that a man who has been justified may thereafter freely choose whether or not he will be at peace with God, Paul could not have intended it. To be justified is to be at peace with God. The Greek verb 'to have' ($\check{\epsilon}\chi\epsilon\iota\nu$), however, 'carries a perfect meaning, viz. I enjoy the possession of something already obtained',[1] so that the subjunctive verb may be interpreted as a brachylogy. Paul means: Since we have been justified we have peace; let us therefore enjoy it.

This is a possible interpretation of Paul's thought; but it may be doubted whether it is correct. The context is not hortatory, but indicative. In the next verse, Paul says 'we have gained our access' and 'we now stand'. Perhaps even more important is the fact that in *vv.* 10 and 11 he says 'we were reconciled', 'we have been reconciled', and 'we have here and now received God's act of reconciliation'. He is not urging his readers to do and be what as Christians they ought to do and be, but reminding them of the facts on which all their doing and being rest. It follows that the reading 'we have' may be preferred, though the textual support for 'let us have' is so strong that a measure of doubt will always remain, since 'let us have' (understood as suggested above) is not theologically impossible, though it is theologically less appropriate than the other reading.

[1] Moule, *Idiom Book*, p. 15; cf. Moulton, *Prolegomena*, p. 110.

If we have peace with God at all it is through our Lord Jesus Christ. **It is moreover through him that we have gained** 2 **our access to this grace in which we now stand.** Paul restates the position mainly with a view to his next forward step, but it is worth noting in passing his use of the word 'access' (cf. Eph. iii. 12—it evokes the picture of a worshipper approaching a shrine or holy place in virtue of a sacrifice), and of 'grace'. The latter is not used in exactly the same way as at iii. 24, because Paul here compresses more into it; he means, 'this state determined by the grace of God', that is, the enjoyment of peace with God. The past and the present thus secure, **looking to the future,** we **exult in our hope of the glory of God.**

Here another grammatical difficulty presents itself. The verb translated 'exult' (καυχώμεθα) could, as far as its form goes, be either indicative (we exult) or subjunctive (let us exult). Only the context can decide between the possibilities; but, as we have seen, the context is clearly indicative.

This Greek verb has earlier (ii. 17, 23; cf. iii. 27; iv. 2) been translated 'boast'. In the earlier passages it was used in a bad sense of men's boastful confidence; but here, used of Christians, it takes a new colour and cannot be satisfactorily translated by the old word. It means a triumphant, rejoicing confidence—in God. The man who has been justified exults in good hope for the future, knowing that he can look forward to nothing less than the glory of God, which all men have lost (iii. 23). For glory as the final eschatological consequence of justification compare viii. 18, 21, 30.

Christian exultation, however, is not merely a matter of hope: **we even exult in our afflictions.** This does not mean that the 3 prospect of glory in the future enables Christians to endure afflictions in the present. It is proper that, when a Christian boasts, or exults, he should do so either in hope, or in his afflictions; in hope, because he knows that he is and has nothing of which he can boast, and hope points to that which is entirely in God's hands (cf. viii. 24); and in afflictions, because they humble him and prevent him from having confidence in himself, so that he trusts in God only, and gives glory to him (cf. 2 Cor. xi. 30). There is a further reason for exulting in afflictions.

Paul believes that the ministry of Jesus inaugurated the last age of world history, which (as many Jews believed) was to be marked by severe affliction for the people of God before the coming of bliss in the kingdom of God. This affliction Jesus had absorbed in his own person on the cross, that his followers might go free; yet this had not been done so completely that they were exempt from bearing their crosses after him. Paul exults therefore in afflictions, because they are a sign of the last age, and mark out the path to glory.

Paul proceeds to work out the same point in another way. We exult in afflictions **because we know that affliction pro-**
4 **duces endurance, and endurance tried character, and tried character hope.** For endurance, cf. ii. 7; also viii. 25. It is not simply the ability to support affliction and distress, but the attitude that looks through affliction and distress to find their meaning in God. Correspondingly, tried character is not simply moral worth. The word ($\delta o\kappa\iota\mu\eta$) is a rare one, formed from a verb which means to test and, if the test warrants it, to approve (see on ii. 18). Testing and approving are clearly in mind here; and it is God who is the judge, and vouches for the tried character of the man who patiently endures affliction. For the word, cf. Phil. ii. 22.

When God's approval is thus given there is room for hope, not because the man of tried character is a strong and trustworthy person but because in his endurance he has learnt to look not to himself but to God. Christian exultation again finds its basis—in hope. And this is a more secure basis than might at
5 first appear. **Our hope is not one that can put us to shame.** The language is based upon Ps. xxii. 5; xxv. 3, 20. Paul means that our hope (of the glory of God (*v.* 2)) will not be disappointed, and that we shall therefore not have to bear the shame of having followed a false hope.

How can we be certain of this? Because **God's love for us has already been poured out in our hearts through the Holy Spirit who was given to us.** The relation between the Holy Spirit who now dwells in the Church and in believers, and the eschatological future, is brought out more clearly and at greater length in ch. viii (see especially viii. 23); but already it appears that the gift of the Spirit now is the pledge that our salvation will eventually be complete. The present sentence is, however, obscure in some points.

God's love for us: the Greek is, literally, the love of God, and the genitive might be objective or subjective. Many interpreters (including Augustine) have preferred 'our love for God'; but in *v.* 8 Paul demonstrates God's love for us, and it is this—not our love for him—which makes us confident in our hope.

The words 'poured out' are generally used of the Spirit; so, for example, at Acts ii. 18, 33; x. 45. All these passages are probably dependent on Joel ii. 28. Paul's meaning would perhaps have been somewhat clearer if he had said that the Spirit had been poured out in our hearts, and that by this means God's love for us had there become fully operative, both in making us aware of its presence, and in transforming us. Those whom he so loves God will not disappoint in the hope they set upon him.

The definite past tense, 'who was given to us', may point to a particular moment at which the Spirit was received; conversion, or baptism, may be in mind. In any case, the gift of the Spirit, like justification (*v.* 1) can be described by a past tense. These are elements in salvation which anticipate salvation itself (xiii. 11).

The next three verses relate the clearest possible proof that God loves men, sinful as they are. The substance of the verses is clear; it is not possible to say so much of their literary arrangement. *V.* 6 enunciates the truth Paul wishes to express; he amplifies it in *vv.* 7 f. In the two clauses of *v.* 7 he virtually repeats himself, as the repeated 'for' (γάρ) shows. It is not impossible that Paul dictated *v.* 7a, thought he could express himself better, and dictated *v.* 7 b. But Tertius (xvi. 22) had now put *v.* 7 a on his paper, and by an oversight it was never removed. God's love can be relied on, **for while we were still** 6 **powerless, at the due moment Christ died for us ungodly men.**

'Powerless' seems rather weak as a synonym of 'ungodly' and 'sinners' (*v.* 8). The point probably is that Christ died for us when we were powerless to help ourselves; we were ungodly and sinful and could do nothing to improve our state.

The 'due moment' is the eschatological moment of the fulfilment of God's promises, 'when the fullness of the time came'
(Gal. iv. 4). God's love, revealed in the death of Christ, is thus
not mere compassion. It means God's freedom in taking the
initiative on behalf of undeserving men, and his faithfulness to
his declared word.

There are many parallels in the New Testament to the statement that Christ died for the ungodly; see especially Mark xiv.
24; John x. 11; xi. 50 ff.; Rom. viii. 32; xiv. 15; 1 Cor. xi. 24;
xv. 3; 2 Cor. v. 15, 21; Gal. i. 4; ii. 20; Eph. v. 2, 25; 1 Thess.
v. 10; 1 Tim. ii. 6; Titus ii. 14; Heb. ii. 9; x. 12; 1 Pet. ii. 21;
iii. 18; 1 John iii. 16.[1] The conviction that Christ died for
sinners (or for sin) was undoubtedly central in the thought of
the primitive Church, but this is not to say that all Christians
understood in the same way how or why he died for sinners. In
the present passage Paul himself is not concerned with a
rationale of the crucifixion; he stresses only the love revealed in
the fact that Christ went to such lengths on our behalf.

He emphasizes the same point by comparing Christ's readiness to die with the unreadiness men would show in more
7   favourable circumstances. **For scarcely will anyone die for a
righteous man,** who might be expected to merit such heroic
action.

Paul breaks off and starts again (see above, p. 105). **For on
behalf of a good man someone might even dare to die.**
'Good man' has the article in Greek; this points out not an
individual but a class.[2] It is also possible, though not probable,
that the word 'good' is neuter, and that Paul means 'for a
good cause someone . . .'. These details, however, are in-
significant; in the next verse Paul drives home the main point.

8   **God proves** (the word used at iii. 5; God 'brings out' the
fact of his love in this way, and at the same time 'brings it
home' to us) **his love for us by the fact that while we were
still sinners Christ died for us.**

'For us' is here taken with 'love'. It is often taken (as 'to us')
with 'proves'. For the ambiguity compare 2 Cor. ii. 8. Paul's

---

[1] In all these passages, as here, the preposition is ὑπέρ, 'on behalf of'.

[2] Moule (*Idiom Book*, p. 111) translates, 'for the good type of man', 'for
your good man'.

usage (see Col. i. 4; 1 Thess. iii. 12; Rom. xvi. 1; 2 Cor. iv. 2; v. 12) strongly supports the view taken in the translation.

The verse can hardly be expounded further. The manifestation of God's love is through a historical event; the application of it is by the Holy Spirit (*v.* 5).

The fact of God's love being now established, Paul returns to the main theme of the paragraph. Since God has already done so much for us we can have a good hope for the future and be confident of final salvation. **Since then we have now been** 9 **justified at the cost of his blood, much more shall we be saved through him from God's wrath.**

As in *v.* 1, justification is presupposed as an event from which conclusions may be drawn. In *v.* 1, the conclusion concerns the present—we have peace; here, the conclusion concerns the future—we shall be saved. Justification has been effected (to translate literally) 'in his blood' (cf. iii. 25). The 'in' may be instrumental ('by means of'), or, reflecting a Hebrew idiom, mean 'at the cost of'. In any case, the reference to blood suggests sacrifice, and this confirms the translation given above. For the thought, see the notes on iii. 25 f.

For Paul's teaching on salvation, see on i. 16; xiii. 11. It belongs essentially to the future, and the verb 'to save' is here, as usual, in the future tense (so at v. 10; ix. 27; x. 9, 13; (xi. 14); xi. 26; at xi. 14 it is possibly in the subjunctive (with future meaning); at viii. 24 it is in the aorist indicative, but qualified by 'in hope'). As 'from God's wrath' shows, it refers to the final deliverance at the last judgement; as such it is already guaranteed by justification, in which God anticipates his favourable verdict. For 'wrath' see on i. 18. It is already revealed in the present age, though not against believers, who are not under law (vi. 15), which produces wrath (iv. 15), and are not being progressively handed over to their own wickedness (i. 24, 26, 28), but promised that sin shall not have dominion over them (vi. 14).

The same truth is now differently expressed in an illuminating parallel. **For if when we were enemies we were reconciled** 10 **to God through the death of his Son, much more, now that we have been reconciled, shall we be saved by his life.** It is important here to notice the introduction of a new term—reconciliation, and the close parallel between this and justification. The two verses (9 and 10) can be set out in outline as follows:

1. Justified	1. Reconciled
2. Through the death of Christ	2. Through the death of Christ
3. We shall be saved.	3. We shall be saved.

Justification and reconciliation are different metaphors describing the same fact. The meaning of the verb 'to reconcile'[1] is determined by the noun 'enemies'; it puts an end to enmity, just as 'to justify' puts an end to legal contention. 'Reconciliation' evokes the picture of men acting as rebels against God their king, and making war upon him; 'justification' that of men who have offended against the law and are therefore arraigned before God their judge.

V. 10 contains two balanced clauses:

> We have been reconciled by Christ's death;
> We shall be saved by his life (literally, 'in his life'; cf. 'in his blood' in *v.* 9).

For the parallelism cf. iv. 25. Here, as there, it is not probable that Paul means to suggest that Christ's death effects one thing, his (resurrection) life another; that is, the contrast is rhetorical rather than substantial. Paul begins by asserting that reconciliation depends upon the crucifixion; but as he argues from reconciliation to salvation he recalls the corresponding truth that the crucifixion was followed by the resurrection.

Christians, then, stand between two decisive moments in God's work of redemption. Because God has manifested his righteousness, to faith, in Christ crucified, they have been justified and reconciled; because they have been justified and reconciled, they will finally be saved when God brings history to a close. To this end they look forward in hope. Paul, however, cannot end his paragraph without emphasizing again that for Christians the present, even though it be a time of tribulation, is 11 a time to exult in God. **Not only have we this hope: we even**

---

[1] 1 Cor. vii. 11 (the reconciliation of husband and wife) is an illuminating parallel. See also v. 11; xi. 15; 2 Cor. v. 18, 19, 20; Col. i. 20; Eph. ii. 16.

exult[1] in God through our Lord Jesus Christ, through whom
we have here and now received reconciliation—that is,
have been reconciled to God.

There is little fresh thought in this verse. For 'exult' see on
v. 2. 'Here and now' (νῦν) describes the anticipation in the
present of God's verdict at the judgement, the peace of the
kingdom of God. Compare iii. 26 (with the note); also 2 Cor.
vi. 2.

14. v. 12-21. ADAM AND CHRIST

(12) Therefore as through one man sin entered the world
(and through sin came that man's death), so also death
came to all men, because they all sinned. (13) For until
the law came, sin was in the world, but where there is no
law sin is not taken into account. (14) All the same, from
Adam up to Moses death reigned, even over those who
had not sinned in such a way as to produce a transgression like Adam's. Now Adam is a type of the Man to
Come.

(15) But the act of grace did not after all correspond
exactly to the act of sin; for if it be true that by the transgression of the One the Many died, much more did the
grace of God, and the gracious gift of the One man Jesus
Christ, abound for the Many. (16) Again, God's gift was
not a mere equivalent of the result that followed from
One who sinned; for from one act of transgression began
the process of judgement which leads to condemnation,
but the act of grace, wrought in the context of many
transgressions, leads to justification. (17) For if, by the
transgression of the One, death reigned through that One,
much more shall those who receive the excess of grace
and of the gift of righteousness reign in life through the
One Jesus Christ.

---

[1] In Greek 'exult' is a participle (καυχώμενοι). It is very unlikely that it is
an imperatival participle (see on xii. 9), or that it should be connected with
v. 10. It is better to suppose that through an accidental slip the construction
is defective; this is not the only imperfect sentence in Paul's writings.

(18) Therefore as, through one act of transgression, the result for all men was condemnation, so also through one act of righteousness the result for all men was justification, which leads to life. (19) For as through the disobedience of the One man the Many were made sinners, so also through the obedience of the One the Many shall be made righteous. (20) The law took its subordinate place in order that transgression might multiply; but where sin did multiply, grace abounded all the more, (21) in order that as sin reigned in death so grace also might reign through righteousness, with eternal life its goal, through Jesus Christ our Lord.

12   The new paragraph opens with **Therefore**; but it is difficult to see how it, or its first sentence, arises logically out of the preceding sentence or paragraph. There are two possibilities of interpretation. (i) 'Therefore' refers to the protasis with which *v.* 12 begins. The sentence would then run: 'For this reason, namely, that sin and death entered the world through Adam, in like manner sin and death became the fate of all men'. This is possible, but strains Paul's language. (ii) Alternatively, 'therefore' is a particle of transition, indicating only a loose relation between what has gone before and what follows. Such a loose relation can be made out, and this seems the best course to take.

In *vv.* 1-11 Paul argued that justification and reconciliation carry with them the certainty of future salvation, in which men may confidently exult. He now supports the same conclusion by a different method. It is through Christ that Christians have their hope of salvation. But Christ is the counterpart of Adam, and we can be as sure that we shall share in the consequences of Christ's acts as that we do already share in the consequences of Adam's. What Christ has done has universal validity.

The thought of this paragraph is complicated, and by no means clearly set out. It will be best to follow Paul patiently through it, and at the end to make an attempt to analyse the position he reaches.

As through one man sin entered the world (and through sin came that man's death), so also death came to all men, because they all sinned.

14. v. 12-21. ADAM AND CHRIST

It need not be said that Paul, a first-century Jew, accepted Gen. i-iii as a straightforward narrative of events which really happened. He also saw in these chapters a theological account of sin which gave him a tool by means of which he could analyse the state of human society and the human heart. But he begins with the narrative. Sin entered the world through the first man, who disobeyed the commandment given him by God. He did this not simply out of longing for a fruit which happened fortuitously to have been forbidden, but in rebellion against his Maker, for the serpent had cast doubt upon God's truthfulness and goodness, and said, 'In the day ye eat thereof . . . ye shall be as God' (Gen. iii. 4 f.). That is, Adam endeavoured to set himself in the place of God (cf. p. 37), and in that moment sin was born. At the same time, Adam fell under sentence of death.

So far Paul has been describing the historical events (as he would deem them) of Adam's career, and established that he was responsible for the entry of sin and death into the world, at least as far as his own person was concerned. But once the connexion between sin and death has been established, Paul moves onward: 'So also death came to all men, because they all sinned'. That is, all men sin (cf. iii. 23), and all men die because they sin; but Paul does not add here that they sin, or that they die, because they are physically descended from Adam. Nowhere, even in *v.* 19, does Paul teach the direct seminal identity between Adam and his descendants which seems to be implied in the nearly contemporary 4 Ezra (especially iii. 7, 21).[1]

Death, then, is the result of sin. But this raises a problem: What if there are men who do not sin? Will they not live for ever? This is not so hypothetical a problem as might appear, for the only means of estimating sin is transgressable law, and where there is no law sin may exist but can give no indication of its presence. Now in fact no law existed between Adam and Moses,[2] and it might be expected that in that period no deaths would take place. This, however, was not so. Paul notes the anomaly, but without offering a formal explanation. **For until** 13

---

[1] The Latin rendering (*in quo*) of the words here translated 'because' could be, and was, understood to mean 'in whom'; that is, all men sinned *in* Adam. But this is certainly not the meaning of the Greek.

[2] Note that Paul takes no account of the 'Noachian precepts'; see p. 52, n. 5.

the law came (with Moses), **sin was in the world, but where there is no law sin is not taken into account** (a
14 commercial term—'put in the ledger'). **All the same, from Adam up to Moses death reigned, even over those who had not sinned in such a way** (that is, against a law) **as to produce a transgression like Adam's.** This, as was said, is not a formal explanation, but the germ of an explanation lies in the distinction which Paul, unsystematically it is true, makes between sin and transgression. Sin is an inward disposition of rebellion against God arising out of exaltation of the self. It has always been in the world since Adam's fall because it is inseparably bound up with man's desire to return to the lost state of bliss and immortality, his will to life in and for himself. This is an unavoidable consequence of man's existence in a world which has once turned away from God. But it is not to be identified with the performance of wicked actions. Sin is turned into transgression, and becomes visible and assessable, only when a law is given.

These observations provide us with important hints for the interpretation of the argument that follows. This is conducted simultaneously on two lines, for Paul deals with both Adam and his counterpart, Christ.

Now Adam is a type of the Man to come.

Paul introduces this remark without warning or explanation; he knew that he was treading familiar ground. In various ways, the first man and the Redeemer had been compared, contrasted, and even identified. An account of these religious speculations would not greatly illuminate the Epistle to the Romans, for Paul takes an independent line. He begins with Jesus, and adopts and adapts such speculative material as he can use.

Adam is a type ($\tau\acute{\upsilon}\pi os$) of Christ. The word means a visible mark left by some object (e.g. John xx. 25). Hence, in metaphor, a type is the mark left in history or nature by the antitype ($\mathring{a}\nu\tau\acute{\iota}\tau\upsilon\pi os$). Paul's use of the word in 1 Cor. x. 6 (cf. x. 11) shows that this precise definition must not be pressed. Paul is using analogy (rather than 'typology'). Adam and Christ were in analogous circumstances and exposed to analogous temptations. Adam fell, Christ did not; but even so the consequences of their acts were analogous. In fact, the best commentary on 'type' is to be found in the series of correspondences, perfect and imperfect, which Paul notes in the following verses.

'The Man to Come' represents a Greek participle (τοῦ μέλλοντος). This may mean no more than the Coming One (cf., e.g., Matt. xi. 3); but the context, and comparison with 1 Cor. xv. 45, suggest that Paul is thinking of Christ as the last Adam. At all events, he proceeds with a series of parallels which throw light on both figures. But a surprise is in store, for where a comparison would be expected (type corresponding to anti-type), we meet with a contrast.

But the act of grace did not after all correspond exactly 15 **to the act of sin.** Paul uses in this chapter three words which, if they stood separately, might all be translated 'sin'. Two have already been considered; one, which represents sin in itself, that which determines man's nature as inimical to God (ἁμαρτία); and another, which means 'transgression', an act of disobedience to a revealed command (παράβασις). The third occurs in this verse, and is here translated 'act of sin' (παράπτωμα); it is scarcely to be distinguished from the second word. Over against the act of sin (committed by Adam) stands the act of grace (performed by Christ). 'Act of grace' represents a word (χάρισμα) closely related to the word grace (χάρις) and having the same grammatical form as the word 'act of sin'. It is used elsewhere in the epistle (i. 11; xii. 6; cf. vi. 23) in a different sense, but there can be little doubt that Paul here uses it to express the actualization of grace, just as the other word represents the actualization of sin. The two words stand in rhetorically effective juxtaposition.

But they do not correspond as exact equivalents. The act of grace does not balance the act of sin; it overbalances it. The point is not simply that grace operates more inclusively and intensively than destruction (Lietzmann). Adam was a man who disobeyed God; Jesus was a man who obeyed God, but he was also more than this. His act was not merely an act of human obedience (though it was this); it was also an act of the grace—of God. In several of the following verses we shall find this fact upsetting straightforward analogies between Adam and Christ. **For if it be true that by the transgression of the One the Many died, much more did the grace of God, and the**

gracious gift of the One man Jesus Christ, abound for the Many.

Here Paul goes further than in *v.* 12; Adam's act of sin is the instrumental cause of universal death. It is true that he says 'the Many died', but by 'many' he can hardly mean anything different from the 'all men' of *v.* 12 (cf. also 1 Cor. xv. 22). This inclusive use of 'many' is Hebraistic; in Old Testament usage 'many' often means not 'many contrasted with all' but 'many contrasted with one or some'.

Adam's act, then, though the act of one man, resulted in the death of the great mass of mankind; over against this, what Christ did, and its effects upon mankind, can only be introduced by means of a 'much more' (cf. 4 Ezra iv. 30 ff.), since these are a matter of divine grace. Paul first describes this as 'the grace of God' (cf. *v.* 20); then he makes another attempt to indicate the actualization of grace, speaking of it this time as 'the gift in grace', a gift, that is, prompted and determined by grace. The content of the gift is not and cannot be defined; it is (like other terms in this passage) simply a convenient way of expressing all that God has done for men through Jesus Christ.

Grace, like death, was for 'the Many'. It cannot be doubted that 'the Many' has the same inclusive sense in both cases; it is occasionally so used in the New Testament of the effects of Christ's death (*v.* 19; Mark x. 45; xiv. 24, and parallels); but it would be as wrong to deduce from these passages a rigid universalism as to suppose that they meant 'many and therefore not all'. The main point is that, like Adam, Christ is the progenitor of a race; only the blessings which the members of the new race derive through their Founder are far greater than the curse which Adam handed down to his children.

In the next verse Paul repeats what is substantially the same thought.

16 **Again, God's gift was not a mere equivalent of the result that followed from One who sinned; for from one act of transgression began the process of judgement which leads to condemnation, but the act of grace, wrought in a context of many transgressions, leads to justification.** The verse is full of obscurities, but this translation gives the probable sense. 'From one act of transgression'

interprets 'from one'. 'From one transgressor' is a possible alternative, but the parallel expression 'in a context of many transgressions' suggests that the deed rather than the doer forms the correct supplement. The process of judgement inevitably began with the first act of transgression, and since the transgression was real and responsible it inevitably led to condemnation. The act of grace, however, could only take place where sin already abounded (*v.* 20).

Judgement led to condemnation; grace led to justification. 'Justification' here renders a word (δικαίωμα) which elsewhere (i. 32; ii. 26; v. 18; viii. 4) calls for different translations. In using it here Paul is governed by rhetorical considerations; it chimes with 'condemnation' (κατάκριμα). There is, however, no question what he means, and it is significant that 'justification' is made to stand out as the opposite of 'condemnation'; each is a verdict pronounced in a court of law.

A third time Paul stresses the contrast between Adam and Christ. **For if, by the transgression of the One, death** 17 **reigned through that One, much more shall those who receive the excess of grace and of the gift of righteousness reign in life through the One Jesus Christ.** The clumsiness of the second part of this verse bears witness to Paul's anxiety to stress the superiority of grace to sin, of Christ to Adam. The 'excess of grace' means that grace more than undoes the effects of sin (cf. *v.* 20). The parallelism of the clauses would have been better maintained if Paul had said not that believers should 'reign in life', but that 'life (not death) should reign'. But the sentence as it stands asserts that they who were reigned over by the tyrant shall themselves reign. The 'gift of righteousness' might mean the conferment of righteousness upon man, or the gift which proceeds from God's righteousness. It is scarcely possible to decide between these alternatives; each presupposes the other.

Having now fully brought out the contrast between Adam and Christ, Paul drops for the moment the language of divine grace, and speaks of Christ as obedient Man, the true counterpart of Adam, or disobedient Man.

Therefore as, through one act of transgression, the result 18 **for all men was condemnation, so also through one act of**

righteousness the result for all men was justification, which leads to life. The sentence as written in Greek lacks verbs, but its meaning is clear. 'Unto condemnation' (εἰς κατάκριμα), and 'unto justification' (εἰς δικαίωσιν), indicate the goal or result of processes which originated 'through one act of transgression' and 'through one act of righteousness' respectively.

'Act of righteousness' translates the troublesome word discussed in the note on *v.* 16. Again, it has come into use for reasons of rhetoric; Paul needs a word of the 'righteous' family to balance 'act of transgression' (παράπτωμα) and this (δι-καίωμα) is the obvious one to choose. But when it is employed in this sense it can no longer (in the same sentence) be used to mean 'justification'; accordingly for this purpose Paul chooses another word (δικαίωσις) which he uses elsewhere only at iv. 25.

Justification, and justification only, leads to life. Paul never attempts to by-pass this step. Man must be found righteous in God's court, even though it be by the grace of the Judge.

'All men' in this verse corresponds to 'the Many' in *v.* 15; but it is significant that the present verse is so phrased that it is impossible to draw from it any simple arithmetical conclusion about the numbers of the saved and of the lost. 'Condemnation' and 'justification' are in their ordinary use ultimate and mutually exclusive terms. At the last judgement, a man is either condemned, or justified (acquitted). Yet Paul says that the result of Adam's act of transgression is condemnation for all, and the result of Christ's act of righteousness is justification for all. There are two possible ways out of this logical difficulty. One is to suppose that when Paul says 'all men' he means 'all men who are "on Adam's side"' and 'all men who are "on Christ's side"'. All who (with Adam) choose sin will be condemned; all who (with Christ) choose righteousness will be justified. The other way out of the difficulty is harder to state but more probably true. There are two ways of looking at men. They may be considered 'in Adam' (cf. 1 Cor. xv. 22); that is, viewed as independent, self-explanatory persons, members of a race which has cut itself off from its Creator and wages war against him. This is the natural way of looking at the race, and the way in which it is natural for the race to consider itself. Viewed and understood in these terms it can have one end only. But it is also possible (by faith, for this is no human possibility) to see mankind 'in Christ' (cf. 1 Cor. xv. 22), the new Man. Men are then clothed in a righteousness which is not their own, and in virtue of it they can and will be justified. Condemnation and justification are thus both of them universal possibilities, and even universal actualities, in the sense that they point to a dialectical truth which is valid for mankind as a whole, and for each individual man. The resolution of this dialectical duality lies ultimately not with man but with the merciful God (cf. xi. 32).

Paul restates his position once more, in the clearest antithesis of all. **For as through the disobedience of the One man the** 19 **Many were made sinners, so also through the obedience of the One the Many shall be made righteous.**

Through Adam's act the Many were *made* sinners; through Christ's they shall be *made* righteous. For the verb, compare Acts vii. 27; it does not mean 'to count' or 'to reckon'. But the words 'sinners' and 'righteous' are words of relationship, not character. Adam's disobedience did not mean that all men necessarily and without their consent committed particular acts of sin; it meant that they were born into a race which had separated itself from God. Similarly, Christ's obedience did not mean that henceforth men did nothing but righteous acts, but that in Christ they were related to God as Christ himself was related to his Father.

So far throughout this paragraph Paul has spoken of Adam and Christ as if there were no intervening stage in religious history. But this is to overlook a most significant event—the giving of the law (cf. *v.* 14). The Jewish interlocutor might well have asked what place Paul could find for this supreme factor in the national religion. Paul answers that the law cannot stand on the same level as the fall of Adam and redemption through Christ. **The law took its subordinate place.** The verb used 20 here is that of Gal. ii. 4 (. . . false brethren privily brought in, who *came in privily*). Paul does not mean to speak ill of the law as he does of the false brethren, but merely to indicate that it came in beside what was already in position, and consequently enjoyed an inferior status.

But why was the law introduced at all? **In order that transgression might multiply.** Compare Gal. iii. 19. As there Paul answers an explicit question, so here he answers an implicit Why? or What? His answer expresses God's purpose in giving the law. Paul has already shown that where there is no law sin is not reckoned (*v.* 13), for only law can turn invisible sin into visible transgression. But men will never see their sin and feel their guilt, and will never therefore have faith, until their sin becomes transgression. It was therefore the wisdom of God to give the law that transgression might multiply (for the expression cf. Ecclus. xxiii. 3). This he could safely, and without prejudice to morality, do, not only because the law was itself holy, righteous, and good, but also because **where sin did multiply, grace abounded all the more.** Again Paul stresses the surplus of grace in Christ over sin in Adam. Man's rebellion cannot be victorious, or God would not be God.

This complicated process of sin, law, transgression, and
21 grace moves to its final purpose: **in order that as sin reigned in death so grace also might reign through righteousness, with eternal life its goal, through Jesus Christ our Lord.**

Most of the elements of this final pronouncement have appeared at some earlier point in the paragraph. In *vv.* 14 and 17 Paul said that death reigned. He here expresses himself more fully. It was sin that reigned, and sin used death (the 'in' is instrumental) as the instrument of its tyranny. Through Christ, however, grace reigns (this is perhaps a more cautious way of expressing what is said in *v.* 17—men do not reign in their own right); because grace reigns righteousness becomes possible, and righteousness leads to eternal life (cf. *v.* 18). Paul uses here the fuller term (eternal life, not life) to emphasize that he is speaking of the life which properly follows (though in Christian belief it may anticipate) the judgement at the end of the age.

This obscure and pregnant paragraph, the difficulty of which has been considerably mitigated by means of the translation but even so remains severe, is at an end. What has Paul said?

His thought goes back to two propositions which are embedded deeply in the gospel tradition. (i) With Jesus the last age, the age of the new creation, has dawned, though it has not been consummated. (ii) Jesus is the Son of man. These two themes

Paul works out with heavy stress upon their moral aspect. The ruin of the old creation, as of the old man, Adam, was sin. Sin could never be a private matter, but corrupted the whole race, which consisted of men born out of true relation with God and condemned constantly to worsen their relationship, whether they carelessly ignored it or self-righteously essayed to mend it. Like planets robbed of the centre of their orbit they could not possibly keep a proper course. The more they sought life for themselves, the more they forsook God and plunged into death. Their lot could only be changed by a new creation, from a new beginning. The new Man instead of seeking to develop his own powers, individuality, and freedom subordinated himself utterly to God, and became obedient even unto death. This was possible because he was at once representative Man and the Son of God. Thus the new manhood was from the beginning joined with God; from this relationship sprang the life which the Man had surrendered in going to the Cross.

As in ch. iii (see pp. 81 f.) Paul's doctrine is in part capable of anthropological development. Two types of manhood are portrayed, and it is of decisive importance that man should recognize the truth of his own existence under the word of God. But there is another aspect of Paul's thought which must not be neglected. Only in virtue of divine action can humanity cease to be what it is and become a new humanity in Christ. The scandal of the Incarnation and the Cross cannot be avoided.

15. vi. 1-14. FREE FROM SIN

(1) What then shall we say? Are we to go on in sin in order that there may be yet more grace? (2) Of course not: how shall we, men who died to sin, go on living in it? (3) Or (if you want further proof) do you not know that we who were baptized into Christ Jesus were baptized into his death? (4) Through this baptism into his death, we were buried with him in order that, as Christ was raised from the dead in a manifestation of the glory of the Father, so we too might come to exist in the new resurrection life.

(5) For if by means of the image of his death we have been joined with his death, then we shall also be joined with his resurrection. (6) And we know this, that our old self was crucified with him in order that our sin-dominated body might be abolished, that we might no longer be slaves to sin—(7) for a dead man is clear from sin. (8) But if we died with Christ, we believe that we shall also live with him, (9) since we know that Christ, now that he has been raised from the dead, can die no more—no longer has death dominion over him. (10) For whereas he died, he died to sin once for all; but whereas he lives, he lives to God.

(11) So do you also consider that you yourselves are dead to sin, but alive to God in Christ Jesus. (12) Let not sin reign in your mortal body so that you obey your body's desires.[1] (13) Do not offer your members to sin, as weapons in the service of unrighteousness, but offer yourselves to God as dead men brought to life, and offer him your members as weapons in the service of righteousness. (14) For sin shall not dominate over you; for you are not under the reign of law, but under the reign of grace.

The juxtaposition in the last verse of ch. v of sin, law, and grace, raises acutely a question already alluded to in iii. 1-8: What is the basis of Christian morality? If justification is by faith, apart from works of the law; if the law (which commands the practice of virtue) occupies only a subordinate place in God's purpose; and if, where sin abounds, grace abounds much more— why should Christians be good? The fact that Paul handles this question at such length shows how seriously his doctrine of 'grace and faith alone' must be taken. It is probable that there were in the Pauline churches antinomians who drew the conclusion that sin might be indulged to the full, and adversaries

---

[1] 'Your body's desires' is supported by B ℵ A C L vg pesh. 'It' (that is, sin) is supported by another strong group of MSS.: P46 D G it Irenaeus Tertullian. The majority of MSS. have a conflate reading—'it (that is, sin) in its (that is, the body's) desires'—which is certainly wrong. The Western reading ('it'), though very early, is probably wrong, since it can be explained as due to assimilation to *vv.* 13, 16, 17, 20.

who alleged that this was the logical outcome of the Pauline system.

In ch. iii Paul answered the question briefly, and on the basis of Jewish presuppositions: God is Judge, and the judge of all the earth will do right. But he has now elaborated the doctrine of justification and redemption, and must give a Christian answer. Throughout this chapter he labours to express it. The answer itself is clear, but Paul does not find it easy to set it out in suitable language.

In the opening verses the style of the diatribe (see p. 43) reappears. Again, it is not impossible that the style reflects questions which had been put to Paul.

What then (in view of what has been said about sin, law, and 1 grace) **shall we say? Are we to go on in sin in order that there may be yet more grace?** 'In order that' (*ἵνα*) expresses purpose. Paul contemplates a course of action directed to the end that there may be more grace. The answer follows immediately. **Of course not: how shall we, men who died to 2 sin, go on living in it?** Paul does not use the ordinary relative (*οἵ*—'we who died') but a specialized form (*οἵτινες*), which gives the sense 'We who in our essential nature, i.e., just because we are Christians, died'. We cannot as Christians go on living in sin because as Christians we have died to sin; as far as sin is concerned, we are dead. The definite past tense, 'we died', points to a particular moment; conversion and (as the next verse shows) baptism must be in mind.

Paul has now stated the basic fact upon which his rejection of the question of *v.* 1 rests. He must still elucidate the manner in which Christians have died, and the clearest way of doing this is by reference to baptism, which he is evidently able to assume as a rite familiar to all his readers.

Or (if you want further proof) do you not know that we 3 who were baptized into Christ Jesus were baptized into his death?

Paul appeals to what is, or ought to be, common knowledge among Christians. How far did this common knowledge extend? To the practice of baptism? To the belief that baptism into Christ involved baptism into his death? To the further conclusions drawn by Paul from the notion of baptism into death?

The answer to this question will depend in large part on the view taken of the origin of Paul's doctrine of baptism. If baptism into Christ's death means what it is taken in this commentary to mean, the idea will probably have originated before and independently of Paul, though beyond question he saw more clearly into its implications than any of his contemporaries.

Baptism was into Christ Jesus. This is probably an abbreviated form of the fuller 'into the name of Christ Jesus', and will therefore have a meaning less mystical than realist. Those who are baptized into the name of Christ become Christ's men (cf. 1 Cor. x. 2; i. 13). Baptized Christians are thus the people of the Messiah, whose death, resurrection, and ascension marked the dawn of the Age to Come. Baptism thus finds its setting in Christian eschatology; but Christian eschatology is no simple matter, for though, in some sense, the Age to Come has come, it is manifest that the present age still persists, and that the general resurrection and renewal of creation have not yet taken place. It follows that baptism is the gateway not to heaven, or to the fully 'realized' kingdom of God, but to a life which is related both to the present age, which is marked by sin and death, and to the Age to Come, which is 'righteousness, peace, and joy in the Holy Spirit' (xiv. 17). This fact lies behind much of the present paragraph; but we must allow Paul to develop it in his own way.

Baptism into Christ means baptism into his death. It has often been argued that the doctrine of initiation by sacramental death and resurrection is of Hellenistic origin; and there are real parallels between the language of Paul and that of some of the Hellenized oriental cults. That Paul knew, and on occasion used, something of their religious terminology is probable, but this is not to say that he drew his doctrine from this source. The 'messianic affliction' (see p. 80) was probably the starting-point of Paul's understanding of the Cross, as it had been for Christians before him. It remained true that before the people of God could enter the Age to Come they must pass through affliction and resurrection; but since Christ had died and been raised from the dead this transition could be in part anticipated by faith through the sacrament of baptism. In this fact lies the root of Paul's doctrine of baptism. It is for this reason that, though baptism always retains for him the double pattern of death and resurrection, he handles the latter element very cautiously. In this chapter, for example, references to the resurrection of Christians are regularly in the future tense or the imperative. There is no sacramental *opus operatum* by means of which Christians can assure themselves, independently of faith and of their own moral seriousness, that they have risen from death to enjoy the life of the Age to Come.

So far (in *v.* 3) Paul has simply used the practice of baptism to support his assertion (in *v.* 2) that Christians have died. The reference to baptism carries him further.

Through this baptism into his death, we were buried 4 **with him** (Paul makes use of the picture suggested by the practice of baptism by immersion) **in order that, as Christ was raised from the dead in a manifestation of the glory of the Father, so we too might come to exist in the new resurrection life.**

For Paul, 'glory' is a word with a predominantly eschatological meaning (e.g. ii. 7, 10; iii. 23; v. 2; viii. 17, 21); glory is that which will be revealed at the last day. When therefore Paul says that Christ was raised from the dead 'through the glory of the Father' he means that the resurrection was an eschatological event, ushering in the time of the fulfilment of God's purpose. Only for this reason can it have as its consequence that we too should (to translate literally) 'walk in newness of life'. This is a Hebraistic expression, a fact which may mean that the thought expressed goes back to the Semitic-speaking Church. The new resurrection life (cf. eternal life, v. 21; vi. 22 f.) is both present (*v.* 4) and future (*vv.* 5, 8, *et al.*).

In the next verse Paul repeats and supports his assertion that baptism means not only death but also resurrection. **For if by** 5 **means of the image of his death** (that is, baptism) **we have been joined with his death, then we shall also be joined with** (that is, share) **his resurrection.**

The word here translated 'joined with' means literally 'grown together with' ($\sigma \acute{v} \mu \phi v \tau o s$). The process of grafting may be in mind (cf. xi. 17 ff. and John xv. 1-5—though the word is not used in either of these passages). The construction is obscure, for a literal rendering of the first clause would run, 'If we have grown together with the likeness of his death'; and it is hard to see how one can grow together with a likeness. One solution is to supply a pronoun, 'him'. The meaning then is, 'If we have grown together *with him* in, or by means of, the likeness of his death', the 'likeness of his death' being baptism. This interpretation, however, is not entirely satisfactory in the context, for the balance of the two clauses requires that one should speak of dying with Christ, the other of being raised with him. The word 'death' must in all probability be repeated, so that the meaning is, 'through the image (or imitation) of his death we have come to be joined with his death'—that is, to die with him. Baptism effects that which it represents.

Of the second clause, Paul writes only 'We shall be of his resurrection also'. The whole framework of the preceding clause must be repeated: Through the likeness of his resurrection (the other aspect of baptism) we shall be joined with his resurrection; that is, we shall be raised with him. Paul breaks the parallelism by using the future. This might be a purely 'logical' future, as in the proposition: If A is true then B will follow. But this would not agree with the undoubtedly temporal future of *v.* 8. In fact, Paul is always cautious of expressions which might suggest that the Christian has already reached his goal, and to say in so many words 'We have died with Christ and we have been raised with Christ' would be to invite if not actually to commit the error condemned in 2 Tim. ii. 18.

So far Paul has simply elicited the fact that Christian existence is rooted in a death and resurrection dependent upon Christ's. He has not yet demonstrated the relevance of this fact to the question of *v.* 1. This he now proceeds to do. *Vv.* 6 f. deal with death, *vv.* 8 ff. with life; in *vv.* 11 ff. he holds the two together and brings out their practical consequences; *v.* 14 is a transition to a new line of argument.

What is the significance of the death Christians die by faith
6 in baptism? **We know this, that our old self was crucified with him in order that our sin-dominated body** (cf. viii. 3) **might be abolished, that we might no longer be slaves to**
7 **sin—for a dead man is clear from sin.** The essential substance of this conviction is clear: death with Christ is an ethical experience, affecting the relation between man and sin.

The 'old self' is literally the 'old man'. Compare Col. iii. 9 f.

(Eph. iv. 22, 24). The interpretation which commends itself by its simplicity is that the 'old man' is the nature of the unconverted man, which upon conversion and baptism is replaced by a new nature, the 'new man'. But careful reading of Col. iii, and of the present passage, makes this interpretation impossible. In Colossians it is Christians who are told to put off the old man, and to put on the new. Here in Romans Christians are told that they must *consider* themselves to be dead to sin and alive to God (*v.* 11). It is much more exact to say that the 'old man' is Adam —or rather, ourselves in union with Adam, and that the 'new man' is Christ—or rather, ourselves in union with Christ. Compare Gal. iii. 27; 1 Cor. xv. 22, 47 ff.

The old, Adamic, self was crucified with Christ. In his crucifixion Jesus endured the messianic affliction, and it is by sharing this affliction in union with Christ that the descendants of Adam participate in the New Creation of which the New Adam is the head. This, however, is no mystical or metaphysical process. Its purpose is the abolition of the sin-ridden body which men have from Adam. From his time, sin and death reigned (v. 14, 17, 21); human nature (for Paul's word 'body' means hardly less than this) correspondingly passed into slavery (cf. *vv.* 6c, 16, 17, 18, 19, 20, 22). Baptismal 'death' accordingly is a step towards the putting out of action of this sin-dominated aspect or element of humanity. The more remote consequence is that 'we' should no longer be in servitude to sin. That is, 'we' are distinguishable from the sin-controlled side of our being.

And (to translate literally) the man who has died has been justified from sin. There are two possible interpretations here. (i) 'Justify' may have its usual forensic meaning: death pays all debts. (ii) 'Justify' means 'to free from sin (actually)'. This meaning does occur (e.g. Ecclus. xxvi. 29; *Corpus Hermaticum* xiii. 9; perhaps Acts xiii. 38 f.; 1 Cor. vi. 11). It is not, however, right to distinguish sharply between these alternatives. The second is suggested by *vv.* 6 and 10; but there follows immediately *v.* 11 (consider yourselves dead). Thus (i) is true absolutely—the man who has died with Christ by faith has been justified; and (ii) ought to be in process of realization.

Paul has thus worked out his point as far as baptismal *death* is concerned. But as in the story of Jesus, so also in baptism and

8 Christian experience, death leads to life. **But if we died with**
9 **Christ, we believe that we shall also live with him, since**
we know that Christ, now that he has been raised from the
dead, can die no more—no longer has death dominion
over him.

For the future tense 'we shall live' compare the future 'we shall be' in *v.* 5. It is primarily a real future and points to the resurrection; but as in *v.* 7 it is important not to make over-sharp distinctions. 'The formula "with Christ" is used in the sacramental (vi. 8; Col. ii. 13, 20) and in the eschatological (2 Cor. iv. 14; xiii. 4; Phil. i. 23; 1 Thess. iv. 14, 17; v. 10; Col. iii. 3, 4) sense' (Lietzmann). This is not surprising if it be true that Paul's view of baptism is primarily eschatological. But it must be noted that the 'we shall live' (whether present sacramental or future eschatological) rests upon 'we believe', whereas the resurrection of Christ is introduced by 'we know' (*v.* 9). The life of the Christian with Christ can be experienced and recognized only by faith; it is not capable of direct observation.

V. 9 emphasizes that the resurrection of Christ was an eschatological event, an anticipation of the resurrection of the last day; hence Christ will not die again. He (and he alone) has begun the resurrection life of the Age to Come; but those who are joined with him in his death and resurrection anticipate it by faith.

We come now to the crucial stage in Paul's argument. The question of *v.* 1 is not yet answered. We must ask, What sort of death did Christ, and do Christians, die? And what sort of life does Christ, and do Christians, live? **Whereas he died, he**
10 **died to sin once for all; but whereas he lives, he lives to**
God. Christ died to sin because he died sinless, because he died rather than sin (by disobeying his Father), and because he died in a context of sin. He was raised from the dead by the glory of the Father (*v.* 4), in order that he might continue to live to God only; he never lived otherwise. He was completely obedient to, and completely dependent upon, God.

So far, Paul has described the death and life of Christ; but all that he has said is, *mutatis mutandis*, applicable to the death and life of Christians. It follows that a Christian (a) is dead as far as sin is concerned; (b) has been raised from the dead to new life;

and (c) in this new life belongs to God. If this be true it is clear at once that any talk of continuing in sin (*v.* 1) is a contradiction of Christian first principles.

It is also of course clear that Christians do not live a sinless and immortal life in heaven with Christ. The sacrament of baptism does not in this life effect its own full meaning. In particular, it leaves room for ethical effort, in which Christians endeavour actually to achieve (with the aid of the Spirit, given in baptism) the life to which baptism points. Paul's next step is to urge his readers to realize in this way that which is already true for them by faith. **So do you also consider that you** 11 **yourselves are dead to sin, but alive to God in Christ Jesus.** The word 'consider' is the same as that used to denote God's 'reckoning' of righteousness to Abraham (Gen. xv. 6; Rom. iv. 3). Christians are no more visibly dead and risen than Abraham was visibly righteous. Outwardly they appear as other men; but *in Christ Jesus* they are newly related to God. It is important to understand what this means for it sums up much of the teaching of this paragraph. 'In Christ' is itself a Pauline phrase of central but disputed significance. It is best explained as originating neither in mysticism nor in the realistic ideas of sacramental communion, nor in the idea of the Church as an institution, but in primitive Christian eschatology. The death and resurrection of Jesus were eschatological events, effecting the transition from this age to the Age to Come. Believers could take advantage of this transition, but the transference from the one age to the other could take place only 'in Christ'. Those who belonged to him by faith passed through death and resurrection and so came to be alive to God. Paul urges his readers to look upon themselves, and to understand their activity, in this light. What this means in practice is expressed in plain terms in *vv.* 12 f.

Let not sin reign in your mortal body so that you obey 12 **your body's desires.** 'In Christ' men are dead to sin and alive to God. This is (if the expression may be allowed) sacramentally and eschatologically true; but neither the efficacy of the sacrament, nor the anticipation of the eschatological future, alters the fact that men in this world have mortal bodies, conditioned by the present age, not the Age to Come; and in these bodies sin is ever at hand. Hence the form of Paul's exhortation; sin must not be allowed to reign; the desires which are naturally engendered in a personality belonging to this age must not be obeyed (cf. xii. 1 f.).

13   **Do not offer your members** (not simply *limbs*, but the various faculties of the mortal body) **to sin, as weapons in the service of unrighteousness** (this word is used in an ethical sense, not corresponding exactly to Paul's most characteristic use of 'righteousness'), **but offer yourselves to God as dead men brought to life, and offer him your members as weapons in the service of righteousness.**

It is impossible to be certain of the translation 'weapons'. The word (ὅπλα) means (i) ship's tackle; (ii) tool, instrument of any kind; (iii) weapon. Compare xiii. 12. Either (ii) or (iii) would make good sense; 2 Cor. vi. 7; x. 4 point to (iii).

Sin, as the parallelism shows (. . . to sin . . . in the service of unrighteousness . . . to God . . . in the service of righteousness), is almost personified. This is not unusual in Paul; see especially vii. 8, 9, 11, 13.

The real force of Paul's injunction lies in the phrase 'as dead men brought to life'. The 'as' is not easy to define. It is neither 'as if you were' nor 'as in fact you are'; or perhaps rather it is both of these. In one sense, Paul's readers have already been raised from the dead. In another, they are still waiting for this to take place. If they had not died and been raised by faith there would be no point in bidding them forsake sin and live to God; if they had already died and been raised up at the last day there would equally, though for another reason, be no point in bidding them forsake sin and live to God. It is because they stand between these two moments in the history of redemption that Christian moral exhortation has its place. It can be given with

14 confidence, because **sin shall not dominate over you; for you are not under the reign of law, but under the reign of grace.**

'Sin shall not dominate over you' (for the future cf. *vv.* 5 and 8) might almost be translated, 'sin shall not be your lord'. For the Christian there is only one Lord, and he has offered himself to God in the service of righteousness (*v.* 13). Sin has lost its power because the Christian does not live under law, in which the strength of sin resides (1 Cor. xv. 56). Law means the upward striving of human religion and morality, and therefore colours all human activity with sin, for it represents man's attempt to scale God's throne. Those who live under the reign of grace, however, have given full scope to God's freedom, since instead of pressing upward towards God they humbly wait for his descent in love. Ultimately, therefore, justification by faith, which means living under grace, though it is rooted in a region of divine-human relations which lies beyond morals, becomes the one hope of a truly moral life. Even so, however, the future 'shall not dominate' remains a future.

The last remark will provide the occasion for a review of the paragraph (vv. 1-14) as a whole. It is a paragraph to which the modern reader is apt to bring his own questions, forgetting that they are not necessarily the questions Paul intended to answer. The modern reader, for example, wishes to know what relation exists between sacrament and faith, and whether, and to what extent, Paul believed that Christians could be free from sin.

When questions such as these are raised, it is particularly important to recall that Paul's thought, like that of primitive Christianity as a whole, was cast in an eschatological mould, and that he believed himself to be living 'between the times', in a world which was swiftly passing; the age in which he wrote formed a bridge between the old world and the new. The death and resurrection of Jesus were eschatological events—the messianic affliction and the manifestation of God's glory. The practice, and the efficacy, of baptism were rooted in these eschatological events; baptism is not simply a religious rite, but springs out of the fact that an hour has struck on the world clock. Christian eschatology is paradoxical, as Jewish eschatology is not; the Christian life, and Christian rites, are paradoxical, as Jewish life and rites are not. It is of the essence of Christian life that men are *simul justi, simul peccatores*, at the same time righteous and sinners. They are righteous in Christ, sinners in themselves (or, in Adam). Because Christ is now hidden from men's eyes in heaven until his *parousia*, the holiness and righteousness of Christians, which are not their own but his, are hidden, and the body of sin is all too clearly visible. In the meantime, however, the 'powers of the age to come' could—

and must—be expressed in ethical terms; here indeed was the only visible indication that Christians belonged to the new age.

Baptism was no contradiction but an expression of the 'obedience of faith' (i. 5). It follows that there is no tension between justification by faith and the recognition of baptism as a sacramental rite obligatory for all Christians. Justification implies the same anticipation of the eschatological future as baptism, and baptism expresses the same new relation with God as justification. But if either is legalized, if, that is, faith is regarded as a virtue or 'work', or baptism as a rite effective in itself without reference to its eschatological setting, the two spring apart, and the Christian faith itself is on the way to disintegration.

16. vi. 15-23. IN BONDAGE TO RIGHTEOUSNESS

(15) What then? Are we to sin because we are not under the reign of law but under the reign of grace? Certainly not. (16) Do you not know that when you offer yourselves to someone as slaves, to obey him, then you are slaves of him whom you obey? This is true, whether the master be sin (slavery to him ends in death), or obedience (slavery to him ends in righteousness). (17) Thanks be to God! You were indeed slaves of sin, but from the heart you gave your obedience to that Christian doctrine to which as slaves you were handed over. (18) You were liberated from sin, and you were made slaves to righteousness. (19) (I am giving all this in a human illustration because your understanding is only human.) The point of the matter is this: Just as in the past you offered your members to uncleanness and iniquity as their slaves (with the result of producing iniquity), so now offer your members to righteousness as its slaves (the result of this will be sanctification). (20) These are mutually exclusive attitudes; for when you were slaves of sin, you were free men in respect of righteousness. (21) (And

**what fruit did you reap of that?—Things of which you
now are ashamed, for their end is death.) (22) But now
you have been freed from sin, and have become slaves
to God. Accordingly your fruit proves to be sanctification, and the ultimate result will be eternal life. (23) For
the wage paid by sin is death; but the gift freely given by
God is eternal life in Christ Jesus our Lord.**

In *v.* 14 Paul found the ground of the Christian's freedom
from sin in the fact that he is no longer under the reign of law.
He had already shown (in ch. v), and is to show again (in ch. vii),
that it is through the law that sin fastens its grip upon men,
because the law awakens desire, and turns all men's striving, and
especially their striving for life and God, into sin. If then for the
law is substituted grace, sin will inevitably lose its hold.

This is Paul's argument; but it could be reversed, and he now,
reverting to the rhetorical style of the diatribe, proceeds to meet
the possible objection. **What then?** It is the law which directs 15
us to do what is right (vii. 12, 14); do away with the law and you
do away with morality. The more sin abounds, the more grace
abounds (v. 20); life under grace invites the multiplication of
sin. **Are we** then **to sin because we are not under the
reign of law but under the reign of grace?**

There could be no more complete misconception of Christian
freedom. It is simply not true that Christians, free though they
are from the law as a means of salvation, are under no obligation to God (cf. 1 Cor. ix. 21). **Do you not know that when** 16
**you offer yourselves to someone as slaves, to obey him,
then you are slaves of him whom you obey?** This is a
general principle, to which no one can take exception. Behind it
probably lies the practice whereby men applied to be taken into
slavery in order to secure a livelihood; but the construction of
the sentence is obscure because the writer has put too much
into it. The obscurity, which is somewhat mitigated in the
translation, arises through the addition of 'obedience' to slavery.
Paul introduces this additional matter because it is important to
him to show that obedience has a place in the system of grace
and faith (cf. i. 5); indeed, it would not be wrong to say that the
whole of ch. vi is an attempt to vindicate that place. In saying

this, however, we have already advanced to the application of Paul's general principle.

This is true, whether the master be sin (slavery to him ends in death), or obedience (slavery to him ends in righteousness).

Paul assumes that men will be slaves, and obedient, to a good master or a bad. Independence is impossible. Fortunately there is no question which side the readers of the epistle have taken.

17 **Thanks be to God! You were indeed slaves of sin** (cf. John viii. 34; also Rom. iii. 19 f.), **but from the heart you gave your obedience to that Christian doctrine** (literally, pattern of teaching—Christian (not Pauline) teaching) **to which as slaves you were handed over.** The last verb is curious but significant. One expects the doctrine to be handed over (the verb—παραδιδόναι—is used for the transmission of traditions; 1 Cor. xi. 23; xv. 3) to the hearers, not the hearers to the doctrine. But Christians are not (like the Rabbis) masters of a tradition; they are themselves created by the word of God, and remain in subjection to it. In fact, though being a Christian means on the

18 one hand emancipation, on the other it means enslavement. **You were liberated from sin, and you were made slaves to righteousness.** Righteousness remains important to the Christian; the only righteousness he has given up is his own, and that in order that he may be in subjection to God's righteousness—which is not less but greater than human righteousness (cf. Matt. v. 20).

Looking forward, perhaps, to *v.* 19 b, rather than backward,

19 Paul inserts an apologetic parenthesis. **I am giving all this in a human illustration** (cf. iii. 5; 1 Cor. ix. 8; Gal. iii. 15) **because your understanding is only human.** The last clause has an exact verbal parallel in Gal. iv. 13 (cf. 1 Tim. v. 23), but the sense there is different. Literally it runs, 'because of the weakness of your flesh'. Paul's use of the term flesh will be considered later (see pp. 137, 146 f.); at this point it has no special theological meaning but simply refers to the frailty of human nature, which cannot grasp profound truth unless it is presented in human analogies. The analogy follows.

The point of the matter is this: Just as in the past you offered your members to uncleanness and iniquity as

their slaves (with the result of producing iniquity), so now offer your members to righteousness as its slaves (the result of this will be sanctification).

This verse adds little fresh substance to what has already been said two or three times in this chapter. Paul as a pastor doubtless knew well that such injunctions cannot be repeated too frequently.

The 'members' are again (as in *v.* 13) the faculties (not the limbs simply). If they are in service to uncleanness and iniquity, the result will be iniquity; if they are in service to (God's) righteousness, the result will be sanctification. The parallel with iniquity suggests that 'sanctification' has here an ethical sense; this agrees with the use of the same word in 1 Thess. iv. 3-7. Submission to the righteousness of God is not itself a matter of ethics, but it has its issue in ethical purity.

Compromise between sin and righteousness is impossible. A man cannot serve two masters. **These are mutually exclusive attitudes** (these words are not in the Greek, but the 'for' ($\gamma \acute{\alpha} \rho$) with which the next sentence begins presupposes some such remark); **for when you were slaves of sin, you were free men in respect of righteousness,** that is, you acknowedged no obligation to it. But this was no advantage to you.

What fruit did you reap of that? Things of which you now are ashamed, for their end is death (cf. *v.* 23; i. 32; v. 12 f.).

There are two ways, both grammatically possible, of punctuating this sentence. The question mark may be placed after 'that', or after 'ashamed'. If the latter alternative is accepted, the answer to the question must be supplied: What fruit did you reap of those things of which you now are ashamed? None; for their end is death. This does not fit the context well and the parallel verse (22) distinguishes between the near and remote consequences of a course of action (the fruit is sanctification, the ultimate result eternal life), thus strongly supporting a similar distinction in *v.* 21, where the translation given here may be confidently accepted.

But now (this may be a logical or a temporal contrast—or perhaps both; cf. iii. 21, and note) **you have been freed from**

sin (as lord; cf. *v.* 14), **and have become slaves to God.
Accordingly your fruit proves to be sanctification** (as at
v. 19), **and the ultimate result will be eternal life.** 'Fruit'
here recalls Gal. v. 22 f. The inward obedience of faith has
visible exterior consequences.

23   **For the wage paid by sin is death; but the gift freely
given by God is eternal life in Christ Jesus our Lord.** For
the contrast, compare iv. 4. Sin is personified, as at *v.* 13.

The 'gift freely given' ($\chi\acute{\alpha}\rho\iota\sigma\mu\alpha$) is not used as at i. 11, or at
v. 15. It is the supreme spiritual gift, the total result of grace, as
far as man is concerned.

The old servitude to sin was under the reign of law, and sin
accordingly paid a wage, as a matter of debt or obligation; the
new servitude to God (a servitude no less serious for this
reason) is under the reign of grace, and God accordingly gives a
gift of grace, namely eternal life.

17. vii. 1-6. FREE FROM THE LAW

**(1) To put this matter of freedom from the law in another
way: you surely cannot fail to know, brethren, for I speak
to men who know the law, that the law has dominion
over a man for such time as he is alive. (2) For (to take an
example) the married woman is bound by law to her
husband as long as he is alive; but if her husband dies, she
is done with the law, as she is done with her husband. (3)
See what this means. If while her husband is alive she
gives herself to another man, she will be styled an
adulteress; but if her husband dies she is free from the
law, so as not to be an adulteress if she gives herself to
another man. (4) So, my brethren, to interpret the illustration: with reference to the law you were put to death
through the body of Christ, that you might give yourselves
to an Other—namely, to him who was raised from the
dead—in order that we might bear offspring to God. (5)
For when we were in the flesh, the passions bound up
with sins and engendered through the law wrought in our**

**members that we might bear offspring to death. (6) But
now we are done with the law since we died to that by
which we were held fast, so that we serve God our master
in a new life marked by the gift of the Spirit, not the
old life, which was marked only by observance of the
written law.**

The paragraph vi. 1-14 concluded with the statement, You
are not under the reign of law, but under the reign of grace. The
next paragraph, vi. 15-23, dealt with an objection: Men who are
no longer under the reign of law will no longer be obliged to
serve God. On the contrary (says Paul), the Christian is bound
to the service of righteousness; indeed he alone, since he is in
subjection to the righteousness of God (not his own), can serve
God fruitfully, and see sanctification and eternal life result from
his service. The present paragraph makes substantially the same
point, by means of a fresh analogy.

To put this matter of freedom from the law in another 1
way: You surely cannot fail to know (for the expression cf. vi.
3), **brethren, for I speak to men who know the law, that the
law has dominion over a man for such time as he is alive.**

It need not be assumed that these words are addressed to
Jews (for the racial constitution of the Roman church see on i.
6). Gentile Christians also knew the law (i.e. the Old Testament)—though it may be that here and elsewhere Paul exag-
gerates their knowledge. Certainly it is the divine law of the Old
Testament which rules over man—till death. The principle
'death pays all debts' was of course widely recognized, but that
the dead are not under obligation to the law was not frequently
expressed in Judaism, though Ps. lxxxviii. 5 (RV: Cast off
among the dead; PBV: Free among the dead) was sometimes
taken to have this meaning.

So far Paul has laid down a fundamental principle: Legal
obligation is discharged only by death. He now proceeds to his
analogy.

For (to take an example) the married woman (the ad- 2
jective—in Greek ὕπανδρος—may itself include the idea of sub-
ordination; cf. Num. v. 20, 29 (LXX)) **is bound by law to her
husband as long as he is alive.** This states fairly the position

of the Jewish wife, not of the Roman. **But if her husband dies, she is done with** (cf. *v.* 6; Gal. v. 4) **the law, as she is done with her husband.** The last words run, literally, 'from the law of the husband'. But the law of marriage was not imposed by the husband but by the appropriate legislative authority. 'The husband' should therefore be taken in apposition with 'the law'; in the analogy as a whole the husband represents the law.

3   **See what this means. If while her husband is alive she gives herself to another man, she will be styled an adulteress; but if her husband dies she is free from the law** (this explains 'done with the law' in *v.* 2), **so as not to be an adulteress if she gives herself to another man.**

In this verse Paul is not simply illustrating the position of the married woman; the 'other man', to whom she cannot legally be joined during the lifetime of her husband, is mentioned in view of the interpretation that follows.

4   **So, my brethren, to interpret the illustration: with reference to the law you were put to death through the body of Christ.** The last phrase means '*both* "through the fact that Christ in his flesh-body died to the law" *and* "through the fact that you now are joined to and are part of that body" '.[1] The latter part of this twofold interpretation should not be pressed since Paul deals with it in the following words ('that you might give yourselves to an Other'). It is important to recall the point which Paul labours in ch. vi; Christ's death is reproduced in the Christian, in particular through his baptism (in which of course he is also incorporated into the Church; on Paul's use of the term 'Body of Christ' see pp. 236f.). The analogy is imperfect. In marriage, the husband dies and the wife is free. In Christian life, the law does not die (as analogy would require); Christ dies, and by faith Christians die with him. All Paul needs for his purpose is a death; but his argument would of course make no sense if he could not assume both that Christ's death on the cross was followed by the resurrection, and that our death by faith in baptism was followed by a new life. Because this is so, Paul can continue: Our relation of bondage to the law has been broken off by a death, **that you might give yourselves to an Other—namely, to him who was raised from**

[1] J. A. T. Robinson, *The Body* (1952), p. 47.

136

the dead—in order that we might bear offspring to God.

The old relation to law has been supplanted by a new relation to Christ. In vi. 21 f. Paul used the image of 'fruit-bearing' in quite general terms, but when he employs it in the present context it can hardly be doubted that he has in mind the birth of children. We are joined to Christ (for he not only died but was raised from the dead), but the children are born 'to God'. This dative is probably due to the careless use of metaphor; but it is the sort of carelessness that is significant. What Christ does is the work of God.

The prospect of fruitful union with Christ prompts Paul to look back at the old condition of union with the law. Again, there is a significant confusion, this time of sin, law, and death.

For when we were in the flesh, the passions bound up 5 with sins and engendered through the law wrought in our members that we might bear offspring to death. (The subject-matter of this verse reappears, at much greater length, in *vv.* 7-25.)

It is implied that we are no longer 'in the flesh'. The same implication is found at viii. 9; Gal. iii. 3; v. 24; but Paul and other Christians are still 'in the flesh' at 2 Cor. iv. 11; x. 3; Gal. ii. 20; Phil. i. 22, 24. It is impossible to escape the conclusion that Paul uses the word 'flesh' (σάρξ) in at least two senses.[1] Here it is used to denote the state in which men are dominated by law, sin, and death. In the terms of this paragraph, it might be described as the state of marriage with the law. The effect of this union was that passions bound up with (due to, or leading to —perhaps both) sins were at work in the organs of our human nature (see on vi. 13). The passions were themselves due to the law (cf. *v.* 9), and in the 'marriage' of man and law (outside the sphere of grace) they resulted in death. 'Death', even if taken to be personified, is not a good parallel to 'God' in *v.* 4; compare, however, vi. 21, 'their end is death'. This is Paul's meaning here.

Such was your state—before Christ and under law. **But now 6** (the contrast is both temporal and logical; cf. iii. 21; vi. 22; xi.

[1] It is also true that, even when 'flesh' is used in a bad sense, Christians are both in and not in the flesh, just as they are both sinful and free from sin. Cf. p. 129.

30) **we are done with the law** (cf. *v.* 2) **since we died to that by which we were held fast.** In the analogy of *vv.* 2 f. the husband died. Freedom through death is the essential point. For the image of men imprisoned by the law cf. Gal. iii. 22 f.

Release through the death of Christ means **that we serve God our master** (no object is expressed in Greek) **in a new life marked by the gift of the Spirit, not the old life, which was marked only by observance of the written law**—literally, 'in newness of Spirit and not oldness of letter'.

The Christian is not exempt from service to God (Paul's verb means service as a slave). Obedience is central in Christian freedom (cf. ch. vi, *passim*).

The meaning of 'newness of Spirit' is clear enough; the life of union with Christ has for its visible mark the fruit of the Spirit. 'Oldness of letter' has been described as a rhetorical imitative formation; but though the choice of 'oldness' is no doubt due to rhetorical considerations, the phrase as a whole is substantial. The old life was marked by subservience to the requirements of the letter of the law. This was of course true preeminently of the Jew, but true also in some degree of every man who practised religion seriously.

18. vii. 7-25. THE LAW AND SIN

(7) In view of this, what shall we say? That the law is sin? Certainly not. Yet it is true that it is only through the law that I came to know sin; for indeed I should not know desire if the law did not say, 'Thou shalt not desire'. (8) But in fact sin seized its opportunity through the law and thereby produced in me every kind of desire—for apart from law, sin is dead. (9) And apart from law I was alive once; but when the commandment came, sin sprang to life (10) and I died; and the very commandment which was intended to produce life resulted for me in death. (11) For sin took its opportunity, deceived me by means of the commandment, and—again by means of it—killed me. (12) So the law then is holy, and the

commandment is holy, righteous, and good. (13) Did then that which in itself is good prove in my case to be death? No indeed. The fact is that sin, in order that it might be shown up as sin, used that good thing to bring forth death for me. Sin did this in order that, by means of the commandment, it might be shown up as exceedingly sinful.

(14) There is no question of the goodness of the law, for we know that it is spiritual; but I am a man of flesh, sold as a slave so as to be under the power of sin. (15) For the works I do are incomprehensible to me, for I do not practise what I wish; on the contrary, I do what I hate. (16) But if I do what I do not wish, then it follows that I agree with the law, admitting it to be right and good. (17) But what in fact is happening is that it is not I that do my works, but sin which dwells in me. (18) For I know that there dwells no good thing in me—I should say, in my flesh. For I can always wish, but never actually achieve, a really good work; (19) for I do not do the good I wish to do; rather, the evil I do not wish to do I practise. (20) But if I do what I do not wish to do, that shows that it cannot be I that do it; it must be sin that dwells in me.

(21) What then does this amount to? That there is imposed upon me, who would do what is good and right, a law, to the effect that evil shall always attend me. (22) For in my inner self I agree with *God's*[1] law, (23) but I observe in my members *another* law which makes war upon the law which rules in my mind and takes me prisoner to the law of sin which is in my members. (24) Wretched man that I am! who shall deliver me from this body of death? (25) Thanks be to God through Jesus Christ our Lord![2]

To sum up then: I myself with my mind serve God's law, but with the flesh I serve sin's law.

[1] Instead of 'God's law', B has 'the law of the mind', harmonizing with *v.* 23. But to say, 'Inwardly I agree with the law of my mind', is tautologous.

[2] There are several variants, of which that adopted in the text is almost certainly right. 'I give thanks to God' (ℵ A ω pesh Origen) is probably due to an accidental mechanical error; 'The grace of God' (D lat) and 'The grace of the Lord' (G) are attempts (based on the fact that Greek uses the same word (χάρις) for 'thanks' and 'grace') to supply a definite answer to the question, 'Who shall deliver me?'.

There is perhaps no chapter in the epistle which has given rise to so many divergent interpretations as this. The most disputed question is, When Paul in this chapter says 'I', what does he mean? Mankind? The Jewish people? Himself as a non-Christian Jew? Himself as a Christian? But it will be well to set this question aside for the moment, partly because it can be answered only on the basis of exact and detailed exegesis, and partly also because to lay too much emphasis upon it is to miss the real intention of the paragraph. Paul does not set out from the question, How may a Christian (or one who is not a Christian) be defined? Still less does he embark upon a psychological account of the feelings and struggles of either regenerate or unregenerate man. He begins from the question, Is the law sin? Earlier passages in the epistle have come near to suggesting that it is; see especially iii. 20; iv. 15; v. 13, 20; vi. 14; vii. 5. No Jew, convinced that the law was the very word of God, could allow such passages to fall from his pen without being compelled to consider whether he was consistent in his opinions. Accordingly Paul makes what is strictly speaking a digression from the main line of his thought (viii. 1 resumes vii. 6), though it is a digression which in the end leads back to the central theme.

One further point must be made before the detailed exegesis begins. It was pointed out above (see p. 84) that often when Paul speaks of 'law' the word might be paraphrased, 'the Old Testament religion'. This equivalence is valid in the present chapter; and what Paul says of the religion of Judaism, the highest of all religions, is true *a fortiori* of all religion. It is in the last resort the meaning of religion that is analysed here.

The question is thrown up bluntly, in the form of the
7 diatribe (see p. 43). **In view of this** (the contrast between the new life in grace and the old life in the letter of the law—*v.* 6), **what shall we say? That the law is sin?** See above. Paul is in no doubt, however, that the answer is, **Certainly not.** This answer is no more to be dismissed as misplaced Jewish nationalism than that of iii. 2. The law is the word of God, a gift of his grace to his chosen and favoured people; see *vv.* 12, 14 below. The law in itself is not sin, but it is impossible to deny a certain connexion between it and sin. **It is true that it is only through the law that I came to know sin.** Compare iii. 20;

v. 13. The inward rebellion against the Creator in the interests of self that is the root of sin exists everywhere, and everywhere there exists enough of the rudiments of religion to make it responsible and blameworthy (cf. i. 19 ff.). But only where the law, religion in the form of the command of the living God, exists, can sin emerge in perceptible and measurable form. The law turns sin into transgression (see p. 112). This, however, does not exhaust Paul's meaning. 'Knowing sin' does not mean merely perceiving its existence, but experiencing it. The law is not simply a reagent by which the presence of sin may be detected; it is a catalyst which aids or even initiates the action of sin upon man. This opinion Paul supports by means of an example.

For indeed I should not know desire if the law did not say, 'Thou shalt not desire'. Paul refers to the tenth commandment, Ex. xx. 17; Deut. v. 21; but he quotes only the verb of the prohibition, omitting the objects which the Old Testament supplies (thy neighbour's house, etc.). The word itself, both noun and verb, is in non-Biblical Greek as neutral in meaning as the English 'desire'; only the context can determine whether it is good or bad. The good sense occurs in the New Testament (e.g. Luke xxii. 15), but the bad predominates; and, ultimately, for the reason Paul exposes by omitting to supply an object of desire. It is of course wrong to desire (covet) one's neighbour's wife; but behind this guilty desire, shown to be guilty by its object, lies a desire which is guilty in itself, independently of its object, and sinful though quite possibly respectable. Desire means precisely that exaltation of the *ego* which we have seen to be of the essence of sin (see pp. 37, 111). Regardless of his place in creation, and of God's command, man desires, and his desire becomes the law of his being. He, rather than God, becomes Lord. This the law cannot tolerate. Its form is God's command, and its basis is God's right as Lord to command. It emphasizes man's creatureliness. It might be summed up in two clauses: Thou shalt not desire—Thou shalt obey; and if both are left without objects their meaning becomes not less but more clear. The inexactness of Paul's quotation is not due to carelessness or to the wish to abbreviate, but is significant.

Another small observation in this sentence will also prove significant. In *v.* 7 b, and *v.* 7 c, Paul uses different verbs, in different tenses, for 'know'. In *v.* 7 b the verb is aorist, in *v.* 7 c, imperfect.[1] The two sentences, if strictly interpreted, should accordingly have different meanings: (a) I should not have come to know sin if I had not come to know it through the law; (b) I should not now know desire, if the law did not now say ... If it were right, either grammatically or theologically, to make a strict temporal contrast, (a) would refer to a pre-conversion event, (b) to a post-conversion state. The very fact, however, that (a) and (b) stand side by side makes such a differentiation difficult. The 'I' in this verse means man, perceiving and participating in sin. The two clauses together amount perhaps to 'I should never have known ...'—no precise limits being attached to this knowledge, whether forward or backward. Men can be religious, and, in particular, they can be Jews, both before and after their conversion.

How does religion, the law, convey knowledge of sin? So far as knowledge means 'perception' the answer is easy. The law provides commandments, and sin shows itself by transgressing them. But if knowledge means 'experience' the answer is not so plain. The law forbids sin; how can it 'engender' it (*v.* 5)? The answer seems to be that it is in the law that man becomes aware of his limitations, and of his status as a creature over against the Creator. Sin is man's reaction against these limitations, his affirmation of himself and of his own will-to-life in the face of the 'Thou shalt not' of the law. The law itself is not sin, but it supplies the raw material of sin. Paul, however, has a different metaphor.

8   The law is not itself sin, **but in fact sin seized its opportunity through the law.** The word here translated 'opportunity' means literally 'point of departure', and is often used in military contexts to denote the origin of a war. Sin and law are clearly differentiated, though closely connected. Sin aimed against man an attack which law never intended, and was able to use law in its approach. It **thereby produced in me every kind of desire,** because law had created the conditions

[1] Strictly speaking, the pluperfect ᾔδειν, used with the force of the imperfect.

in which desire (see above) could operate. Apart from law, the desire would not have been apparent, **for apart from law, sin is dead**—that is, inactive; sin was present, but not counted (v. 13); indeed, not countable.

The allusion to v. 13 suggests one possible interpretation of this verse, and of *vv.* 9 ff. They may be understood as pointing to the story of Adam; indeed, if Paul is not actually telling this story he is at least using it to bring out his point. Sin—the serpent—was in the Garden even before man, but had no opportunity of attacking the man until the command 'Thou shalt not eat of it' (Gen. ii. 17) had been given. It was precisely by means of this command, the prototype of all law and religion, that the serpent tempted man. The command marked out the difference between man and God, creature and Creator, which is the theme of religion. The serpent was able to represent this as humiliating to man. 'The difference is not ultimate; transgress the command and you shall be as God' (Gen. iii. 4 f.). Man's will to live was thus turned into sin, and from sin into transgression. The woman, soon joined by the man, saw that the forbidden tree was 'to be *desired*' (Gen. iii. 6).

It is possible that Paul is not simply describing the fate of Adam, which he had read in the Old Testament, but telling his own story in the light of Genesis. The tenth commandment proved to be the psychological means by which sin was stirred to activity within his own experience. It has often been pointed out that to prohibit some course of action is to awaken desire to pursue it. It may be therefore that Paul is thinking of an occasion in his youth when the legal prohibition awakened revolt within his soul.

The next verse looks even more like autobiography. **Apart** 9 **from the law I was alive once; but when the commandment came, sin sprang to life and I died.** 10

The autobiographical interpretation would run as follows. In the first innocence of youth Paul was alive. Death is the consequence of sin, and there was at that time no sin to incur it. Life is from God, and there was nothing to interrupt the child's natural and instinctive communion with him. Then came the moment when the Jewish boy became a 'Son of the Commandment', and assumed responsibility before the law. With this new legal responsibility sin took its place in the boy's experience. The forbidden world appeared upon his horizon, and he longed to enter it. He desired to gratify himself and to achieve independence of the God who placed unwelcome restraint upon him. This was death.

When we turn back to the narrative of Gen. iii, all that need be added is precise reference to the warning, 'In the day that thou eatest thereof thou shalt surely die' (Gen. ii. 17; cf. iii. 19).

The process may be summarized: **the very commandment which was intended to produce life resulted for me in death.** The command of Gen. ii. 17 was intended to maintain life, for it was directed against a course of action which could only lead to death. The law also, under whose sway the Jewish boy entered, was intended to give life (e.g. Ecclus. xvii. 11; *Aboth*, ii. 7: The more study of the law the more life). Life is that to which religion points, when it directs man to be content with the place in creation that God has accorded him. But all these well-intentioned institutions have produced a race under sentence of death, and already the cancer of corrupting bondage (viii. 21) is felt and seen in human affairs; it suffices to refer to i. 18 – iii. 20.

But the commandment achieved this unintended result not because of a defect in itself, but through the attack, and the
11 deceitfulness, of sin. **For sin took its opportunity** (cf. *v.* 8), **deceived me by means of the commandment, and—again by means of it—killed me.** This is almost a quotation from Gen. iii. 13, to which Paul alludes again at 2 Cor. xi. 3 (cf. 1 Tim. ii. 14). It was the commandment which gave the serpent his opportunity. The commandment singled out the forbidden tree, and its property of giving divine knowledge; and this last in turn made it easy to twist the warning, Ye shall surely die. Law and religion, which begin by drawing attention to the gulf that separates man from God, are shaped by men into a bridge across the gulf. This is man's misuse of religion (see p. 55); in particular, it is the Jew's boasting in the law that condemns him.

12 To say this, however, is to absolve the law itself. **The law then is holy, and the commandment is holy, righteous, and good.** Scripture is holy (i. 2) because it comes from God;

whatever may be true of other religions and of other codes of morals, those in the Old Testament are the word of God himself. The 'commandment' suggests the special enactments of the Mosaic code (and perhaps Gen. ii. 17). These too are holy; they are righteous, in that they command what is right (cf. Gal. iii. 21); and they are good, that is, beneficent in their intention. Paul's argument hitherto has evidently been intended to vindicate this holy, righteous, and beneficent character of the law.

What then is wrong? **Did that which in itself is good** 13 (Prov. iv. 2 was sometimes made the basis of an identification of the law with 'the good') **prove in my case to be death?** The question must be asked, because death has in fact resulted (*vv.* 10 f.). But the answer is clear: **No indeed.** The fault does not lie with the law *in itself*. **The fact is that sin, in order that it might be shown up as sin, used that good thing** (the law) **to bring forth death for me.** The fault lies entirely with sin, which here is almost personified (cf. vi. 12 ff., etc.). The means by which sin took advantage of the situation created by law have already been brought out in the preceding verses and need not be repeated now. It is to be noted that this verse betrays not the least interest in psychology; Paul simply states that sin led to death—the doom of creation separated from the Creator; and that this happened in order that sin might stand out in its true colours. The serpent had promised (Gen. iii. 5) that men should be as God; but the rebellion begun with the highest conceivable hope ended in condemnation and death. Sin might appear as human progress, or in any other attractive guise; but death proved it to be—nothing but sin. The most damning feature of its disclosure was the fact that sin had used in its death-dealing work God's good gift, the law. **Sin did this in order that, by means of the commandment, it might be shown up as exceedingly sinful.** The second purpose clause is parallel to the first, but goes further. Sin, in its deceitful use of law and commandment, is revealed not merely in its true colours but in the worst possible light. The purpose was God's (cf. v. 20; also Gal. iii. 19).

One point in Paul's argument is not perfectly clear; he has not shown whether law precedes sin (as the condition in which it appears), or follows it (with the intention of unmasking its true character). It is, however, unfair to expect perfect clarity here, where clarity could be attained only by plunging more deeply into mythological speech than Paul intends to do. He has brought out the subtle interrelation of law and sin; the holiness of the former and the exceeding sinfulness of the latter. It is not too much to suppose that it was precisely these points that he intended to bring out.

But he has not yet done with the matter. Law and sin are still engaged in conflict, and their battle-ground is human life. Their mutual relations may be observed further in this field.

14 **There is no question of the goodness of the law** (this clause, which is not in the Greek, is to be understood as the necessary antecedent of the 'for' (γάρ) that follows), **for we know that it is spiritual**, that is, in its origin; it is from God. This was axiomatic in Judaism (e.g. *Sanhedrin*, x. 1: These are they that have no share in the world to come: he that says . . . that the law is not from heaven [God]). Because it is spiritual in origin, the law is spiritual in character, and in its mode of contact with men. Those to whom it is merely a matter of 'letter' (vii. 6) cannot understand it; neither can they who are not themselves spiritual.

It is here that difficulty arises. **I am a man of flesh, sold as a slave so as to be under the power of sin.** It will be noticed that Paul no longer speaks in the past tenses of *vv.* 7, 8, 9, 10, 11, 13, but in the present; this continues to the end of the chapter.

We have already seen (p. 137) that Paul uses the word 'flesh' in at least two senses; sometimes it merely describes the physical aspect of human life, and sometimes it takes on a darker tone, and describes a proclivity to sin by which all men are affected. From this Christians are delivered, but their deliverance is never in this life so complete that Paul finds it unnecessary to warn them against the flesh, and exhort them not to live in accordance with it. In baptism, flesh (in the bad sense) is destroyed in principle; but the process of destruction has still to be completed in fact.

What flesh (in the bad sense) means appears clearly in this verse. I have been sold (as a slave) in such a way as to come under the power of sin. Sin has dominion over me (cf. vi. 14). This dominion is given vivid rhetorical expression in the next

verses; for the moment we may recall that Paul is still emphasizing the central point: the law is not at fault. Not the
spiritual law, but carnal, sin-dominated man is the cause of
death. This even sinful man must admit. **For the works I do** 15
are incomprehensible to me (not, 'I do not know what I am
doing', for Paul knows only too well; but 'I do not recognize
and approve'), **for I do not practise** (it is doubtful whether
Paul means to distinguish between 'practise' and 'do'; cf. i. 32)
what I wish; on the contrary I do what I hate. But if I do 16
what I do not wish, then it follows that I agree with the
law, admitting it to be right and good (one adjective only in
Greek, not that of *v.* 12).

Commentators usually quote in illustration of these verses
Ovid's words (*Metamorphoses*, vii. 20 f.), *uideo meliora proboque,*
deteriora sequor. There is an even closer verbal parallel in
Epictetus (II. xxvi. 4): (the thief) does not do what he wishes.
Neither Ovid nor Epictetus, however, says exactly what Paul is
saying here. It is assumed that the measure of Paul's actions is
the law, and that they do not conform to this standard. Unless
his words are simply tautologous, he must mean that there is
within himself an independent authority which confirms the
judgement of the external law. But Paul has already spoken of
such an independent (though allied) authority, namely, the
conscience (see ii. 15). The very fact that I am unhappy about
my own deeds confirms that the law is just and good. Is the law
sin? Certainly not; it is confirmed by conscience.

A further point now emerges. We find man in a state of rebellion against God, and under sentence of death. For this unhappy situation the law is not to blame. But neither, it now
appears, am 'I', for I agree with the law, and disapprove of the
sins which I myself commit. Who then is to blame? **What in fact** 17
is happening is that it is not I that do my works, but sin
which dwells in me. Sin is personified as an evil power which
takes up its residence within human nature, and there controls
man's actions.

Having come upon this fresh point in the course of an argument directed to a different end (that of exonerating the law),
Paul proceeds to develop it through the next three verses, coming
back in *v.* 20 to the conclusion he has already announced in *v.* 17.

18 The fault must lie with sin, **for I know that there dwells no good thing in me** (he must correct himself, for he has just said that 'I' agree with the law and wish to do what is good)—**I should say, in my flesh.**

It is important to note here the distinction between the 'I' and the 'flesh'. Here at least, and at *v.* 25, the flesh is radically evil; it corresponds to the 'evil inclination' of Rabbinic Judaism, which constantly draws man in the direction of sin. Whether Paul identified this evil principle with the material constituent of human nature, and regarded it as evil because it was material, are difficult questions, which we are not yet in a position to answer. Here it must suffice to note that there is an element in human nature so completely under the power of sin that not only is there no good in it, it corrupts all man's activity. How do we know that this is so? By observing (as in *vv.* 15 f.) the sheer moral incompetence of man: **For I can always wish, but**
19 **never actually achieve, a really good work; for I do not do the good I wish to do; rather, the evil I do not wish to**
20 **do I practise.** The conclusion is the same as that of *v.* 17: **But if I do what I do not wish to do, that shows that it cannot be I that do it; it must be sin that dwells in me.**

The effect of this reiterated conclusion is to emphasize the distinction between the true self—'I'—and the sin-dominated flesh, which has its way and carries out actions of which 'I' disapprove, and does not carry out the good actions of which 'I' approve.

Paul has now advanced beyond his original proposition (that the law so far from being sin is in all respects good) in two matters. (a) Equally blameless with the law is the conscience, which, in agreement with the law, condemns evil behaviour. (b) Evil behaviour is caused by sin, a personal power residing in and dominating the flesh. The digression is coming to its close, and in *vv.* 21-5 Paul sums up its meaning. It is unfortunate, in the interests of clarity, that in doing so he introduces new metaphors and psychological terms.

21 **What then does this amount to? That there is imposed upon me, who would do what is good and right, a law, to the effect that evil shall always attend me.** This verse describes in fresh terms the state described in *vv.* 15 f., 18 b-20 a;

but it is complicated by the use of the word 'law'. Of this, several interpretations have been given; the most important are the following.

(i) Throughout the chapter 'law' means the law of Moses. This verse then means, 'This is what I find the law—a life under the law—to come to in my experience: when I wish to do good, evil is present with me' (Denney). This interpretation finds support in *vv.* 8, 11.

(ii) 'Law' (*νόμος*) means 'rule' or 'principle'. For this suggestion and an objection to it see on iii. 27.

(iii) 'Law' here stands for a law-like rule, which as an evil double of the Mosaic law can bear the same name. Thus there are *two* laws; the true law of Moses, and the base imitation of this which is the work of sin. This interpretation is strikingly confirmed by *v.* 23, where two 'laws' are mentioned side by side.

Of these interpretations, (i) and (iii) are perhaps not as far apart as at first sight appears; but the sharp antithesis of *v.* 23 requires (iii), or something very much like it. It must be remembered that Paul, in these concluding verses of the chapter, is closing the last gaps in his argument that the law is not in itself responsible for the evil state of mankind. He has asserted that the law is holy. He has shown that this is attested by the conscience. He has accused sin of being the corrupting influence which takes advantage of the law to attack men. Yet, when all this is said, the law still looks like an enemy. It is under the rule of law that sin and death flourish. It would have been simpler for students of the epistle if Paul had here reverted to the language of ch. ii, and shown that the trouble arises not through the use but through the abuse of the law, and that the law ministers to sin only when men instead of being humbled by it use it as an instrument of self-glorification. But Paul does not do this. He says (*v.* 23) that sin produces a counterfeit law, which makes war upon the true law, takes man captive and so works its will with him. Religion which, especially in its Old Testament form, ought to keep man in a state of humble dependence before the Creator becomes (in its perverted form) the watchword of his revolt.

As often happens, Paul states his case first, and then proceeds to support it with a 'for' sentence.

22, 23 **For in my inner self I agree with** *God's* **law, but I observe in my members** (cf. vi. 13) *another* **law which makes war upon the law which rules in my mind** (evidently the same as God's law which is approved by my inner self, *v.* 22) **and takes me prisoner** (as a prisoner of war) **to the law of sin** (the 'other law') **which is in my members.**

The two laws mentioned in these verses have already been discussed, but attention must be given to the psychological terms introduced.

The 'inner self', or 'inward man' (ὁ ἔσω ἄνθρωπος), is a term which recurs in 2 Cor. iv. 16 (cf. Eph. iii. 16). In these passages it refers to the interior Christian life. Its meaning cannot be substantially different here; it is synonymous, or almost synonymous, with the 'I' that would do good and hates evil (*vv.* 14-17, 19 f.), and the 'mind' of *vv.* 23, 25. 2 Cor. iv. 16, however, gives a further pointer, for it is set in an evidently eschatological context. The 'inward man' belongs to the Age to Come, just as the 'outward man' belongs to the present age, and is therefore doomed to perish. That is, the 'inward' or invisible man is also the 'new man' implied by vi. 6. It is the new creation, which in faith and sacramentally Christians have experienced, and which ethically they must continually be instructed to put into practice; in fact, it is Christ himself, whom Christians have 'put on' (Gal. iii. 27), and whom they must still 'put on' (xiii. 14). 'Paul takes over the language of the Hellenistic-dualistic way of thinking but remoulds it to modes of expression of his own anthropology which is Christian, and determined on soteriological-eschatological lines'.[1]

Little would be gained by an attempt to distinguish between the 'mind' and the 'inner self'. Again, Paul is dependent on Hellenistic terminology, but even where he appears to borrow most he is in fact writing independently. So far from the intelligence being essentially good, it can become 'unfit' (i. 28).

On the 'members' see on vi. 13. This term provides a clear way of saying, 'in my actual corporeal existence', in which I am determined by the conditions of life in this (fallen) world; or, better, in this present age.

To sum up: the mind is able to conceive a pure religion, in

[1] J. Behm, in *T.W.N.T.*, ii. 697.

which all life is ordered in accordance with its proper place in creation. In a covenant of law man recognizes his indebtedness to, and his total dependence on, God, whom he loves and serves with all his heart and soul. But this is not religion as it exists, even within Judaism and the Old Testament. For sin has taken possession of the law ('the law of sin', *v.* 23), and made out of it a subtle perversion of law. If by 'law' the inquirer means this perversion, then the law is sin; and from it there is no visible means of escape.

No wonder that Paul cries out: **Wretched man that I am!** 24 **who shall deliver me from this body of death?** 'The body of this death' is grammatically possible but scarcely makes sense. Paul means the body or human nature which through sin and law has fallen under the dominion of death.

The source of Paul's wretchedness is clear. It is not a 'divided self', but the fact that the last hope of mankind, religion, has proved to be a broken reed. Through sin, it is no longer a comfort but an accusation. Man needs not a law but deliverance.

Paul writes as a Christian, and he knows the answer to his own question—knows it so well that with unstudied dramatic aposiopesis he does not express it in words. **Thanks be to God** 25 **through Jesus Christ our Lord!** Christ, and Christ alone, is the answer.

Those who interpret this paragraph on psychological lines almost always feel obliged to transfer *v.* 25 b to a different place, or to omit it altogether. These, however, are expedients to which resort may be had only if the words in question prove quite unintelligible where they stand. But this is not so. They are an apt summary of the paragraph. There are two laws; there are two parts of human nature. The mind recognizes the law of God, the flesh—human nature living in and for this age—recognizes the law which sin has fashioned for this age.

To sum up then: I myself with my mind serve God's law, but with the flesh I serve sin's law.

We must return to the questions posed at the beginning of our discussion of this paragraph, but it will be necessary first to recall three important facts.

(i) In passages where Paul certainly describes his life before his conversion there is no trace of spiritual conflict or of a 'divided self'. Gal. i. 13 f. and Phil. iii. 4 ff. depict a Jew practising his religion more successfully than any of his contemporaries, blameless in his observance of the law, and entirely satisfied with his own righteousness.

(ii) Ch. vi has already made clear the ambiguous position of the Christian in this world. In baptism, by faith, he has died with Christ to sin, and been raised with him to live a new life. Yet, true as this is, it is still necessary for the apostle to urge him to do what he has already done—to die to sin, and to offer himself to God as one whom God has raised from the dead. He is, and he is not, free from sin; he lives, and he does not live, for God; he is at the same time a righteous man and a sinner (cf. p. 129). This ambiguous personal position reflects the eschatological situation. The Age to Come has dawned, in the life, death, and resurrection of Jesus; but the present age has not passed. The two exist uneasily side by side, and Christians still look earnestly for the redemption of the body (viii. 23), knowing that they have been saved in hope (viii. 24).

(iii) 'The use of the 1st and 2nd person singular as representing any one in general, in order to express some truth of general validity in vivid style by using the example of a single person, as though he were present, is not as common in Greek as in other languages, and in literature seems first to occur in the late classical period (as a peculiarity of vivid colloquial speech). In the New Testament Paul presents a few examples; especially Rom. vii. 7 ff. belongs to this class. . . .' (B.D. pp. 126 f.).

In addition to these facts it must be remembered that, as the exegesis has brought out, the primary question in Paul's mind here is not psychological or anthropological, but concerns the meaning of law and religion. Is the law sin? If not, how came it to be so closely connected with sin? How did God's good gift, and man's highest achievement in understanding and feeling, prove to be man's death sentence?

In answering these questions Paul is incidentally involved in an analysis of human nature. It is true that the analysis is not merely academic; Paul wrote what he smartingly did feel. But it is human nature, and not Paul's nature, with which he deals; and it is human nature on earth, and not in heaven, that he describes. The insights of this paragraph are Christian insights.

The paragraph itself does not tell the whole story of the Christian life, but it is written from within the Christian life to account for the role of religion in man's experience. So far as Christianity is a 'religion', what is true of other religions is true of it also, and in pre-eminent degree; so far as Christians are religious men, what is true of other religious men is true of them also, and in pre-eminent degree: We ourselves also, who have the first-fruits of the Spirit, we ourselves also groan inwardly, while we still look forward to our adoption as God's children, the redemption of our body (viii. 23). Thus the digression comes back to the main theme of redemption in Jesus Christ.

19. viii. 1-11. LIFE IN THE SPIRIT

(1) It follows therefore that those who are in Christ Jesus fall now under no condemnation whatever. (2) For the religion which is made possible in Christ Jesus, namely that of the life-giving Spirit, liberates[1] from the old religion which is abused by sin and leads to death. (3) For this liberation, which the law could never effect because it was weak through the flesh, God brought about when, by sending his own Son in the form of flesh which had passed under sin's rule, and to deal with sin, he condemned sin in the flesh, (4) in order that the law's requirement (that we should be righteous) might be fulfilled in us, whose lives are determined not by the flesh but by the Spirit. (5) For those whose lives are determined by the flesh set their minds on the affairs of the flesh,

[1] Many of the best MSS. (B ℵ G it pesh) have 'liberated thee'; the majority of MSS. (A C D ω vg sah) have 'liberated me'; some have 'liberated us'; and there is slight evidence (mainly from Origen) for the use of the verb without any object pronoun. (If, as here, this reading is adopted, it is best to take the verb as a kind of gnomic aorist and translate it by an English present.) The reading 'us' is almost certainly a generalization, intended to make clear that Paul's words apply to all Christians; it is therefore secondary. 'Thee' is undoubtedly a harder reading than 'me', for the latter harmonizes better with ch. vii; 'thee' should therefore be preferred. But 'thee' may well be due to accidental repetition of the last syllable of 'liberated' ($\dot{\eta}\lambda\epsilon\upsilon\theta\acute{\epsilon}\rho\omega\sigma\epsilon$). The reading with an object is easier than that without, and accordingly there is much to be said for the short text, notwithstanding its slight attestation.

while those whose lives are determined by the Spirit set their minds on the affairs of the Spirit. (6) This contrariety is absolute; for to have one's mind set on the flesh results in death, but to have one's mind set on the Spirit results in life and peace. (7) A mind set on the flesh results in death, because it is in a state of enmity against God, for it is not in subjection to the law of God, nor indeed can it be. (8) It follows that those who are in the flesh cannot please God. (9) But you are not in the flesh but in the Spirit, if, as is indeed the case, the Spirit of God dwells in you. And if anyone has not the Spirit that comes from Christ, he is not Christ's. (10) But if Christ is in you, the body on the one hand is dead on account of sin, but the Spirit on the other is at work giving life because you are righteous before God; (11) and if the Spirit of him who raised up Jesus from the dead dwells in you, then he who raised Christ Jesus from the dead will quicken your mortal bodies too, through his Spirit, who dwells in you.

1   **It follows therefore**—not from the excursus of vii. 7-25 but from vii. 6—**that those who are in Christ Jesus fall now** (cf. the 'now' of vii. 6, with the note) **under no condemnation whatever.** It is the law that leads to condemnation, both because sin fastens its grip upon man through the law, and because judgement takes place on the basis of law. Christians, however, are dead to the law and therefore escape judgement. They are dead to the law not because they have decided to ignore it, but because they have died with Christ (vi. 3); hence it is those who are in Christ who are not condemned. Compare v. 16, 18: the act of the first Adam leads to condemnation, but the act of the new Adam leads to acquittal (justification). For the phrase 'in Christ' see vi. 11 and xii. 5, with the notes. Christians share the death and resurrection of Christ and so pass in him into the Age to Come. This observation is of fundamental importance. Paul does not say that Christians are free from condemnation because they are sinless, but because they are in Christ; that is, he is still speaking of justification and its consequences. Among these consequences, hardly mentioned in the epistle up to this point (but

see vii. 6, which is in fact the beginning of this paragraph) is the gift of the Spirit.

That it is their freedom from the law which releases Christians from condemnation is confirmed by the next verse. **For the** **religion** (literally, law) **which is made possible in Christ Jesus, namely that of the life-giving Spirit, liberates from the old religion** (literally, law) **which is abused by sin and leads to death.** Two 'laws' (for the translation 'religion' see above, p. 84) are mentioned in this verse; compare the two laws of vii. 23, 25. The second is, literally, the 'law of sin and death'. This is evidently the law of Moses, seized and perverted by sin and consequently leading to death. The first (literally, the 'law of the Spirit of life in Christ Jesus') is a rhetorical rather than a substantial parallel to the second. Its meaning can only be understood when the several parts are taken separately. The 'law' itself means a religion, a way of life. This is characterized by the gift of the Spirit, which is the distinguishing mark of the Christian. The Spirit produces life (cf. *v.* 6), just as law and sin produce death; and the whole process is put into effect and operates in Christ.

The new way liberates from the old, which acts as a tyrannical master; compare vi. 18, 22; vii. 3, 24. It is evident that this liberation could never have been won for men by the law of Moses, which was not able to give life (Gal. iii. 21), and had itself passed under the control of sin. To attempt to use it as a way of salvation was to misapply it, and to fall into sin. Liberation could only come through a new and creative act of God. **This liberation, which the law could never effect because** **it was weak through the flesh, God brought about.** The flesh was committed to 'sin's law', and was bound therefore to paralyse the divine law. 'Brought about' has no equivalent in the Greek, but some such supplement is required in order to complete the construction, which Paul breaks off when he reaches the word 'God', going on to say at once what it was that God had done.

God effected liberation **when, by sending his own Son in** **the form of flesh which had passed under sin's rule, and** **to deal with sin, he condemned sin in the flesh.**

Jesus Christ was *sent* by his Father; he was neither a man who discovered the truth about God, nor a heavenly rebel, like Prometheus, but a divine envoy, whose authority resided not in himself but in him who sent him. Paul's assertion here contains the root of the doctrine of the Incarnation; but as he continues he raises acutely one of its most difficult problems. If Jesus Christ was on the one hand God's own Son, on the other he was man. But in what relation did he stand to the humanity he came to redeem? Paul's words, literally translated, are that Christ was sent 'in the likeness (ὁμοίωμα) of flesh of sin'. Paul certainly does not mean that Christ was sinful like the rest of mankind (2 Cor. v. 21), or that he was a man only in appearance —his insistence upon the Cross as a real event makes it impossible to think that he believed in a docetic Christ. One possible suggestion is that Paul distinguished between flesh as it was created by God, and 'flesh of sin', that is, flesh which had fallen under the dominion of sin. Christ (on this view) had perfect, unfallen flesh, which nevertheless was indistinguishable in appearance from 'flesh of sin'; he came in flesh, so that the incarnation was perfectly real, but only *in the likeness* of 'flesh of sin', so that he remained sinless.

It is doubtful, however, whether this is what Paul means. The word 'form' or 'likeness' (ὁμοίωμα) has already been used several times in the epistle (i. 23; v. 14; vi. 5), and in none of these places does it mean simply 'imitation'. Compare also Phil. ii. 7, where Paul certainly does not mean to say that Christ only appeared to be a man. We are probably justified therefore in our translation, and in deducing that Christ took precisely the same fallen nature that we ourselves have, and that he remained sinless because he constantly overcame a proclivity to sin.

The Son of God was sent 'to deal with sin'; compare iii. 25. As in iii. 25 there may be a reference to the lid of the Ark, and to the Day of Atonement, so here there may be an allusion to the Old Testament sin-offering. Paul uses a simple prepositional phrase (περὶ ἁμαρτίας) which means 'concerning sin'; but this phrase was sometimes used in the LXX to translate a Hebrew word which means sometimes 'sin' and sometimes 'sin-offering'. On the whole it seems more probable that Paul means here nothing more precise than in Gal. i. 4.

The work of Christ was the beginning of the fulfilment of God's eschatological purposes; for this reason its effect could also be described as the condemnation of sin (not of sinners, *v.* 1). Judgement has begun, and the Cross left no doubt of the attitude of God towards sin (cf. iii. 25 f., and the note). But the judgement was not merely negative; it was made **in order that the law's requirement (that we should be righteous) might be fulfilled in us, whose lives are determined not by the flesh but by the Spirit.** 'The law's requirement (that we should be righteous)'—the same word is used here as is discussed on i. 32; ii. 26; v. 16, 18. The closest parallel to the present use is ii. 26 ('righteous requirement'). Here the thought is not so much that what the law requires is righteous, as that what the law requires is righteousness. The law tells us that God has the right to summon us to his court, and that he requires that we be found righteous.

Paul would be consistent with what he has written earlier if he wrote here that this requirement is fulfilled in us who rely not on works of law but on faith. But now he is looking at the same truth from a different angle, and describes the same contrast in terms of flesh and Spirit.

Those whose lives are determined by the flesh set their minds on the affairs of the flesh, while those whose lives are determined by the Spirit set their minds on the affairs of the Spirit. This verse is a definition. To have one's life 'determined by the flesh' is not simply to live a corporeal existence (Christ himself did this) but to have one's gaze focused upon all that flesh means, and limited thereby to this world; 'to have one's mind set' (for this meaning of the word cf. Mark viii. 33; Rom. xii. 16; Phil. iii. 19; iv. 2) upon existence apart from God. Correspondingly, to be determined by the Spirit is to have one's gaze focused upon that which cannot be seen, upon that invisible Other who alone gives meaning and authority to existence. Compare ii. 7 f.

The consequence follows at once. **This contrariety is absolute** (this supplement is required by the 'for' ($\gamma\acute{\alpha}\rho$) which follows); **for to have one's mind set on the flesh results in death, but to have one's mind set on the Spirit results in life and peace.** To confine oneself within the circle of this world is inevitably to cut oneself off from the only source of life, and therefore to court death. To be determined by that which is God and not oneself means life and peace, not only as subjective experiences but as objective relationship with God.

7   Further, **a mind set on the flesh results in death, because it is in a state of enmity against God, for it is not in subjection to the law of God** (true, not perverted, religion; cf. vii.
8   23), **nor indeed can it be. It follows that those who are in the flesh cannot please God.** For the flesh to be obedient to God is a contradiction in terms, for 'flesh' in this context means a mind from which God is excluded. It is certain that in v. 8 'those who are in the flesh' means 'those who are determined by the flesh'. Elsewhere Paul uses the expression otherwise; so, for example, at i. 3; ix. 5; 2 Cor. iv. 10; x. 3; Gal. ii. 20. But v. 9 shows beyond dispute that it cannot here mean 'living a bodily life'. The present verse almost amounts to, 'Those who are living to please themselves (not simply in a "carnal" sense) cannot also please God'.

The word 'please' is itself significant. It is wrong to 'please oneself' (xv. 1, 3); 'pleasing men' is dangerous and often wrong (1 Cor. vii. 33 f.; Gal. i. 10; 1 Thess. ii. 4), but we ought to please God and our neighbour (xv. 2; 1 Cor. x. 33; 1 Thess. ii. 15; iv. 1). 'Being in the flesh' may almost be defined as 'pleasing (not God but) oneself'.

What has just been said does not apply to the Christian
9 readers of the epistle. **You are not in the flesh** (that is, you are not determined by the flesh) **but in the Spirit, if, as is indeed the case, the Spirit of God dwells in you.** Paul is in process of developing a new definition of the Christian life. When he speaks of dying and rising with Christ, and of justification, he is using terms eschatological in origin; now he speaks of the Spirit, contrasting the invisible activity of God himself with the visible world of the flesh. Christians are men whose lives are directed from a source outside themselves. This leads to a fundamental definition: **if anyone has not the Spirit that comes from Christ, he is not Christ's.** It is idle to seek a distinction between 'Spirit of God' and 'Spirit of Christ'. Each is a correct description of what Paul means. The Spirit is the Spirit of God; and it is only through Christ that the Spirit is known and

received. A more serious question is raised in the next verse, where Paul continues, **But if Christ is in you, the body on the one hand is dead on account of sin, but the Spirit on the other is at work giving life because you are righteous before God.** In *v.* 9, The Spirit of God dwells in you; in *v.* 10, Christ is in you. Some interpreters of the epistle have maintained that Paul here simply identifies, because he cannot distinguish, the Spirit and the heavenly Christ (cf. 2 Cor. iii. 17, where the same confusion is sometimes said to occur). But the identification is not demanded by Paul's words, and is flatly contradicted by the words 'Spirit of Christ' in *v.* 9. What Paul means is that 'Spirit in you' is impossible apart from 'Christ in you'. Union with Christ is the only way into the life of the Age to Come, of which the distinguishing mark is the Spirit.

If Christ is in you, two consequences follow. On the one hand your body is dead. 'Your body' is 'you', and you are dead; for this see vi. 2-11; vii. 1-6. Of course it remains true that this baptismal death must be constantly realized (vi. 11) and may well be experienced in persecution (viii. 36). Compare also *vv.* 12 f., where Paul finds it necessary to warn his readers against living under the authority of the flesh.

On the other hand, while the body is dead, the Spirit (of God) is life-giving. Paul does not mean that the (human) spirit is alive, and imply thereby a strict dichotomy of body and spirit. If he had meant this he would have said, 'The spirit is alive', not 'the spirit is life' (a literal rendering of his words). Compare the contrast of 1 Cor. xv. 45.

The human self is dead—to sin; the Spirit is able to give life—because of justification, because, that is, man is now rightly related to God in whose gift the Spirit lies. All the graces of the Christian life are the consequences of, and depend upon, justification. And the vista of life in the Spirit extends as far as the general resurrection. **If the Spirit of him who raised up Jesus from the dead dwells in you, then he who raised Christ Jesus from the dead will quicken your mortal bodies too, through his Spirit, who dwells in you.**

The resurrection of Christ was an eschatological act (see on vi. 4), which marked the beginning of the Age to Come. This age was running to its close, and at its end death would be destroyed

(1 Cor. xv. 26). The first event was the pledge of the last, and they were connected by the presence and activity of the Holy Spirit (see further on *v.* 23), who brought the life-giving activity of God to bear upon every stage of the intervening period (cf. 2 Cor. iii. 18), so that even our *mortal* bodies (cf. vi. 12; 2 Cor. iv. 11) are transformed and quickened.

20. viii. 12-30. THE HOPE OF GLORY

(12) In consequence of this, brethren, we are men under obligation; but our obligation is not to the flesh, to allow our lives to be determined by it. (13) For if you do live under the authority of the flesh you are doomed to death; but if by the Spirit you put to death the activities of the body, you will live. (14) For those who allow themselves to be directed in this way by the Spirit of God are the sons of God. (15) For the Spirit you received was not one which brings into bondage and reduces you again to a state of fear. No, it was the Spirit which anticipates our adoption as sons, the Spirit in which we cry out, Abba (Father). (16) The Spirit himself in this way bears witness with our spirit that we are children of God; (17) and if children, then heirs too—heirs of God and joint-heirs with Christ, if (as is true) we suffer with him that in turn we may be glorified with him.

(18) The glory is as sure as the suffering, for I consider that the sufferings of the present time are not worthy to be compared with the glory that is to be revealed in and for us. (19) So great is this glory that the whole created world is looking eagerly forward to the disclosure of the sons of God. (20) For the creation was subjected to a vain life under inferior spiritual powers. This was not creation's own choice, but was done by the One who subjected it, and qualified by hope; (21) because the creation itself also shall be liberated from the corrupting bondage in which it lies, to attain the freedom which springs from the glory of the children of God.

(22) For we know that the whole creation with one consent groans and travails up to this moment. (23) And not the creation only: we ourselves also, who have the first-fruits of the Spirit, we ourselves also groan inwardly, while we still look forward to our adoption as God's children, the redemption of our body. (24) For we were saved in this hope. And hope really means *hope*; for a hope you can see is no hope at all—for why does anyone endure patiently for what he can see?[1] (25) No; if we hope for what we cannot see, then we wait for it with patient endurance. (26) In the same way, the Spirit also helps us in our weakness; for we do not even know what are the proper prayers to offer, but the Spirit himself intercedes on our behalf with groans that do not need expression in speech. (27) For God who searches men's hearts knows without words what the Spirit means, for he intercedes for the saints as God himself wills. (28) And we know that all things co-operate[2] for good to those who love God, to those, that is, who are called in accordance with his purpose. (29) For those whom he foreknew, he also fore-ordained to bear the same image as his Son, so that he might be the eldest in a large company of brothers; (30) and those whom he fore-ordained he also called; and those whom he called he also justified; and those whom he justified he also glorified.

The last paragraph moved to the same absolute distinction between life and death as is found, for example, in vi. 4. As there, so here also Paul finds it necessary to make clear to his readers that conversion and baptism are not an end but a beginning. Dying and rising with Christ are not an *opus operatum* working automatically to produce a sinless and immortal Christian. 'You are not in the flesh but in the Spirit' (*v.* 9);

---

[1] The text here is very confused and has been transmitted in at least six forms. The text translated is probably correct (see Lietzmann); but the general sense of the passage is in any case not in doubt. Hope must not be glossed, or robbed of its full force by sight.

[2] Some excellent authorities (P46 B A sah Origen) supply 'God' as the subject of the verb 'to co-operate'. Others (including ℵ C D G ω) omit. Two translations of the short text are possible: (i) He (that is, God) co-operates in all things; (ii) All things co-operate. See the commentary.

but this fact must be expressed in a series of choices and decisions, which, of course, can only be made in the Spirit. Final glory is guaranteed by the present co-operation of the Spirit.

12 **In consequence of this, brethren, we are men under obligation**—not 'debtors', for no actual debt is involved; see on i. 14. We are under obligation as men raised from the dead; compare vi. 13. **But our obligation is not to the flesh, to allow our lives to be determined by it.** So far in this chapter the flesh has been constantly referred to. The variety of phrases used shows that we are not dealing with a technical term in the proper sense, yet the fundamental meaning remains constant. Life determined by the flesh is life in and for itself, apart from

13 God. Such life can have only one end. **For if you do live under the authority of the flesh you are doomed to death.** Paul does not use the simple future, You will die, but a word often used to denote an 'event which will surely happen in consequence of God's decision';[1] compare iv. 24; 1 Thess. iii. 4. He who seeks his life shall lose it; he who does not die by faith will die eternally. **But if by the Spirit you put to death the activities of the body, you will live.** 'The activities of the body' are the same as 'your members which are upon the earth' in Col. iii. 5. To put these to death is truly to 'consider oneself dead to sin' (vi. 11; cf. vii. 4), and can be done only 'by the Spirit'. This is the way that leads from the resurrection of baptism to the resurrection at the last day—'you will live'.

Throughout the rest of this long paragraph Paul is concerned with this way. He begins here with an injunction to his readers to follow the way of life, and not the way of death, and proceeds to give them an assurance of the certainty of final salvation, and to comfort them in the afflictions that must precede it.

14 **Those who allow themselves to be directed in this way by the Spirit of God are the sons of God.** Paul does not often speak of direction (literally, 'being led') by the Spirit, but there is a close parallel in Gal. v. 18. The word (ἄγειν) is not infrequently used of the passions. Again it is only rarely that Paul describes Christians as sons of God—apart from this verse, only at *v.* 19; 2 Cor. vi. 18 (a quotation of 2 Sam. vii. 14); Gal.

[1] W. Bauer, *Wörterbuch, s.v.* μέλλω.

iii. 26; iv. 6 f. The last of these is a close parallel. Paul is interested in sons as heirs (see further on *v.* 17), and in sonship as a relationship which guarantees future salvation, and is established in the present through the Holy Spirit, who anticipates the future (see on *v.* 23). The actual process of begetting does not interest him; unlike some New Testament writers he does not describe conversion and baptism in terms of regeneration.

The argument of this verse is not carried forward until *v.* 17; the next two verses (15, 16) confirm the fact that we are God's sons.

For the Spirit you received was not one which brings 15 **into bondage and reduces you again to a state of fear.** Paul does not mean that there exists such a 'spirit of bondage'; the phrase is a rhetorical formation based upon 'Spirit of adoption', which is mentioned shortly. The old life was marked by fear. The contrast is not so much between those who look upon God as master, tyrant, or judge, and those who approach him as Father with the confidence of children, as between those who have no hope for the future, and those who can confidently look forward to life and glory.

No, it was the Spirit which anticipates our adoption as sons, the Spirit in which we cry out, Abba (Father). *V.* 23 makes quite clear that our adoption (a legal term belonging to the Hellenistic age, but not found in the LXX, doubtless because the Jews did not practise adoption; cf. ix. 4; Gal. iv. 5; Eph. i. 5) lies in the future. The 'Spirit of adoption' is therefore not 'the Spirit which actually effects adoption' but 'the Spirit which anticipates adoption', which brings forward into the present what is properly an eschatological event. We may compare justification, which is properly the verdict at the last judgement but is anticipated by faith through God's manifestation of his righteousness.

It is in the Spirit that we cry out to God as Father. The word Abba (Mark xiv. 36; Gal. iv. 6) is Aramaic, but a word commonly found not in liturgical but in colloquial use. That it occurs twice in Paul's Greek writings is a striking fact, which may be due to the impression made by Jesus' direct and unconventional approach to the Father. It corresponds exactly to the opening of the Lord's Prayer in the Lucan form (Luke xi. 2), and Paul's reference here may be to the use of this prayer in Christian worship—the very fact that you can address God as Abba proves that the Spirit is at work among you and that you are God's children. Alternatively, he may refer to Spirit-inspired prayers (cf. 1 Cor. xiv. 15). This is supported by the use of the violent word, 'cry out'. But the contrast between a liturgical prayer and a free prayer spontaneously inspired by the Spirit may well have been less marked in the first- than in the twentieth-century mind. Certainly the Spirit was at work in both; how else could men ad-

16 dress God as their Father? Thus **the Spirit himself in this way bears witness with our Spirit that we are children of God.**

In *vv.* 15 and 16 it is possible to put a full stop after '. . . as sons'; the translation would then continue, 'In that we cry out, Abba (Father), the Spirit himself . . .'. Whether or no this be the correct construction, it gives the sense. The prayers of the Church (cf. *v.* 26) confirm the personal conviction of the Christian. The word 'to bear witness with' is used at ii. 15 and ix. 1; both of the conscience. The content of the Spirit's witness is that we are God's children; this word is hardly more frequent than 'sons'; *vv.* 16, 17, 21; ix. 8; Phil. ii. 15. It serves to bring

17 Paul back to his main theme: **if children, then heirs too.** Paul is still concerned to demonstrate the certainty of future salvation, and argues that if we are heirs of God our inheritance is secure. Of course the analogy is imperfect. Ordinarily an heir enters upon his inheritance only at the death of the testator; but the language of inheriting can be adopted here because in the Old Testament the word 'inheritance' is regularly used of that which God gives to his people (especially the land of Israel).

We are not God's heirs in our own right but only as **joint-heirs with Christ.** The explanation of Paul's point here is to be found in his treatment of Abraham in ch. iv, and, still more clearly, in his discussion of the same theme in Gal. iii. 6 – iv. 7. In the latter passage it is argued (see especially iii. 16) that Christ alone is the true 'seed of Abraham'—the heir of the promise. Others may become sons of God *in Christ Jesus* (iii. 26); this is effected by putting on Christ in baptism (iii. 27). Thus believers become the seed of Abraham, and heirs according to promise (iii. 29).

That we are joint-heirs with Christ appears **if (as is true) we**

suffer with him that in turn we may be glorified with him.
It is important to notice how the basic principle of vi. 8 is
expanded here. Christ by enduring the messianic affliction made
it possible for men to enter the messianic kingdom by sharing
his sufferings by faith, and, especially, in baptism, where they
die and rise again with him. But this sacramental union with
Christ's death does not exhaust the matter. We have just seen
(v. 13) that Christians must put to death the activities of the
body by renouncing a life directed by the flesh; Paul now implies that the suffering of tribulation and persecution may also
be indicative of union with Christ (cf. Col. i. 24). The process
initiated in common suffering cannot but end in common glory.

Here is a firm basis for consolation and encouragement. **The** 18
glory is as sure as the suffering (this supplement is required
by the 'for' (γάρ) which follows), **for I consider that the
sufferings of the present time** (cf. iii. 26—this is the unique
moment of eschatological time anticipated in the present) **are
not worthy to be compared with the glory that is to be
revealed in and for us.** For 'glory' as a description of the
future see on p. ii. 7; iii. 23; v. 2; it is preceded by the time of
affliction, in which Christians are allowed the privilege (Phil. i.
29) of sharing. Paul now goes on to describe the interim period,
showing how Christians should take courage both from the prospect of glory and from the assistance already given them by the
Holy Spirit.

So great is this glory that the whole created world is 19
**looking eagerly forward to the disclosure of the sons of
God.** 'Disclosure' is the noun cognate with the verb translated
'reveal' in v. 18. When it does not mean 'vision' it refers to an
eschatological revelation (ii. 5; xvi. 25; 1 Cor. i. 7; 2 Thess. i. 7).
Usually it is Christ who is revealed; but compare 1 Thess. iv.
16 f.; 1 Cor. xv. 23; also Deut. xxxiii. 2, and the apocalyptic
passages dependent on it (e.g. Zech. xiv. 5 (LXX); 1 Enoch i. 9,
quoted in Jude 14). Paul introduces the point here because his
main object in mentioning the creation is to emphasize the
certainty of future salvation for Christians. He is not concerned
with creation for its own sake, but evidently feels that the matter
requires some further explanation.

For the creation was subjected to a vain life under 20

inferior spiritual powers; literally, to vanity (ματαιότης). The English reader recalls at once passages such as Eccles. i. 2, but in the LXX this and related words sometimes refer to the gods of the heathen (e.g. Ps. xxxi. 6). Paul would doubtless agree that creation apart from Christ could have only an unreal existence, but would himself express this more concretely as subjection to what he describes as the 'elements of the world' (e.g. Gal. iv. 9). Thus the whole universe needed redemption. Paul's language here may owe something to current gnosticism and astrology, according to which all creation lying below the planetary spheres was enslaved to the celestial powers which moved above it; but he makes no concession to dualism. **This was not creation's own choice, but was done by the One who subjected it, and qualified by hope.** Creation always remained under the control of the supreme God, and was therefore never without

21 hope. **Because the creation itself also** (that is, in addition to Christians) **shall be liberated from the corrupting bondage in which it lies, to attain the freedom which springs from the glory of the children of God.**

'Corrupting bondage' is, literally translated, 'bondage of corruption'. Creation is in bondage because it was subjected (*v.* 20); it is not exactly in bondage *to* corruption (though it is not impossible that Paul personifies 'corruption'); it is in bondage to corrupt powers, and this bondage is inevitably corrupting. Compare 1 Cor. xv. 42, 50.

Over against this corrupting bondage stands (again, to translate literally) the 'freedom of the glory of the children of God'. This string of genitives is inelegant, but 'of glory' is not to be taken as adjectival. The 'glory of the children of God' is an independent concept (see on *v.* 18), which can be contrasted with corruption (cf. 1 Cor. xv. 43). Out of this (eschatological) glory arises freedom (from corruption, death, and sin).

Paul now begins to move back from creation to the Church.

22 **For we know that the whole creation with one consent groans and travails up to this moment** (the decisive moment, when God's purposes are fulfilled; cf. *v.* 18). For 'groaning' cf. *v.* 23 and 2 Cor. v. 2, 4); the cognate noun is used in *v.* 26. It is tempting to translate 'groans and travails *with us*'; but this would make nonsense of *v.* 23.

And not the creation only: we ourselves also, who have 23
the first-fruits of the Spirit, we ourselves also groan in-
wardly, while we still look forward to our adoption as
God's children, the redemption of our body. Creation can
do nothing but wait and hope—and groan. We too wait and
hope and groan, even though we have an advantage denied to
creation; we have the Spirit. How the Spirit helps us will be
hinted at in *vv.* 26 f. For the moment it is important to note that
the Spirit is described as *first-fruits* (for the word, cf. xi. 16; xvi.
5), the first portion of the harvest, regarded both as a first
instalment and as a pledge of the final delivery of the whole. The
Holy Spirit is thus regarded as an anticipation of final salvation,
and a pledge that we who have the Spirit shall in the end be saved.
(Cf. the use of the similar word *earnest* in 2 Cor. i. 22; v. 5).

Possession of the Spirit is a great privilege, but it is not God's
final gift, for which Christians still look eagerly forward. Adoption is evidently (cf. *v.* 15) our final acceptance into God's
family, and of this the redemption of our body must be a
synonym. For the word 'redemption' compare iii. 24; 1 Cor. i.
30; Col. i. 14. In none of these passages is 'of the body' attached.
It may be doubted whether the 'reference is to the whole mass
of fallen human nature in which we share as men';[1] the parallel
in 2 Cor. v. 4 suggests rather an individual interpretation. Paul
certainly does not mean 'the redemption of the Church', for
the Church is never the body *of us* but the body *of Christ*. The
deeds of the body must be put to death (*v.* 13); but in the end
the body will be redeemed.

We were saved in this hope. The verb 'to save' is almost 24
always used in the future; see on v. 9. The past tense used here
is possible only because it is immediately qualified by hope. The
hope, of course, is no forlorn, but a confident, hope, supported
by the Holy Spirit. Yet it is true that we have not been saved
absolutely, but only in hope. Paul underlines this. **And hope**
really means *hope*; **for a hope you can see is no hope at all**
—for why does anyone endure patiently for what he can
see? The point here is clear, notwithstanding the textual confusion mentioned above (p. 161, n. 1). It is, however, significant
(if we may rely on the text) that Paul uses the words 'endure

[1] J. A. T. Robinson, *op. cit.* p. 30.

patiently'; see on ii. 7. The attitude of hope means that Christians put no confidence in themselves but look steadily beyond themselves to find the fulfilment of their own selves and actions in

25 God. **No; if we hope for what we cannot see, then we wait for it with patient endurance.** To live as a Christian is to walk by faith, not by sight (2 Cor. v. 7), to find the meaning of life in God's future, rather than in the present.

26 But even in the present we are not abandoned. **In the same way, the Spirit also helps us in our weakness.** Paul proceeds to an example of the Spirit's aid. **We do not even know what are the proper prayers to offer, but the Spirit himself intercedes on our behalf with groans that do not need expression in speech.** Why does Paul choose this example? Possibly because prayer is the most elementary of religious duties: we are so weak that we do not even know how to pray. This may be the correct answer, but a different one will account for more of Paul's words, some of which recall (Lietzmann, *ad loc.*) the language of gnostic religion. Man does not know the secret prayers which alone can give him access to God; when he has been initiated, the divine Spirit speaks through his mouth the correct formula, which may never be communicated to, and indeed would not be understood by, the public. It is certain that Paul does not mean what the gnostics meant; for him, prayer is no formula, nor are men saved by repeating unintelligible words. He borrows at most the notion of an indwelling God described as Spirit, and so introduces the notion of prayer as the Spirit's activity. The Spirit actually makes intercession for us. It is uncertain whether Paul means *unspoken* or *unspeakable* groans. Compare 2 Cor. xii. 4. There may be a reference here to speaking with tongues (1 Cor. xii, xiv), but it seems on the whole more probable that the point is that communion between Spirit (-filled worshipper) and God is immediate and needs no spoken

27 word. This is supported by the next verse. **For God who searches men's hearts** (cf. e.g. Jer. xvii. 10) **knows without words what the Spirit means, for** (or, namely that) **he intercedes for the saints** (see on i. 7) **as God himself wills** (cf. *v.* 26; and 2 Cor. vii. 9 ff.).

The activity of the Spirit on our behalf points to the ultimate security in God of those whom he has chosen. The presence of the Spirit, the first-fruits, is a proof that the Age to Come has dawned, and that its consummation cannot be long delayed. **We know that all things co-operate for good to those who love God.** On the text of this passage see p. 161, n. 2. We have to choose between two different ways of taking the sentence. (i) With those who love him God co-operates in all things for good. (ii) For those who love God, all things co-operate for good. The latter, the construction of AV, has been attacked as attributing to Paul an evolutionary optimism foreign to his thought; but it is less harsh as a rendering of the Greek,[1] and though Paul was not an evolutionary optimist he did believe that Christ had overcome and was overcoming (*vv.* 35, 38 f.; 1 Cor. xv. 24-8; Col. ii. 15) the powers of evil, and that the last period of world history was speeding to a close which would bring salvation to the elect (xiii. 11).

Paul does not often describe Christians as 'those who love God'. For him, love generally describes the relation of God to men, while for the relation of men to God he reserves the term faith. In this he displays an accurate use of words, for men can never love God (who is altogether worthy of our regard) in the sense in which God loves us, his enemies (v. 8). It is evidently appropriate to speak of love for God, and both Testaments provide examples; it is a grateful, trustful love. But Paul cannot allow himself to leave the impression that men may exercise an initiative which properly belongs to God alone. Those who love God are more searchingly defined as **those who are called in accordance with his purpose.**

For 'called' see on i. 1, 6. 'Calling' is the realization in history of God's eternal *purpose* (cf. ix. 11; also Eph. i. 11; iii. 11). It is here, in God's purpose, that the ultimate assurance of salvation rests. This purpose and its realization are analysed in the next two verses. *V.* 29 deals with what may be called the pre-temporal (or extra-temporal) aspects of the process, *v.* 30 with the temporal, though it also looks beyond history to the final glory.

Those whom he foreknew (cf. xi. 2), **he also fore- 29 ordained to bear the same image as his Son, so that he might be the eldest in a large company of brothers.**

[1] See W. L. Knox, *St. Paul and the Church of the Gentiles* (1939), p. 105, n. 2.

It is not easy to distinguish between 'foreknew' and 'fore-ordained'; God's knowledge must surely involve ordination, since men and things must be and become what he knows them to be. The slightly ambiguous phraseology may serve as a warning that we are not dealing here with a rigidly thought out and expressed determinist philosophy, but with a profound religious conviction. To say this, however, does not mean that pre-destination is to be emptied of its meaning.[1] The history and personal make-up of the Church are not due to chance or to arbitrary human choices, but represent the working out of God's plan. Only here can peace and security be found. Our own intentions, like our own virtues, are far too insecure to stand the tests of time and judgement.

God's intention is that Christ shall be the eldest (cf. Col. i. 18; i. 15 is less close) of many brothers, who become joint-heirs (cf. *v.* 17) with him, and so enter with him into his inheritance. This picture of Christ as the eldest in the family explains what is meant by 'bearing the same image as his Son'. 'Image' is for Paul primarily an eschatological word (though this is not inconsistent with its origin in Gen. i. 27). Compare 1 Cor. xv. 49; 2 Cor. iii. 18; iv. 4; Col. i. 15; iii. 10. When God's purpose is fully realized we shall share Christ's glorious body in God's likeness. At present we are conformed (συμμορφιζόμενοι) to his death (Phil. iii. 10); we shall be conformed (σύμμορφοι, used by Paul in the present verse) to the body of his glory (Phil. iii. 21).

30 Predestination is worked out in time: **those whom he fore-ordained he also called.** See above on *v.* 28; also i. 1, 6. In human terms, calling is conversion; compare 1 Cor. vii. 18; Gal. i. 6; Col. iii. 15; 1 Thess. iv. 7. Man becomes aware of the pre-destinating love of God. **Those whom he called he also justified,** because they responded in faith to his call. Life and glory are impossible apart from the righteousness conferred in justification (see pp. 29 f.). With justification Paul has reached the present; but so sure is his confidence, and so certain the purpose of God, that he can go on to describe a future event in a past tense: **those whom he justified he also glorified.** For glory as the final consummation of God's saving purpose, see pp. 46 f. Beyond this there is no more to say.

[1] On this subject see especially chs. ix-xi.

Predestination is the most comfortable of all Christian doctrines, if men will accept it in its biblical form, and not attempt to pry into it with questions which it does not set out to answer. It is not a 'quantitative limitation of God's action, but its qualitative definition',[1] the final statement of the truth that justification, and, in the end, salvation also, are by grace alone, and through faith alone.

21. viii. 31-9. ASSURANCE

(31) In conclusion, then, what shall we say of all these things? If God is on our side, who is against us? (32) God did not spare his own Son, but on behalf of us all delivered him up; how then can he fail to bestow upon us all things, with him? (33) Who can bring a charge against God's elect? God—who justifies us? (34) Who condemns us? Christ Jesus—who died, or rather was raised, who is at the right hand of God, who actually is interceding on our behalf? (35) Who shall separate us from the love of Christ? Shall affliction, or anguish, or persecution, or famine, or nakedness, or danger, or the sword? (36) These things are foretold as our lot, as it is written, 'For thy sake we are put to death every day, we were reckoned as sheep due for slaughter'. (37) True; but in all these things we are more than conquerors through him who loved us. (38) For I am confident that neither death nor life, neither angels nor their princes, neither things present nor things to come, nor spiritual powers, (39) whether above or below the level of the earth, nor any other created thing, shall be able to separate us from the love of God which is in Christ Jesus our Lord.

From the beginning of ch. v, though not without digressions, Paul has set out the grounds of Christian hope, and indicated the corresponding lines of Christian action in the present. He now draws the matter to a close, and in the opening verse of

[1] K. Barth, *The Epistle to the Romans* (English translation by E. C. Hoskyns, 1933), p. 346.

the present paragraph, which is in the rhetorical style of the diatribe, and full of passionate eloquence, he states the essence of his argument.

31 **In conclusion, then, what shall we say of all these things? If God is on our side, who is against us?** The question is not whether we are on God's side, but whether he is on ours. If he is, we may be exposed to perils and pains of every kind, but none can ever endanger our salvation. That God is 'for us' is proved by the fact of Jesus Christ, and it is to him that we must cling, as the pledge that God will give us every
32 good thing. **God did not spare his own Son, but on behalf of us all delivered him up; how then can he fail to bestow upon us all things, with him?**

In these words Paul seems to allude to the story of Abraham and Isaac (see p. 99). See especially Gen. xxii. 16 (where the LXX uses Paul's word 'spared'). This allusion is at least as likely as that to the Suffering Servant (Isa. liii. 12 (LXX)). In the Cross God displays such love (v. 8) that we cannot doubt his willingness to give us any good thing.

In the next two verses Paul expresses himself in the forensic language of the earlier chapters of the epistle. Their general drift is clear—those whom God justifies, through Christ crucified and risen, no accuser can imperil; but the construction is obscure. The translation adopted here, prompted by the many rhetorical questions in the context (*vv.* 31, 32, 35), assumes that
33 each clause is to be punctuated with a question mark. **Who can bring a charge against God's elect? God—who justifies us?**
34 **Who condemns us? Christ Jesus—who died, or rather was raised, who is at the right hand of God, who actually is interceding on our behalf?**

There are two alternative possibilities. (i) There are two questions, with two ironical answers, thus: Who can bring a charge? God—who justifies! Who condemns? Christ—who died! (ii) The words 'God who justifies; who condemns?' may have been drawn from Isa. l. 8 ff., and should therefore be taken together. We now have one major question with two answers. Who can bring a charge? God, who justifies (who then can condemn?)! Christ, who died! Of these, (ii) seems unnecessarily complicated, and the irony of (i) is scarcely Pauline.

The details of the two verses require little comment. If 'Who shall bring a charge?' is to have a positive answer, Satan must be meant; the scene is that of the last judgement. The 'elect' is not a common Pauline description of Christians; elsewhere only at xvi. 13 (in a different sense) and Col. iii. 12. Election, however, is presupposed by calling.

In his account of Christ in v. 34 Paul may be dependent on a Christological formula; this is suggested by the parallel participles (died—was raised) and by the balanced relative clauses. Paul has already shown that the Spirit intercedes within us (v. 27); in heaven, Christ (who is also judge; see ii. 16) intercedes for the elect. Paul here reflects Jewish ideas of the Messiah as an intercessor.[1]

To speak of Christ in this way suggests the rhetorical questions of v. 35. **Who shall separate us from the love of** 35 **Christ** (that is, Christ's love for us)? **Shall affliction** (in which we exult, v. 3), **or anguish, or persecution, or famine, or nakedness, or danger, or the sword?** Should it be inferred from these words that persecution had already fallen upon the Roman church? It is not impossible that the expulsion of the Jews under Claudius, when they rioted 'at the instigation of Chrestus', was in some way connected with the foundation of the church (see Introduction, p. 6); but it is more probable that Paul's words reflect his own experiences (though, of course, he had not yet experienced the sword) and the general insecurity and unpopularity of Christians. But such perils can never separate us from the love of Christ. Why, **these things are** 36 **foretold as our lot** (these words, not in the Greek, must be added as the presupposition of the quotation that follows), **as it is written, 'For thy sake we are put to death every day, we were reckoned as sheep due for slaughter'.** The quotation is from Ps. xliv. 22. The sufferings of Christians, like those of Christ, were foretold. The probable inference is that they formed part of the messianic affliction (see pp. 80, 122). It is noteworthy that Paul makes no cross-reference to Isa. liii. 7.

Suffering and persecution are not mere evils which Christians must expect and endure as best they can; they are the scene of the overwhelming victory which Christians are winning through

[1] See Nils Johansson, *Parakletoi* (1940).

37 Christ. **True** (we suffer constantly); **but in all these things we are more than conquerors** (Paul uses a somewhat uncommon verb to intensify the idea of victory) **through him who loved us.**

In his final affirmation of God's love Paul turns to what his readers probably regarded as their chief and most dangerous enemies, the astrological powers by which (as many in the Hellenistic world believed) the destiny of mankind was controlled. Not even these lords of destiny (Paul asserts) can

38 separate the Christian from the love of God. **For I am confident that neither death nor life** (Paul was not certain that all Christians would have to face death before the return of Christ; see 1 Thess. iv. 15; 1 Cor. xv. 51 f.), **neither angels nor their princes** (for the last word—ἀρχαί—see 1 Cor. xv. 24; Col. i. 16; ii. 10, 15), **neither things present nor things to come, nor**

39 **spiritual powers, whether above or below the level of the earth** (here Paul uses technical astronomical—or astrological—terms), **nor any other created thing, shall be able to separate us from the love of God which is in Christ Jesus our Lord.**

Of course not; for Christ Jesus is—the Lord. He is Lord over all spiritual powers, for he has triumphed over them in the Cross (Col. ii. 15); he is Lord over life and death, for he was crucified, and raised from the dead; he is Lord over things present and things to come, for it was in him that God elected us in love, and it is with him that we shall enter into God's glory beyond history. In Christ Jesus, God is *for us*; and it is in Christ Jesus that we know him and trust him.

22. ix. 1-5. THE UNBELIEF OF ISRAEL

(1) I am speaking the truth in Christ; it is no lie; my conscience bears me witness in the Holy Spirit (2) when I say that I feel in my heart great grief and ceaseless pain. (3) For I could wish that I myself were separated by a curse from Christ if that would benefit my brethren, my human kinsmen (4)—the Israelites. They were made God's sons, they were shown his glory, with them he

made the covenants,[1] to them he gave the law and the temple worship and the promises;[2] (5) to them belong the fathers of the race and from them (on the human side) springs the Christ himself—Blessed for ever be God, who stands over the whole process!

That viii. 38 f. forms the impressive close of one division of the epistle, and that ix. 1 opens a new theme, cannot be disputed. But the connexion between chs. i-viii and chs. ix-xi is much closer than is sometimes recognized; for chs. i-viii are not so much concerned with an 'experience of salvation' as with the character and deeds of God who is the source of salvation, and chs. ix-xi are not at all concerned with Paul's patriotic sentiments but with the character and deeds of God who elected the Jews and now calls the Gentiles. In the second as in the first half of the epistle Paul writes about God and his strange mercy in offering to men justification on the basis of faith alone, but his portrayal of divine freedom and grace is determined by somewhat different sets of circumstances.

The basic fact which, though it is never actually mentioned, lies behind every verse in the opening paragraph, and sets in motion the whole long argument of chs. ix-xi, is that, notwithstanding her privileges, and his apostolic labour, Israel has rejected the Gospel Paul preached. The movement of his thought is clear. In the last verses of ch. viii he sings with moving eloquence the love of God bestowed freely and invincibly upon sinful man from foreknowledge to glory. The dictation is ended; and in the silence he reflects: He came unto his own, and they that were his own received him not. Disappointed and bitter, he continues: **I am speaking the truth in 1 Christ; it is no lie; my conscience bears me witness in the Holy Spirit when I say that I feel in my heart great 2 grief and ceaseless pain.**

Perhaps as the Jewish 'apostle of the Gentiles' (xi. 13) he

[1] There is very strong evidence (P⁴⁶ B D G it) for the singular, 'the covenant', and this may be the original reading: but the plural is the harder reading, and on that ground may be preferred. On the meaning of the two readings see the commentary.

[2] There is some evidence ((P⁴⁶) D (G)) for the singular, 'the promise'. See the commentary.

had been accused of indifference to the fate of his compatriots; perhaps the vehement assertion of truthfulness is no more than a mark of the energy and feeling with which he writes (cf. 2 Cor. i. 23; ii. 17; xi. 31; xii. 19; Gal. i. 20). His conscience is clear in the matter; compare ii. 15, where, as here, conscience is mentioned as a joint-witness. Evidently Paul thought of the conscience as an almost independent party in any dispute, capable of standing over against a man to accuse or acquit him of falsehood. Paul does not, however, simply appeal to what is, after all, part of himself. He speaks the truth *in Christ*, and his conscience bears witness *in the Holy Spirit*. In comparison with these divine witnesses (viii. 26, 34) the verdict of his own conscience is unimportant (1 Cor. iv. 4).

So far from being an unfeeling apostate, Paul is racked with pain at the thought of Israel's unbelief. Further, like the best of all Jews, Moses (Ex. xxxii. 31 f.), he is willing to sacrifice him-3 self for his people's good. **I could wish that I myself were separated by a curse from Christ if that would benefit my 4 brethren, my human kinsmen—the Israelites.** The grammatical construction of the sentence shows that Paul recognizes that his wish is scarcely capable of fulfilment.

'Separated by a curse from Christ' is literally 'anathema from Christ'; compare 1 Cor. xvi. 22; Gal. i. 8 f. The word *anathema* is found in the LXX as the equivalent of *ḥerem*, 'thing or person devoted (to destruction or sacred use and therefore secluded from profane use)'.[1] Here, of course, destruction is in mind; to be separated from Christ is to be consigned to damnation. Similar forms of speech were current among the Rabbis; for example, *Negaim*, ii. 1: R. Ishmael says: The children of Israel (may I make atonement for them!) are . . .

The Jews are Paul's kinsmen, but only *on human terms*, for Paul has now been born into a new family (cf. Mark iii. 34 f.). The qualification is significant, and we shall meet it again in the next two verses, in which Paul sets out the privileges of Israel. It supplies too the clue (though this becomes evident only when the whole of chs. ix-xi are taken into account) to the otherwise insoluble problem raised by the defection of Israel. Why should

[1] L. Koehler and W. Baumgartner, *Lexicon in Veteris Testamenti Libros* (1953), *s.v.*

those upon whom so many privileges had been showered reject the manifestation of God's righteousness in Christ? Precisely because they were content to evaluate their privileges on a purely human level. Thus, for example, the law was their proud possession, of which they could boast; they failed to see that in it was written their own judgement before God (cf. ii. 17-29). Similarly the temple worship became a monument of self-congratulation; they did not consider that it spoke to them of the holiness of him who was God and not man. Even the Messiah was to be one of their own children, whom—provided he was a good Jew—they would be pleased to approve. All this is not explicit, but it can be read between the lines of *vv.* 4 f. Those who seem now to have been rejected by God **were made God's sons, they were shown his glory, with them he made the covenants, to them he gave the law and the temple worship and the promises; to them belong the 5 fathers of the race and from them (on the human side) springs the Christ himself—Blessed for ever be God, who stands over the whole process!**

'They were made God's sons' by adoption. The word is used in viii. 15, 23, in a different sense. The sequence of privileges described in these verses suggests that Paul here thinks of sonship as a status conferred upon Israel at the Exodus; compare Ex. iv. 22; Hosea xi. 1.

The glory of God also suggests the Exodus. It was manifested in the pillars of cloud and fire at the crossing of the Red Sea, which was a glorious act of deliverance (Ex. xv. 6, 11) and in the theophany at Mount Sinai (Ex. xxiv. 16 f.; xxxiii. 18). When the tabernacle was built it was filled with the glory of the Lord (Ex. xl. 34 f.).

If the singular 'covenant' (see p. 175, n. 1) is read the reference is evidently to the covenant made at Mount Sinai. This makes excellent sense, for this covenant was of course the basis of Israel's national and religious life. The plural, however, also makes good sense. There were several covenants—with Adam, with Noah, and with Abraham, as well as with Moses—and it is possible that Paul refers to these; but it is more likely that (like other Jewish writers; see S.B. iii. 262) he distinguished three covenants within the great covenant of the Exodus—a covenant at Horeb, a second in the plains of Moab, and a third at Mounts Gerizim and Ebal.

The bestowal of the law and the establishment of the temple cultus were the pre-eminent privileges of Israel. 'By three things is the world maintained: by the law, by the temple worship, and by deeds of loving-kindness' (*Aboth*, i. 2). These two gifts accompanied the establishment of the covenant.

Along with these provisions Israel was given also the promises (or 'the promise', singular, summarizing the many predictions —see p. 175, n. 2) of an even more glorious future. Promises understood as messianic are no doubt intended. It is worth noting that all the privileges mentioned in *v.* 4 can be understood as promises. For adoption and glory see viii. 15, 23; ii. 7. The past covenants point to the new covenant (Jer. xxxi. 31; 1 Cor. xi. 25). The temple worship suggested the language of iii. 26, and the law itself, rightly understood, pointed forward to the Gospel, as did the patriarchs (see especially ch. iv).

Last in the list of privileges comes the fact that the Messiah himself, so far as human descent goes, was to be a Jew. For the same fact, and the same limitation, compare i. 3. This sums up the fact that God had chosen Israel to be the scene upon which his saving purpose should be worked out. This was what made the fact of Israel's present rejection doubly offensive. What was evidently God's purpose seemed to have failed altogether in its effect. It is not Jewish nationalism, but a glaring theological paradox which sets in motion the argument of chs. ix-xi (cf. on iii. 1 f.).

Before, however, we can turn to this argument we must consider one of the most difficult questions of exegesis in the epistle.

As it is here translated the doxology with which the paragraph concludes is independent of the preceding sentence and refers to God the Father. It would, however, be grammatically easier to unite it with the preceding words as a relative clause referring to Christ, thus: From them . . . springs the Christ himself, who is God over all, blessed for ever. A third possibility is to introduce a stop within the doxology itself, and render: . . . Christ, who is over all. Blessed be God for ever. It is very hard to decide between these possibilities.

The objection to the first is grammatical and stylistic. Pauline doxologies are usually connected with the context and do not stand (as does this one, in our translation) in complete asyndeton. At Rom. i. 25; 2 Cor. xi. 31, for example, where doxologies are addressed to God the Father, they arise out of the preceding words. Moreover, if Paul wished to say 'Blessed be God', he should have placed the word 'blessed' (εὐλογητός) first in the sentence, as he does not.

The objection to the second is theological. Nowhere else in any epistle does Paul call Christ God. Even Phil. ii. 6 is not a real parallel. In fact, Paul, 'high' as his Christology is, is reserved in the use of strictly divine titles for Christ. Is it likely that he would here run counter to his general practice and use the word God? It may not be likely but it cannot be held to be impossible; this verse might be an extension of the partial parallel in i. 3 f. Perhaps Paul wishes to say that Christ was in human terms a Jew, but in fact God.

The third possibility has little to commend it, but there is a proposed emendation of the text which is worth consideration. By a very slight alteration of the Greek (substituting ὧν ὁ for ὁ ὤν) it is possible to obtain, '*Whose is* the supreme God, blessed for ever'. This has the advantage of giving a clause parallel to those that have preceded: Whose is the adoption . . . whose are the fathers . . . of whom is the Christ . . . whose is God. . . . It is true that Paul has denied that God is God of the Jews only (iii. 29) but the Old Testament itself declares that 'they shall be my people, and I will be their God' (e.g. Jer. xxiv. 7), and a special relationship with God was both the foundation and the consummation of Israel's privilege. The emendation is attractive; but the text of the MSS. is not so difficult as to be impossible, and it is wise to retain it, leaving open the question whether the doxology refers to Christ or to God the Father.

23. ix. 6-13. GOD'S ELECTIVE PURPOSE

(6) But it is not as though the word of God itself had failed. For not all who are descended from Israel are truly Israel. (7) Nor are all the children of Abraham counted

**as his seed; rather, as Scripture says, 'Your descendants
through Isaac shall be called your seed'. (8) That is, it is
not the children of Abraham's flesh, born in the course
of nature, who are children of God; it is the children who
come by promise who are counted as his seed. (9) For
the promise runs thus: 'I will come at this time and
Sarah shall have a son'. (10) Further: when Rebecca conceived through intercourse with one man, Isaac our
father, (11) before the two children had been born, before
they had done anything good or evil, in order that God's
elective purpose might stand firm, (12) resting as it does
not on works but on God who calls, it was said to her,
'The greater shall serve the less'; (13) as again it is
written, 'Jacob I loved, but Esau I hated'.**

The introductory paragraph (*vv.* 1-5) has sharpened the
problem. Since God has so clearly given Israel a position of
unique privilege, does not Israel's defection mean that God's
intention has broken down? The word of promise has been
proved false by history. Paul's blunt negative answer to this
question is supported by an analysis of the meaning of Israel.

6 **But it is not as though the word of God itself** (cf. iii. 2)
**had failed. For not all who are descended from Israel are
truly Israel.** If the word Israel is understood in a mechanical
sense it cannot be disputed that the majority of Israel have, to
all appearance, set aside God's word, which has accordingly (at
least for the present) failed. But Israel is not a term like Ammon,
Moab, Greece, or Rome. 'Israel' cannot be defined in terms of
physical descent, or understood simply 'on the human side'
(*v.* 5); it is created not by blood and soil, but by the promise of
God, and therefore exists within the limits of God's freedom.
If he were bound by physical descent, he would be unfree, and no
longer God. But he is not so bound, as Scripture itself proves—a
vital point to Paul. Consider first Abraham, the father of the race.

7 **Nor are all the children of Abraham counted as his
seed; rather, as Scripture says, 'Your descendants through
Isaac shall be called your seed'.**

The first part of this verse, like the last of *v.* 6, is ambiguously
phrased in Greek, but there can be no question that here 'seed'

should be taken as predicate; in both clauses the phrase with 'all' is subject. Paul is denying a universal assertion: it is not true that all who appear, or claim, to be Israel are truly the seed of Abraham.

For 'seed of Abraham' compare iv. 13, 16, 18; Gal. iii. 16, 19, 29; (2 Cor. xi. 22). The passages in Galatians are particularly important, for they show that though Paul recognizes 'seed' as a collective term he believes that it is focused upon the one descendant of Abraham, Christ. That is to say, behind the difficult theological development of *vv.* 6-13 lies thought that is fundamentally Christological and soteriological. The 'seed' arose through promise (*v.* 8), and accordingly to the 'seed' belongs the promise made to Abraham (iv. 13; Gal. iii. 16). It is *in Christ* that the promises of God are fulfilled. Thus the thought of *v.* 4 receives a severe qualification: the promises do indeed belong to Israel, but—what is Israel?

Paul proceeds to illustrate his point by quoting Gen. xxi. 12, which means that for purposes of inheritance the divine promises made to Abraham shall operate on the line proceeding from him through Isaac. **That is, it is not the children of Abra-** 8 **ham's flesh, born in the course of nature, who are children of God; it is the children who come by promise who are counted as his seed.**

Abraham had several children in addition to Isaac (Gen. xxv. 1-4); here it is Ishmael who is in mind (cf. Gal. iv. 21-31).

The word 'counted' is of fundamental importance in this epistle. It has already occurred in several contexts, but especially in the quotation from Gen. xv. 6 (Rom. iv. 3). It points to the creative freedom of God, who creates 'righteousness' by 'counting' it, and annuls sin by not 'counting' it (iv. 6, 8). He can raise up sons to Abraham out of stones (Matt. iii. 9; Luke iii. 8), and freely determines what is 'seed' and what is not.

'Seed', thus understood in the light of the creative freedom of God, is necessarily bound up with 'promise'. Ishmael was a true son of Abraham, with as much of his father's blood in his veins as Isaac had; but he was a child of the flesh, not of promise. Isaac's birth, which took place in the context of human death and sterility (iv. 19), depended entirely upon God's gracious promise.

9 As a footnote, Paul adds a precise reference: **For the promise runs thus: 'I will come at this time and Sarah shall have a son'** (Gen. xviii. 10).

So far Paul has based his argument upon the story of Abraham; and it is open to an objection. Ishmael and Isaac (it could be argued) had one father, but Ishmael's mother was the bondwoman Hagar, Isaac's the princess Sarah (cf. Gal. iv. 21-31). This difference could account for the fact that Abraham's seed was reckoned through the one and not the other. Paul answers this objection by proceeding to the next generation.

10 **Further: when Rebecca conceived** (Gen. xxv. 21) **through intercourse with one man** (the *one* is emphatic), **Isaac our father** (for the patriarchs as 'fathers' cf. *v.* 5),

11 **before the two children** (Esau and Jacob) **had been born, before they had done anything good or evil, in order that**

12 **God's elective purpose might stand firm, resting as it does not on works but on God who calls, it was said to her** (Gen. xxv. 23), **'The greater shall serve the less'** (the original Hebrew could be correctly translated, 'The elder shall serve the younger' (so RV); the Greek could not in itself mean

13 this, and Paul probably gave it its proper meaning); **as again it is written** (Mal. i. 2 f.), **'Jacob I loved, but Esau I hated'** (the Hebrew idiom means, 'I preferred Jacob to Esau'; but Paul may again have taken the words literally).

In this story, as in that of Abraham, we have to do with two brothers. Not only have they the same father; they have also the same mother, and their origin goes back to the same moment of conception. The distinction between the twins is expressed between conception and birth. God's freedom is absolute. No antecedent ancestry, and no subsequent virtue or sin, controls it. Whatever happens, God's purpose, which operates on the basis of election, stands firm. This marks out the theme of chs. ix-xi. God has a purpose; it works by a process of election; and it cannot fail. When viewed from the human side this means that not works but the call of God is decisive. Works and calling are correlative here, just as, earlier in the epistle, works and faith are correlative. Evidently calling and faith correspond; faith is the answer to God's call—as the example of Abraham makes clear. Not works but faith leads to justification; not works but God's call admits to the promise. These are different ways of expressing the same truth.

So far Paul has simply established his argument in terms of events which happened in remote antiquity; but the first-century Jew—and the twentieth-century Christian—cannot escape the consequences of the argument. For what Paul has established is the freedom of God in grace. It is impossible for his Jewish interlocutor to reply: Very well! I am descended from Abraham, through Isaac (not Ishmael), and Jacob (not Esau); therefore I must stand within the promise. To argue in this way is to say: God was free in the days of the patriarchs, but he is no longer free now—which is absurd. God, if he be still God, still operates on the basis of his 'elective purpose'. The Church can never draw a simple boundary line between itself and the world, nor can it connect itself with the divine promise by means of a simple line of succession.

It is important to recall here that the seed of Abraham contracted till it became ultimately Christ, and was subsequently expanded to include those who were in Christ (see on vi. 11). This means that election does not take place (as might at first appear from Paul's examples) arbitrarily or fortuitously; it takes place always and only *in Christ*. They are elect who are in him; they who are elect are in him (cf. Gal. iii. 29). It is failure to remember this that causes confusion over Paul's doctrine of election and predestination. But the point must be pursued in the next paragraph.

24. ix. 14-29. GOD'S SOVEREIGNTY

(14) What then shall we say? Is there unrighteousness in God's dealings? No, indeed. (15) For he says to Moses, 'I will have mercy on whomsoever I do have mercy, and I will pity whomsoever I do pity'. (16) So then everything depends, not on man who exercises his will or like an athlete runs to a goal, but on the merciful God. (17) For God in Scripture says to Pharaoh, 'For this very purpose

did I raise thee up, namely that in thee I might demonstrate my power, and that my name might be proclaimed in all the earth'. (18) So then he has mercy on whom he wills, and whom he wills he 'hardens'.

(19) Of course you will say to me, If this is so,[1] why does he still make complaints? For who can resist his will? (20) Yes, but,[2] my dear sir, who are you to answer back to God? What, will the model say to the modeller, Why did you make me like this? (21) Has not the potter a right over the clay, to make out of the same lump one vessel designed for noble, one for ignoble use? (22) But what if God with great long-suffering 'endured the vessels of wrath', 'prepared for destruction', because he wished to show forth his wrath and to make known his power, (23) and moreover did so in order to make known the wealth of his glory for the vessels of mercy, which beforehand he made ready for glory—(24) us, those whom he called, not only from among the Jews but from among the Gentiles too? (25) That this calling of Gentiles as well as Jews was intended is shown in Scripture, as God says in the book of Hosea: 'That which was not my people I will call my people, and her that was not beloved I will call beloved'; (26) 'and it shall come to pass that in the place where it was said to them, You are not my people, there shall they be called sons of the living God'. (27) And Isaiah cries out concerning Israel, 'Though the number of the children of Israel should be as the sand of the sea, yet it is the remnant of them that will be saved, (28) for the Lord will bring his word to pass upon the earth, accomplishing it and determining it'. (29) This accords further with what Isaiah said earlier, 'If the Lord Sabaoth had not left us a seed, we should have become like Sodom, and we should have been made like Gomorrah'.

---

[1] 'If this is so' is an addition made in the translation to bring out the sense. It could be regarded as a translation of 'then' (οὖν) if this word be read ('Why *then* does he . . .?'), with P46 B D G.

[2] 'Yes, but' represents the Greek μενοῦνγε. This is read before 'My dear sir' (ὦ ἄνθρωπε) by the majority of MSS. (ω), and after it by ℵ A (B); it is omitted altogether by P46 D G lat—perhaps rightly.

Paul resumes his argument in the question-and-answer style of the diatribe, as he often does when an objection has to be faced. If the fundamental fact (see p. 181) that Christ is the seed of Abraham, and that men are elected in him, is lost sight of, the assertions of *vv.* 6-13 are open to objection. To distinguish between unborn twin infants, to love the one and hate the other, even to prefer the one to the other, is unjust. This is the verdict of the conscience, and if Paul can appeal to conscience when it suits his case he is bound to listen to it when it does not. It seems therefore to follow that, on Paul's showing, God is unjust. This is unthinkable, and the objector will infer that the argument which leads to such a conclusion is false. **What then shall we say? Is there unrighteousness in God's** 14 **dealings?** Paul is as eager as any man to deny such a suggestion. **No, indeed.** But how can the objection be met?[1]

Paul defends his position in *vv.* 15 f.; at least, he appears to do so, but it is often held that in fact he does no such thing, but merely reiterates his offensive views in shriller tones. But this judgement fails to do justice to Paul. He begins with an Old Testament quotation: **For he** (the subject must be God, as 15 *v.* 14 suggests; cf. *v.* 17) **says to Moses, 'I will have mercy on whomsoever I do have mercy, and I will pity whomsoever I do pity'** (Ex. xxxiii. 19). From this assertion of the divine freedom and initiative Paul concludes, **So then every-** 16 **thing depends, not on man who exercises his will or like an athlete runs to a goal, but on the merciful God.**

The point to note is that these verses emphasize not only the freedom of God, but his mercy. If God does anything at all for sinful man, it is of his mercy. If he does nothing, he is not unjust, for man deserves nothing. Mercy (ἔλεος; verb, ἐλεεῖν) is the key-note of chs. ix-xi, as will appear at point after point in the commentary. Here, where the word first occurs, it may suffice to point onwards to the last occurrence: God has shut up all men to disobedience, in order that he may deal with all men in mercy (xi. 32). In chs. i-viii Paul has dealt with the divine act of grace and redemption by virtue of which men may be justified, and in the end saved, through faith alone. Behind this

[1] It is worth noting that Paul finds it necessary to demonstrate that God is righteous. See iii. 26, and the notes.

process lies an attitude or attribute of God which is occasionally described as love (v. 8) but more characteristically as *mercy*. It is because God is merciful that justification by faith is possible. And God is determined to treat men on the basis of mercy; indeed, if he treated them otherwise none would survive. But if his dealings with them are to be governed by his mercy they cannot be determined by man's will, or earnest striving towards a goal. Elsewhere (1 Cor. ix. 24, 26; Gal. v. 7; Phil. ii. 16; (iii. 12)) Paul uses the metaphor of running a race (common in the Stoic diatribe) in a good sense—Christians must run so as to win the prize; but never in such a way as to suggest that salvation, or the mercy which grants salvation, rests upon man's achievement. Everything depends (one might almost say, God's mercy depends), not upon man, but only upon the merciful God.

So far, then, Paul has argued that his conception of the absolute predestinating sovereignty of God is necessary, if God's dealings with men are to be seen to rest solely upon his mercy. He now presses his point further still on the basis of another text in Exodus.

17 **For God in Scripture** (literally, Scripture—the written word being almost personified) **says to Pharaoh, 'For this very purpose did I raise thee up, namely that in thee I might demonstrate my power, and that my name might be proclaimed in all the earth'**. Paul's quotation follows neither the Hebrew nor the Greek of Ex. ix. 16 exactly, but gives their substance.

The new quotation allows two fresh points to be made. Pharaoh, who doubtless thinks himself master of the situation in Egypt, has in fact been brought on the scene by God for two purposes: (i) in order that God may manifest his power; (ii) in order that God's name may be universally proclaimed. Pharaoh exists not to further his own ends, but God's; and God's ends are the carrying out of a mighty act of salvation, and the publication of this act of salvation among all men. Historically, Pharaoh supplied the occasion for the deliverance of the people; if there had been no 'Pharaoh of the oppression' there would have been no Exodus, and the proclamation of the Exodus (in Scripture, and in the Passover service) would never have taken place. Paul's interpretation of this history is as clear as the history itself, though it involves the transference of imagery from Pharaoh to Israel. In the present time, Israel (like Pharaoh in his) exists for a double purpose, (i) to provide the occasion or context for a divine act of deliverance—that in which men are freed from the law, and thereby from sin and death; (ii) to act so as to cause the publication of God's act of deliverance through all the world —which took place precisely because Israel rejected the Gospel (xi. 11, 15, 19, 25). Thus, as Pharaoh's plans were overruled to God's ends, so Israel's self-will is to be overruled to God's ends; and his ends are merciful.

Paul sums up the position reached so far: **So then he has** 18 **mercy on whom he wills, and whom he wills he 'hardens'** (this word is suggested by the story of Pharaoh, and occurs at Ex. iv. 21; vii. 3; ix. 12; xiv. 4, 17). It is true that 'hardening' introduces a sharpness which was not apparent in *vv.* 15 f.; but it cannot be understood apart from the thought of *v.* 17, which has just been explained. It does not necessarily imply final rejection, but points out the way in which God has, in his wisdom, decided to work out his purposes, which are governed from first to last by mercy.

Nevertheless, 'hardening' is an offensive word, and objection again breaks out. **Of course you will say to me, If this is so,** 19 **why does he still make complaints? For who can resist his will?** (cf. Wisd. xii. 12). The gravamen of the objection lies not in the injured national sentiment of the Jew, but in the implication that the moral government of the universe is at fault. If God treats men as Paul supposes, they have no moral responsibility; God himself has no business to condemn as a sinner a man whom he himself has hardened. Paul replies in more Old Testament imagery.

Yes, but, my dear sir, who are you to answer back to 20 **God?** Man's sense of moral responsibility has not the ultimate value he attaches to it; it gives him no right to question God's dealings. He can never be anything other than God's creature, and his wisest course is not to pass judgement upon his Creator, but to accept his position with humility. **What, will the model say to the modeller, Why did you make me like this? Has** 21 **not the potter a right over the clay, to make out of the same lump one vessel designed for noble, one for ignoble**

use? In these verses, there are echoes of Isa. xxix. 16; xlv. 9 f.; Wisd. xii. 12; compare also Jer. xviii. 1-6. 'Vessel' ($\sigma\kappa\epsilon\hat{v}os$) in *v*. 21 is used literally, of a vessel made by a potter; but the transition to the metaphor of *vv*. 22 f. is easy, since the corresponding Hebrew word (and the Greek word in Judaizing Greek) has a very wide range of meaning, including persons and even abstract ideas.

Paul argues that, just as a potter may fashion his clay as he pleases, so God has perfect liberty to make what he wills of the humanity he has created, and man has no more right to answer back than the potter's clay. 'It is a well-worn illustration. But the trouble is that a man is not a pot; he *will* ask, "Why did you make me like this?" and he will not be bludgeoned into silence. It is the weakest point in the whole epistle' (Dodd, p. 159). But the argument is perhaps not so weak, or the analogy so remote, as at first appears. Of course man is not a pot, and obstinate questionings arise in his mind. It is because the mind asks questions about the divine government of the universe that works like Romans are written. To stress this point, however, is to emphasize a detail in the analogy instead of the major comparison, which is between the final responsibility of the potter for what he produces, and the final responsibility of God for what he does in history. 'Everything depends, not on man who exercises his will . . . but on the merciful God' (*v*. 16). The question of *v*. 19 is wrongly framed, for God is not making complaints against men who have had no opportunity of being good, but commending his love to wilful rebels in the death of his Son (v. 8). The doctrine of apparent double predestination implies not a crude numerical division within the human race but a profound definition of God and of his purpose for men in terms of mercy (cf. p. 171).

It is to be noted further that in *v*. 21 Paul speaks of vessels designed for noble and ignoble use respectively. This distinction seems to reflect the different roles played by Israel and Pharaoh respectively in the story of the Exodus; and it is not unimportant that Pharaoh (as *v*. 17 already implies) is regarded as standing within God's purpose, which is a purpose of mercy. His place in it may be an ignoble one, but it is within and not outside it. Once more, however, the following verses, with their reference to 'vessels of wrath, prepared for destruction', sharpen the contrast.

The next three verses (22 ff.) raise very difficult linguistic questions, which must be attended to before an exposition can be attempted. In the translation, one view of the construction is adopted; in the notes an attempt will be made to justify it.

But what if God with great long-suffering 'endured the 22 **vessels of wrath' (cf. Jer. i. 25, LXX), 'prepared for de- struction' (cf. Isa. liv. 16, LXX), because he wished to show forth his wrath and to make known his power, and more-** 23 **over did so in order to make known the wealth of his glory for the vessels of mercy, which beforehand he made ready for glory—us, those whom he called, not** 24 **only from among the Jews but from among the Gentiles too?**

Three separate problems may be distinguished here. (i) The whole passage is in the form of a conditional sentence with a protasis (if-clause) but no apodosis. This is not a serious diffi- culty. Greek sometimes expresses by means of an if-clause what in English we express by saying 'What if . . .?' (e.g. John vi. 62). The construction is rhetorical in style, 'What if this is so?' being used for 'Why should this not be so?'; that is, 'This is in fact so, and there is no reason why it should not be so'.

(ii) *V.* 24 is loosely attached to what precedes, but here again there is no serious difficulty. The two relative clauses ('which he made ready' and 'us, those whom he called') are both in explanatory apposition to 'vessels of mercy'.

(iii) The main difficulty lies in the participle ($\theta\acute{\epsilon}\lambda\omega\nu$) here translated 'because he wished', and in the conjunction ($\ddot{\iota}\nu\alpha$) here translated 'in order to'. (a) The participle may be causal ('because he wished') or concessive ('though he wished'). The latter has been supported by a reference to ii. 4: God wished to show forth his wrath and make known his power, yet instead displayed long-suffering to the vessels of wrath with a view to bringing them to repentance. But it will be recalled that the whole of i. 18 – iii. 20 describes the eschatological manifestation of God's wrath (see especially on i. 18-32), mitigated in such a way—by God's long-suffering—that sinners are not instantly consigned to destruction. The former way of taking the participle may therefore be preferred, especially because it also makes possible the better explanation of the conjunction, and the most convincing interpretation of 'to show forth his wrath and to make known his power'. (b) If the participle is taken as concessive, it becomes necessary to couple the conjunction (καὶ ἵνα) with 'with great long-suffering' ('. . . with great long-suffering and with the intention of making known'). This is very awkward grammatically and does not seem to make good sense. Alternatively, if the participle is causal the conjunction (expressing purpose) will be parallel to it ('. . . on the one hand wishing to show his wrath upon A, . . . and on the other to make known his mercy upon B'). This seems preferable on every ground.

It remains to ask what Paul means by these three verses. It is important to bear in mind several facts which have already been established. (i) Paul represents the present as an eschatological age, in which God, through the death and resurrection of Jesus, is manifesting his righteousness in such a way as to anticipate the last judgement. A verdict of 'Guilty' is expressed in the hardening of the unbelieving, and of 'justified' in the peace and joy of those who have faith. (ii) Paul has used the example of Pharaoh (vv. 17 f.), whom God raised up and hardened in order to show forth his power and to cause his name to be proclaimed in all the earth. (iii) What is said about Pharaoh is transferred to Israel, whose hardening and unbelief have furnished the occasion for a demonstration of God's power and for the worldwide publication of the Gospel.

It is in the framework of these facts that vv. 22 ff. must be understood. They may be outlined thus: (a) God endured . . . (b) because he wished . . . (c) in order to . . . Clause (c) is comparatively easy to understand. What God has done, he has done in order to show his mercy towards those whom he calls, both Jews and Gentiles. Clause (a) also can be fairly readily understood. God's endurance and long-suffering refer to the fact that he has not yet instituted the last judgement and brought in the day of wrath (ii. 5); he seeks to lead men to repentance (ii. 4). His long-suffering applies to all, for all (iii. 20) would fare ill if judgement according to works (ii. 6) were set up at once. 'Vessels of wrath prepared for destruction' may apply as well to Jews as Gentiles (vv. 27, 29). Between these fixed points, clause (*b*) seems to mean that God wished to reveal both his wrathful judgement against sin, and his saving power. But this is precisely what Paul has already said in iii. 26. What then if this is the purpose that lies behind God's election? In glory and in wrath he is manifesting his righteousness, and all his actions are rooted in the mercy with which alone he will deal with men.

The remaining verses of this paragraph do not require lengthy exposition. Paul uses a series of Old Testament quotations to prove (i) that God means to call Gentiles, and (ii) that he calls only a remnant and not the whole of Israel.

First come two passages from Hosea. **That this calling of** 25 **Gentiles as well as Jews was intended is shown in Scripture** (a supplement, to explain the following 'as'), **as God says in the book of Hosea: 'That which was not my people I will call my people, and her that was not beloved I will call beloved'** (Hosea ii. 23, somewhat loosely quoted); **'and** 26 **it shall come to pass that in the place where it was said to them, You are not my people, there shall they be called sons of the living God'** (Hosea i. 10). Paul of course refers mainly to the call of Gentiles; it is, however, possible that he is also thinking (as Hosea did) of the temporary lapse of Israel and their subsequent return.

Two passages from Isaiah follow. **Isaiah cries out con-** 27 **cerning Israel, 'Though the number of the children of Israel should be as the sand of the sea, yet it is the remnant of them that will be saved, for the Lord will** 28 **bring his word to pass upon the earth, accomplishing it and determining it'** (Isa. x. 22 f.). **This accords further** 29 **with what Isaiah said earlier, 'If the Lord Sabaoth** (this word is a transliteration, used by the LXX as by Paul, of the Hebrew word for 'hosts') **had not left us a seed, we should have become like Sodom, and we should have been made like Gomorrah'** (Isa. i. 9).

It is unlikely that Paul quoted the word 'seed' without remembering the use he had made of it elsewhere (see p. 181). The remnant and the seed alike were reduced to one—Jesus Christ; henceforth the elect people of God were elect *in him*. This fact reminds us that behind Paul's discussion there lies the

historical background formed by the ministry of Jesus; his rejection and crucifixion by Israel, which thereby disavowed its own
place in God's plan; and the election of a new Israel in Christ to
take the place of the old. These were the events of the last age,
which reflected the mind and character of God; but they were
not the end itself. God remained hidden behind a veil of
'mythological' event. The time is still to come when men shall
know as they have been known (1 Cor. xiii. 12).

25. ix. 30-33. WHY ISRAEL STUMBLED

**(30) What then shall we say? This, that Gentiles, who do
not make righteousness their aim, have attained righteousness—the righteousness, of course, which rests on
faith; (31) but that Israel, whose aim is a law purporting
to give righteousness, never reached that law. (32) Why?
Because they did not pursue their aim by faith, but as if it
could be reached by works. They stumbled against the
stone set for stumbling—(33) as it is written, 'Behold I lay
in Zion a stone for stumbling and a rock for tripping; and
he who believes upon it[1] shall not be put to shame'.**

The facts have now been laid bare. God, in the pursuit of his
elective purpose, has caused the partial rejection of Israel, and
the election into the messianic people of the last age of a
number of Gentiles. So far Paul has been content to say that
God has the right to treat men in this way, and that what has
happened was in fact predicted in the Old Testament; but the
question cannot fail to be asked, How did Israel come to make
the astounding blunder of rejecting the Messiah? The answer is
first stated in this paragraph, and then developed in ch. x,
before Paul returns in ch. xi to consider the full meaning of
God's elective purpose.

30   **What then shall we say?** The sum of the matter is **this,
that Gentiles** (not *the* Gentiles—as RV; there is no article in
the Greek, and the Gentiles as a whole were not yet included

---

[1] The Greek pronoun (αὐτῷ) could equally be translated 'him'.

in the Church), **who do not make righteousness their aim, have attained righteousness—the righteousness, of course, which rests on faith.** 'Righteousness' here is not moral righteousness, but the harmonious relation with God from which alone life and salvation can spring. This relation was not a concern of the Gentile world, though its inharmonious and sinful life bore witness—to those who had ears to hear—to the lack of it. It was only under the preaching of the Gospel that they had discovered faith, stumbling upon it unexpectedly.

So much for the Gentiles. Of the Jews it must be said **that 31 Israel, whose aim is a law purporting to give righteousness, never reached that law.** Paul does not say that Israel made *righteousness* their aim, but (to translate literally) a *law of righteousness*. The law of Moses was itself righteous (vii. 12), and it could have produced righteousness (a) if it had been done (Gal. iii. 10), and (b) if it had been able to give life (Gal. iii. 21). These two conditions amount to much the same thing, and they mean that the law, though good, is misused if treated as a means of attaining righteousness. This was the mistake made by the Jews. It is proper to seek righteousness, that is, a proper relation with God; and the law itself is a good thing. But to seek righteousness by means of works done in obedience to the law, may produce at most human righteousness, not God's (x. 3).

In fact, Israel did not even reach the law after which they strove. **Why? Because they did not pursue their aim** (Paul 32 now means, their aim of achieving righteousness) **by faith, but as if it could be reached by works.** Here is the second of the two great keys to the mystery of Israel's rejection. The first is that God willed it; the second, that Israel sought the right goal by the wrong means. Paul cannot bring himself to say, They sought it by *works*; this is to him so manifest an absurdity that he says, *as if it could be reached by works.* To seek righteousness by works is not merely contrary to Paul's own doctrine; it is contrary to the true meaning of the law itself—see x. 6 ff. Thus Israel, in their ill-directed search for righteousness, **stumbled against the stone set for stumbling.** Paul returns to the fundamental explanation of Israel's defection: it was willed by

God. It may be possible to give a psychological or anthropological account of what took place, but this would only describe the mechanism used by God, who provided the stone for Israel to trip over.

The 'stone of stumbling' is a phrase drawn from the Old Testament; but in providing the reference Paul combines two

33 passages. **As it is written, 'Behold I lay in Zion a stone for stumbling and a rock for tripping** (cf. Isa. viii. 14); **and he who believes upon it** (see p. 192, n. 1) **shall not be put to shame'** (Isa. xxviii. 16, LXX).

Isa. xxviii. 16 is quoted again at x. 11; and a similar composite quotation occurs in 1 Pet. ii. 6 ff. (where Ps. cxviii. 22 is also included). This fact has led some to think that Paul and the author of 1 Peter may both have drawn upon a Testimony Book (or collection of Old Testament proof-texts) in which the passages were already combined. This may be so; but Paul was not unfamiliar with the Old Testament, and it must be supposed that he knew what he was doing when he used the composite quotation, which contains in germ the argument developed in x. 1-13. Three points may be distinguished.

(i) It is the man who has faith who is not put to shame. This *sola fide* was, historically speaking, the primary source of scandal to the Jews (cf. 1 Cor. i. 22 f.). They preferred the way of law, by means of which they hoped to establish their own righteousness, and to avoid submitting to God's (x. 3). Here we are driven back to the theme of God's mercy, for only faith is the proper response to mercy.

(ii) The stone is Jesus Christ himself, who has the double effect of creating both offence and faith (see 1 Cor. i. 18; 2 Cor. ii. 15; and the notes on i. 18). He himself is the 'seed of Abraham'; election and rejection are both in him, and it is impossible for men to glimpse God's eternal purposes apart from him.

(iii) All these truths, as the quotation itself shows, have the authority of Scripture. The Jews' own Bible proclaims the offensive Christ, whose obscurity and suffering scandalized his own people (*v*. 5), just as it commends, even through the law, the way of faith.

There is no need to develop these themes here, since they are continued in ch. x.

26. x. 1-13. THE RIGHTEOUSNESS OF MEN AND THE RIGHTEOUSNESS OF GOD

(1) Scripture or no Scripture, brethren, my own heart's will, and my supplication to God, are on their behalf, and are that they may be saved. (2) For I bear them witness that they have an enthusiasm for God, but it is not informed with understanding. (3) For precisely because they did not understand God's righteousness, and sought to establish their own, they did not submit themselves to the righteousness of God. (4) For Christ, by realizing righteousness for every believer, proves to be the end of the law.

(5) For Moses writes of the righteousness which has its root in the law, that 'the man who has done it shall live by it'. (6) But the righteousness which has its root in faith speaks thus: 'Do not say in your heart, Who shall ascend into heaven?' (that is, to bring Christ down); (7) 'or, Who shall descend into the abyss?' (that is, to bring Christ up from the dead). (8) No; what does it say? 'The word is near you, in your mouth and in your heart' (that is, the word of faith which we preach). (9) And the word is to this effect, namely, that if 'with your mouth' you confess Jesus as Lord, and if 'with your heart' you believe that God raised him from the dead, you shall be saved. (10) For faith works in the heart to produce righteousness, and confession in the mouth to produce salvation. (11) For Scripture says, 'No one who believes in him will be put to shame'. (12) For there is no distinction between Jew and Greek; the same Lord is Lord of all, and he abounds in wealth to all who call upon him. (13) For 'whosoever shall call upon the name of the Lord shall be saved'.

How did the most religious of all peoples come to reject their own Messiah, for whose coming they had so long waited? Paul has already given his answers to this question (see p. 193); now he analyses them further. But first of all he emphasizes afresh (cf. ix. 1 f.) his own longing for the salvation of Israel.

1 **Scripture or no Scripture** (this supplement is an attempt to bring out the meaning of the particle (μέν) which opens the paragraph, and means 'so far as it depends on my wish'[1]), **brethren, my own heart's will** (this rather than 'wish' seems to be the meaning; cf. Eph. i. 5), **and my supplication to God, are on their behalf** (taking 'on their behalf' as a predicate—with the Vulgate, *fit pro illis*), **and are that they may be saved.** The last word looks beyond (and therefore includes) the process of justification up to the salvation of Israel at the last day. Nothing Paul has said about God's sovereign electing grace, and no Scripture prediction that only a remnant of Israel shall be saved, can alter his desire for the salvation of all Israel.

2 **For I bear them witness** (cf. 2 Cor. viii. 3; Gal. iv. 15; Col. iv. 13) **that they have an enthusiasm for God, but it is not informed with understanding.** The words of Judah b. Tema, Be strong as the leopard and swift as the eagle, fleet as the gazelle and brave as the lion to do the will of thy father which is in heaven (*Aboth*, v. 20), are no more than characteristic of Judaism at its best. No nation had given itself to God with such devoted and courageous zeal as Israel; yet it was also true that the eternal decree which had determined Israel's unbelief could be traced in sins and errors for which Israel was responsible—an interplay of predestination and human responsibility characteristic of the Bible, and not to be disposed of in the interests of simplicity on the one side or the other.

3 Israel's religious enthusiasm is misdirected. **For precisely because they did not understand God's righteousness, and sought to establish their own, they did not submit themselves to the righteousness of God.** There is a close parallel to this verse in Phil. iii. 9, which strongly suggests that, in Romans, the genitive 'of God', and the genitive substitute 'their own' (τὴν ἰδίαν), denote *origin*. There is a righteousness which comes from God as his gift, and there is (or, at least, there may be thought to be) a righteousness which men evolve out of themselves in obedience to the law.

Now the Jews have rightly perceived (cf. ix. 31) that religion is a matter of righteousness—man cannot stand in the presence

[1] B.D., p. 204.

of God the righteous judge without righteousness; but they have not seen that, if their own beliefs are to be taken seriously, the only righteousness which can be of the slightest use is God's own. Man can never make himself God, and can never produce a righteousness capable of satisfying God's requirements. It is true that God had given the Jews a law, but in thinking that their own obedience to it could secure their standing in God's court they misunderstood God's intention. What was required was not that they should be perfectly obedient to the law and so 'establish their own righteousness', but that they should 'submit to God's righteousness'; that is, acknowledge him as the righteous and merciful God and leave their fate in his hands. Here again is the contrast between 'works' and 'faith', for man's 'own righteousness' can be nothing other than a righteousness based on works of law, and God's righteousness can be accepted only by faith. The man who seeks to establish his own righteousness, however virtuous he may be, can be only a rebellious creature of God, for he is pressing himself into the Judge's throne; the man who accepts God's verdict and submits to God's righteousness thereby automatically harmonizes himself with the universe, since he falls into his appointed place as a dependent creature.

Yet this is not the whole truth. The contrast of the principles of faith and works can up to a point be expressed in anthropological terms, but Paul never (cf. pp. 81 f., 119) supposes that these terms can express it completely. Man does not of himself decide to put an end to his legal relation with God and to live henceforth by faith. This can take place not at man's choice, but only through God's initiative. **For Christ, by realizing right-** 4 **eousness for every believer, proves to be the end of the law.** 'Christ' means God's act in history, by which he introduced the Age to Come, and brought to an end the old order of relations between God and man, since it is in Christ that men are henceforth related to God. Hence Christ is the 'end of the law'. The word 'end' ($\tau\acute{\epsilon}\lambda os$) means not only 'termination', but also 'purpose', or 'intention', and the key to the present passage is to be found in the words 'by realizing righteousness' (literally, 'unto righteousness'—'unto' expressing purpose, or goal). Christ is the end of the law, with a view not to anarchy but righteousness. He puts an end to the law, not by destroying all that the law stood for but by realizing it. The law never was an effective means of attaining righteousness, but, since it was righteous (vii. 12), it did always bear witness to God's righteousness. This, however, has now actually been manifested in Christ (i. 16 f.; iii. 21).

Thus Christ is the end of the law; but he is the end of the law —for every believer. We saw that the opposites, 'works' and 'faith', do not simply lie within human choice; it was necessary that a divine act should take place. Yet the corresponding truth is also valid. The divine act, when once it has taken place, is appropriated by faith. The second pair of opposites, law and Christ, does not form a simple chronological sequence, for, as the story of Abraham shows (ch. iv), faith was possible 'before Christ', and, as the story of the Jews constantly pressed home upon Paul, allegiance to the principle of works remained possible 'after Christ'. Apart from Christ, and apart from faith, the curse of the law (Gal. iii. 13; cf. Rom. iv. 15) still holds sway.

The next nine verses (5-13) are devoted to a contrast between the righteousness which comes through the law, and that which is based on faith. As Paul has pointed out already (see p. 73), the law itself points to a non-legal righteousness; in the present paragraph Paul develops this point.

Law itself is inextricably bound up with works, for a law
5 exists only to be obeyed (cf. ii. 25 ff.). **For Moses writes of the righteousness which has its root in the law, that 'the man who has done it shall live by it'.** The same quotation (from Lev. xviii. 5) is used at Gal. iii. 12. Paul no doubt found it a convenient way of summarizing, in the law's own words, what he understood the law to mean. But also the new righteousness, which is by faith, is mentioned in the law itself, and Paul proceeds to quote Deut. xxx. 12 ff., with interspersed and appended comments.

In this passage, the Deuteronomic writer claims that the law is not too difficult to fulfil. Like the author of Leviticus (see *v.* 5), he too speaks of 'doing', and adds that there is no reason why the law should not be done. In point of fact, it is doubtful whether he did think of the law in a strictly 'nomistic' way; Deuteronomy is full of the notion that God's relations with his people rest upon grace. Paul, however, strikes out a fresh interpretation of the passage which seems to have no Jewish parallel, though it is worth noting that in 1 Bar. iii. 29 f. the words of Deuteronomy are taken to apply to Wisdom. So here, Paul supposes that they refer to Christ, though he takes the speaker to be the righteousness of God (*v.* 6), here described as the righteousness which has its root in faith.

But the righteousness which has its root in faith speaks 6 **thus: 'Do not say in your heart, Who shall ascend into heaven?' (that is, to bring Christ down).** 'Bringing Christ down from heaven' means to precipitate the Incarnation. This has already taken place; the Messiah has appeared, and it is therefore impossible to hasten his coming (as some devout Jews thought to do) by perfect obedience to the law and penitence for its transgression. The divine act of redemption (iii. 24) has already been performed, not as a reward for legal righteousness but as an act of sheer grace.

It is equally wrong to say, **'Who shall descend into the** 7 **abyss?' (that is, to bring Christ up from the dead).** Paul's words here differ from all known forms of the text of Deut. xxx. 13. His freedom suggests that he is not using his quotation as a rigid proof of what he asserts, but as a rhetorical form. The variation in the quotation was no doubt suggested by the interpretation of the previous clause. The counterpart of bringing Christ down from heaven is not crossing the sea, but bringing Christ up from the underworld (the abode of the dead). This also is sheer impossibility, since the resurrection has already happened and Christ has ascended into heaven. This means that the eschatological conditions have been realized; the Age to Come has dawned; the Gospel has become possible in the manifestation of God's righteousness (i. 17; iii. 21).

The righteousness of faith, then, does not mean that man must initiate the process of salvation, or, by good works or repentance, induce God to act. **No; what does it say? 'The** 8 **word is near you, in your mouth and in your heart' (that is, the word of faith which we preach).** Faith, as a divine possibility, is an immediate possibility. That which man might seek in heaven and hell in vain is at his side. Faith alone is what God seeks, and that he himself provides. The 'word of faith' means the Gospel, as preached by Paul; compare Eph. v. 26; vi. 17; Heb. vi. 5; 1 Pet. i. 25 b; if, as is possible, *v.* 9 suggests baptism, the first of these parallels may be the most relevant. But the 'word of faith' does not itself refer (as is often supposed) to a baptismal confession of faith, for it is something 'we preach'—that is, the Gospel message itself, not the summary of this message in a symbol. It follows that the first word (ὅτι) of the next sentence is to be translated not 'for' but 'that'; the good news is that (v. 13) everyone who calls upon the name of the Lord shall be saved.

9 **The word** of faith **is to this effect, namely, that if 'with your mouth' you confess Jesus as Lord, and if 'with your heart' you believe that God raised him from the dead, you shall be saved.**

The formulation of this verse is due to Deut. xxx. 14 (in thy mouth and in thy heart). No distinction is to be drawn between the confession and the faith; the confession is believed and the faith confessed. The Old Testament passage also suggests (though it certainly did not create) the content of faith—Christ the heavenly Lord, Christ crucified and risen.

The word 'confess' (ὁμολογεῖν) has several meanings in New Testament Greek, as in modern English. Here evidently it means to 'declare', 'profess', 'avow', 'proclaim'. For the double accusative (Jesus *as* Lord) compare John ix. 22; for similar use of the verb see, for example, 1 John iv. 2, 15; for the cognate noun, Heb. iii. 1; iv. 14; x. 23; 1 Tim. vi. 12. The verb suggests that Paul may be using a recognized formula, and this is confirmed by 1 Cor. xii. 3. The form of the sentence, 'If thou shalt confess . . . and believe . . . thou shalt be saved' suggests that the formula may be a baptismal confession.

The profession 'Jesus is Lord' is undoubtedly one of the oldest expressions of Christian belief. It has been suggested[1] that it arose in time of persecution as the Christian reply to the insistence of the state religion that 'Caesar is Lord';[2] but this seems improbable. (i) The Aramaic-speaking Church seems to have called Jesus Marana, our Lord (1 Cor. xvi. 22; *Didache*, x. 6).

[1] O. Cullmann, *Die ersten christlichen Glaubensbekenntnisse* (1943), pp. 22 f.
[2] Cf. *Mart. Pol.* viii. 2: What harm is there in saying 'Caesar is Lord' and in sacrificing and in the accompanying rites, and so being saved (διασώζεσθαι)?

At first, during the life of Jesus, this may well have meant no more than 'Teacher'; but as soon as Christians, after the resurrection, said, 'Marana *tha*' (Our Lord, *come*), begging their absent *Mar* to return from heaven, they were addressing not a Rabbi but a heavenly being. (ii) In the non-Jewish world, the word 'Christ' ($X\rho\iota\sigma\tau\delta s$) was unintelligible, and speedily became (as it already is in the Pauline epistles) scarcely more than a proper name. The notion of divine kingship (more or less bound up with Messiahship) was now expressed by Greek-speaking Jews and Gentiles alike by the term Lord ($\kappa\dot\nu\rho\iota os$). (iii) Lord ($\kappa\dot\nu\rho\iota os$) was the natural correlative term for men who knew themselves to be slaves ($\delta o\hat\nu\lambda o\iota$); compare i. 1 and the note.

Along with the first article, Jesus is Lord, goes the second, God raised him from the dead. This provides a very important qualification, or corrective. In the Hellenistic world it was very easy for the figure of Jesus, as the divine Lord and Saviour, to become assimilated to the 'gods many and lords many' (1 Cor. viii. 5) which peopled that world; he might well seem no more than another 'divine man', the centre of yet another oriental-Hellenistic cult. By insisting upon this second clause, Paul does two things. (i) He emphasizes again the true Christian subordinationism (see pp. 20 f.). Christ is not an independent demigod, but one who was what he was only in virtue of his ordination by and unbroken union with the Father. His ministry, and his death, had their effect only through the seal laid upon them when God raised him from the dead. The Christian faith therefore is not one cult among many, nor is Christ one 'lord' among many; he is, and the Church accordingly rests upon, the one unique act and self-revelation of God. (ii) At the same time, Paul reasserts the primitive Christian eschatology. The significance of Jesus is that in him God began to put into effect the Age to Come. Jesus is confessed and believed as one who stands both within and outside history; not primarily as a teacher (Paul shows no interest in him in this role) but as the source of supernatural life.

Hence he adds: You shall be saved. For Paul's conception of salvation see pp. 27 f., 107; as usual, the verb 'to save' is used in the future tense. Paul means that believers, already justified, will be saved at the last day; though, of course, he does not deny that preliminary effects of salvation are already apparent through the work of the Holy Spirit.

The shape of *v.* 10, like that of *v.* 9, is determined by Deut. xxx. 14; the distinction between faith and its effect, and con-

10 fession and its effect, is rhetorical only. **For faith works in the heart to produce righteousness, and confession in the mouth to produce salvation.** In this neat rhetorical summary of *vv.* 6-9, Paul uses some of his key-terms (faith, righteousness, salvation), and works back to the theme, central to his argument in this chapter, that righteousness is by faith only, so that the Jews who sought it by means of the law were doomed to failure

11 and rejection. This is supported by another quotation: **For Scripture says, 'No one who believes in him will be put to shame'.** The passage is taken from Isa. xxviii. 16, already used at ix. 33; here Paul has slightly modified it (by adding πᾶς—'all' —in Greek) so as to make it more universal in scope. He does this perhaps under the influence of the words he is about to quote in *v.* 13, but also because his argument requires it. In the back of his mind, the dominant question is still, Why have the Jews been rejected? And a major part of the answer to this question is (see ch. xi), In order that the Gospel may be preached to *all*, Gentiles as well as Jews. Paul proceeds to emphasize this.

12 **For there is no distinction between Jew and Greek** (that is, Gentile); **the same Lord** (confessed in the Christian faith, *v.* 9) **is Lord of all** (cf. iii. 29 f.), **and he abounds in wealth to all who call upon him.** At iii. 22 Paul spoke of the absence of 'distinction' between Jew and Greek in a negative sense—all without distinction have sinned. Here he makes the corresponding positive statement—all without distinction have the same Lord, and enjoy the rich resources of his goodness and glory (cf. ii. 4; ix. 23: God's 'wealth' is a favourite thought of Paul's; cf. xi. 33; 1 Cor. i. 5; Phil. iv. 19; Col. i. 27; iii. 16). 'Calling upon God' implies, and is the outward expression of, faith (cf. *v.* 14). Paul draws the word from the quotation used in the next verse, which is already in his mind.

13 **For 'whosoever shall call upon the name of the Lord shall be saved'.** Compare *v.* 11 and the note—Paul has in mind

the extension of the Gospel beyond Judaism. Here there is no
need to modify the Old Testament material, and Paul quotes
exactly the LXX version of Joel ii. 32.

27. x. 14-21. ISRAEL'S UNBELIEF INEXCUSABLE

**(14) This, however, evokes a new series of problems.
How are they to 'call upon' one in whom they have not
believed? How are they to believe in one whom they have
not heard? How are they to hear without someone to
make proclamation? (15) How shall men make proclamation unless they are sent? Yes, but, as it is written,
'How beautiful are the feet of those who bring good news
of good things!' (16) Yet not all became obedient to the
good news. For Isaiah says, 'Lord, who believed what
they heard from us?' (17) Faith then comes as a result of
hearing, and hearing comes through the word of Christ.
(18) Yes, but I say, Did they not hear? Why, listen: 'Their
utterance has gone out into all the earth, and their words
have come to the end of the world'. (19) But I say, Did
Israel really not know? First Moses says, 'I will stir you
up to envy with that which is not a nation, by means of a
senseless nation I will provoke you to anger'. (20) And
then Isaiah makes bold to say, 'I was found by those who
did not seek me, I appeared to those who did not inquire
for me'. (21) But of Israel he says, 'I stretched out my
hands all day to a disobedient and contradicting people'.**

'Whosoever shall call upon the name of the Lord shall be
saved' (*v.* 13). This, as an Old Testament pronouncement, was
beyond dispute. The trouble was, that Israel had not called upon
the name of the Lord (by which title Paul, though not of course
Joel, understands Jesus). Where did the fault lie? Paul seeks an
answer to this question by constructing a chain of connecting
links, and inquiring which link fails.

This evokes a new series of problems (a supplement 14
necessary for the understanding of the following sentences).

How are they to 'call upon' one in whom they have not believed? How are they to believe in one whom they have not heard? How are they to hear without someone to make proclamation? How shall men make proclamation unless they are sent?

15 Most of the links in this chain are self-evident and require no comment. It goes without saying that men will only call (for salvation) upon one in whom they believe. In the next clause it is right to translate strictly, 'whom (not *of whom*) they have not heard'. Christ must be heard either in his own person, or in the person of his preachers, through whom his own word (*v.* 17) is spoken; otherwise faith in him is impossible. Further, those who 'make proclamation' must, if they are to speak the word of Christ, come not of their own choice or on their own authority, but because they are sent. The verb 'sent' (ἀποσταλῶσιν) is cognate with the noun 'apostle' (ἀπόστολος). For the ideas involved see on i. 1. Christian missionaries act under and with the authority of him who sent them. The chain of argument is at an end. Men call on the Lord because they believe; they believe because they hear; they hear because others preach; these preach because they are sent—by the Lord, with whom the whole process begins, as it ends with him.

Paul next shows, from Scripture, that God did not fail to send out authorized preachers (*v.* 15), and adds, a little later, that Israel did not fail to hear and know what was said (*vv.* 18 f.). He anticipates the vital conclusion in *v.* 16. The break in the chain occurs at the link of faith.

How can there be preachers if they are not sent? **Yes, but, as it is written, 'How beautiful are the feet of those who bring good news of good things!'** Some commentators regard this quotation (in which Paul is nearer to the Hebrew than to the LXX version of Isa. lii. 7) as a mere ornament, but it is better to take it as a step in the argument. If there had been no preachers, Israel could not have been blamed for unbelief; but in fact Scripture itself shows that there are those who preach the Gospel (bring good news), and since their existence is noted in Scripture, and with approval, it cannot be doubted that they are true apostles.

In the next verse Paul leaps to his conclusion, though it might

more appropriately have been placed later. **Yet not all became** 16
obedient to the good news. The break in the chain consisted
only in Israel's unbelief, for which Israel was responsible, since
she had not only heard but also known (*vv.* 18 f.) God's plan.
That 'disobedience' means unbelief is shown by the quotation
that follows; compare i. 5 and the note. **For Isaiah says,**
'Lord, who believed what they heard from us?' (Isa. liii. 1).
The prophetic and the apostolic witness to Christ have gone
unheeded.

Faith then comes as a result of hearing, and hearing 17
comes through the word of Christ. Paul here uses the word
'hearing' in the sense it commonly has in his writings, though,
the same word is differently employed (as 'report', that is, 'what
they heard') in the previous verse, where Paul's usage is determined by the Old Testament. The preachers speak the word *of*
Christ; see on *v.* 14.

It has often been remarked that this verse (17) would come
more appropriately after *v.* 15 a. It is undoubtedly true that a re-
arrangement would improve the logic of the paragraph, for *v.* 17
summarizes the chain of connexions given in *vv.* 14 f., and so
would prepare the way for *v.* 16, with its disclosure that the
chain was broken in the link of faith. This, however, is not a
sufficient reason for rearranging the text. Paul leaps ahead to his
main point, and then returns to fill up a gap in the argument. He
will fill up more gaps in *vv.* 18 f.

Yes, but I say, Did they (Israel) **not hear?** If it could be 18
established that they did not, they would at once be exonerated
from the guilt of not believing. But this is not so. **Why, listen:**
'Their utterance has gone out into all the earth, and their
words have come to the end of the world'. Ps. xix. 4 refers
to the witness of God's creation. Paul takes it to apply to the
Christian mission, and to be already fulfilled. For this 'universal'
preaching of the Gospel, compare xv. 19, 23; also Mark xiii. 10;
xiv. 9. Israel has heard the Christian message of salvation; no
excuse for her unbelief can be found here.

Paul can go further. Israel ought to have understood the
theme of God's righteousness and mercy, for first the law (*v.* 19)
and then the prophets (*vv.* 20 f.) declared it.

But I say, Did Israel really not know? First Moses says, 19

'**I will stir you up to envy with that which is not a nation, by means of a senseless nation I will provoke you to anger**' (Deut. xxxii. 21). That is to say, unbelieving Israel will be put to shame by believing Gentiles. This theme will prove to be an important part of the argument of ch. xi; see especially xi. 11 f., 28.

20 After the law, the prophets. **And then Isaiah makes bold to say** (perhaps, *grows even bolder*—than Moses—*and says*), '**I was found by those who did not seek me, I appeared to those who did not inquire for me**', that is, the Gentiles; com-
21 pare ix. 30. The quotation has an apt continuation. **But of Israel he says, 'I stretched out my hands all day to a disobedient and contradicting people'.** The reference is to Isa. lxv. 1 f. The paradox of the Gentiles' faith will be matched by the paradox of Israel's disobedience. Through his Son, both in his own incarnate person and by means of his apostles, God has pleaded with Israel, and met with nothing (or little more than nothing—see xi. 5) but rebuffs. Both the pleading and the rebuffs, as the reference to Scripture shows, formed part of his eternal purpose.

28. xi. 1-10. THE REMNANT

(1) With all this in mind, I am bound to ask this question, Has God cast off his people?[1] **Certainly not. Why, I myself am an Israelite, of the seed of Abraham, of the tribe of Benjamin. (2) God has not cast off his people, whom he foreknew. Do you not know what the Scripture says in the story of Elijah, how he appeals to God against Israel? (3) 'Lord,' he says, 'they have killed thy prophets, they have digged down thine altars, and I alone am left; and they seek my life.' (4) But what does the divine oracle say to him? 'I have left myself 7000 men, who have not bowed the knee to Baal.' (5) So also at the present time there has come into being such a remnant, based on a gracious act**

[1] P46 A D* add 'whom he foreknew'. This reading is an assimilation to *v*. 2, and incorrect.

of election. (6) But note that if this act is done by grace it does not depend on works; otherwise grace would no longer be grace.[1] (7) What then? What Israel seeks after, Israel did not attain—but the elect remnant attained it, while the rest were hardened, (8) as it is written, 'God gave them a spirit of slumber, eyes not to see and ears not to hear, up to this day'. (9) And David says, 'Let their table become a snare and a trap, an offence and a recompense to them; (10) let their eyes be darkened so as not to see; bow down their backs for ever'.

If Israel is a disobedient and contradicting people (x. 21), totally unresponsive to God's appeals, it might seem that God has no recourse but to wash his hands of her. And at first glance this appears to be what has happened, for the rejection of Israel has been shown to be no accident of history but God's eternal plan, foretold in Scripture. But this would be far too simple a reading of the circumstances. The Old Testament contains far more than predictions of Israel's fall.

With all this (x. 14-21) **in mind, I am bound to ask this question, Has God cast off his people?** The language of this verse (and of *v.* 2) is based on Ps. xciv. 14. The question is raised again at *v.* 11, and is similar to that of iii. 3. The answer here is as clear as there: **Certainly not.** It may be established on theological grounds (as in iii. 3), but here Paul bases it upon a simple matter of fact, **Why, I myself am an Israelite, of the seed of Abraham, of the tribe of Benjamin.**

It is possible that by these words Paul means, 'God cast off his people? How could I, a Jew myself, even entertain such a thought?'; but it is much more likely that he means, 'God cannot have cast off his people (as a whole), for I myself am both a Jew and a Christian; this proves that Christian Jews may exist'.

In other passages Paul speaks of his Jewish origin: 2 Cor. xi. 22; Phil. iii. 5 f.; also Gal. i. 13 f.; ii. 15. Compare also Acts xxii. 3; xxiii. 6; xxvi. 5. He mentions it here, without boasting (ii. 17), as a fact relevant to his argument. The word 'seed' is used

[1] The text translated here is that of P[46] ℵ A D G lat. B ω pesh add 'But if it depends on works it is no longer grace; otherwise the work is no longer work (B has, no longer grace)'. This is almost certainly a secondary expansion, intended to complete the sense but in fact obscuring it.

without the special sense it has in ix. 7; Paul means simply, 'descended from Abraham'.

The existence of Jewish Christians, such as Paul, proves that 2 **God has not cast off his people, whom he foreknew.** For God's foreknowledge compare viii. 29. Paul refers to the many passages in the Old Testament which speak of God's election of Israel to be his own people in a special sense (see on ix. 5). God will not go back on his ancient choice (cf. *v.* 29).

The existence of Jewish Christians is not a full answer to Paul's problem, since they are a small minority of the nation as a whole. This very fact, however, suggests a line for advance. There are important Old Testament precedents for the presence of such a minority within an apostate people. Of these, Paul quotes only one. As early as the time of Elijah and the national apostasy under Ahab there remained a faithful remnant.

Do you not know what the Scripture says in the story of Elijah (literally, *in Elijah*, a curious expression which reflects a usage of Rabbinic Hebrew), **how he appeals to God** (Paul's word, ἐντυγχάνειν, often has the sense 'to intercede' (e.g. viii. 27, 34); but in itself it means only 'to have dealings with', and 3 takes its sense from the context) **against Israel? 'Lord,' he says, 'they have killed thy prophets, they have digged down thine altars, and I alone am left; and they seek my life.'** Paul gives the sense of 1 Kings xix. 10. So far the story seems to speak of a uniformly successful revolt against God. Only Elijah has resisted it, and he will soon be dead. But this, though it was Elijah's own impression of the situation, was false. 4 **What does the divine oracle say to him? 'I have left myself 7000 men, who have not bowed the knee to Baal.'** Again Paul gives the sense, rather than the words, of 1 Kings xix. 18. Elijah was not alone; 7000 other Israelites were as faithful as he. The nation was not totally apostate; a substantial proportion had kept faith.

So much for the historical illustration. The application is 5 clear. **So also at the present time** (see on iii. 26) **there has come into being such a remnant.** It is impossible to bring out in English the fact that the Greek word for 'remnant' (λεῖμμα) is cognate with the verb 'to leave' (*v.* 4, κατέλιπον); in the translation, the word 'such' is introduced in order to make the connexion. The body of Jewish Christians, exceptions to the general unbelief of their race, form a group analogous with the 7000 who refused to worship Baal.

At this point Paul introduces a brief parenthesis (*vv.* 5 b, 6) because he sees an opportunity of emphasizing his primary contention, that God's dealings with men are based not upon works but upon grace. The remnant was **based on a gracious act of election** (literally, according to election of grace). For election, see on ix. 11. The existence of a remnant—a nation within a nation—can be due only to an act of choice (ἐκλέγεσθαι), and the choice (ἐκλογή) must therefore have sprung from God's freedom, or grace. Thus 'remnant' is a word that spells grace, as the distinction (see ch. ix) between Isaac and Ishmael, Jacob and Esau, spells mercy. In itself the remnant is not 'better' than the rest of Israel, any more than Isaac was 'better' than Ishmael, or Jacob than Esau; but it consists of the 'vessels of mercy' (ix. 23), whom God chose as the vehicles of his glory.

But note (Paul, as we saw, is making a note in passing, for 6 his readers' better understanding of the whole matter) **that if this act is done by grace it does not depend on works; otherwise grace would no longer be grace.** As the last clause shows, Paul is here defining his terms rather than offering a constructive argument. If you confuse such opposites as faith and works, then words will simply lose their meaning. Paul does not, of course, deny that the remnant had performed 'works of law'—he had performed many himself (Gal. i. 14; Phil. iii. 6) —but insists that the election was not *dependent* upon them, since God's choices are eternal as he is eternal, and the election is therefore antecedent to all works. That is why it is by grace. Thus the logical basis of the latter part of the verse ('grace would no longer be grace') may be said to rest upon a time-sequence: election cannot take place both before and after the performance of works.

But it is time to return from the parenthesis and resume the main argument. **What then?** Paul pulls himself back into line 7 with a rhetorical question. **What Israel seeks after, Israel did not attain—but the elect remnant attained it, while the rest were hardened.** The object of 'seeks after' and 'attained' is nowhere expressed, but may be supplied from ix.

30 ff.; x. 3; it is presumably righteousness, the proper relation between man and God (or, people and God), in which alone are life and salvation. Paul has already said that Israel as a whole has, through seeking it by means of works, failed to achieve this goal, though the Gentiles, who, in the nature of the case, could reach it by faith alone, had achieved it. He now adds to the Gentiles, and subtracts from the people as a whole, the elect remnant, who also, like the Gentiles, attained it just because they did not (*ex hypothesi*) attempt to attain it, but received it as part of the act of grace by which they were constituted.

The rest of Israel (that is, Israel less the remnant) stood outside this relation and consequently were 'hardened'. For this important biblical word compare *v.* 25; ix. 18 (a different word in Greek); and Isa. vi. 10. It is incorrect to stress the use of the passive voice—'they were hardened'—as if Paul were unwilling to commit himself to the view that God himself had hardened men. If they were hardened, it was because someone hardened them, and there is no doubt who is the subject of the active verb in the next verse. Moreover, the use of a passive instead of an active verb with God as subject is a common Jewish reverential expedient for avoiding the use of the divine name. It is impossible here to distinguish between 'hardened because disobedient' and 'disobedient because hardened'; the two processes are concurrent. Because those Israelites who were not of the remnant stood outside the relation of grace, the more they sought righteousness (as all Jews did—x. 3) the further they fell away from it. Their religious enthusiasm was turned to sin. Paul does not shrink from the conclusion that it was God's will (determined ultimately by his mercy) that this should be so, and confirms the conclusion by Old Testament quotations.

8 They were hardened, **as it is written, 'God gave them a spirit of slumber, eyes not to see and ears not to hear, up to this day'.** Paul sharpens Deut. xxix. 4 by placing the negative with the infinitives, instead of with 'gave'.

9 **And David says, 'Let their table become a snare and a**
10 **trap, an offence and a recompense to them; let their eyes be darkened so as not to see; bow down their backs for ever'** (Ps. lxix. 22 f.). It was no doubt the reference to unseeing eyes that attracted Paul to the passage, and he probably

understood the obscure words about their 'table' and their 'backs' in a corresponding sense. Their table is their table-fellowship: the unity and interrelatedness created by the law and so highly valued in Judaism were no more than a delusion since they were a union in sin (iii. 20), not righteousness. The bent back is a symbol of bondage; compare Gal. iv. 25.

29. xi. 11-24. THE UNFOLDING OF GOD'S PLAN

(11) I must repeat my question then: Did they stumble so as to fall altogether? Certainly not. What has happened is this. By their stumble, salvation has come to the Gentiles, in order to provoke them (the Jews) to envy. (12) But if their stumble has thus come to mean the wealth of the world, and the cutting down of their numbers has led to the wealth of the Gentiles, it will mean so much more when their numbers are again brought up to full strength.

(13) Now I am speaking to you Gentiles. Precisely because I am a Gentile-apostle, I make much of my office, (14) to see if I may provoke to envy my own flesh and blood, and so save some of them. (15) For if their rejection has resulted in the reconciliation of the world, what will their acceptance be but life from the dead? (16) If the first-fruit is holy, so also is the lump; and if the root is holy, so also are the branches.

(17) But if some of the branches were broken off, and you, a wild olive, were grafted in among them and became a partaker in the rich root of the olive tree,[1] (18) do not boast over the branches; and if you do boast, it is still true that it is not you who bear the root, but the root that bears you. (19) You may say, 'Branches were broken off that I might be grafted in'. (20) True enough: it was for unbelief that they were broken off, and it is by faith

---

[1] 'In the rich root of the olive tree'; literally, this is 'of the root of the richness of the olive tree'. This string of genitives was too much for many copyists. Some MSS. have 'of the richness of the olive tree' (P46 D G it Irenaeus), others 'of the root and of the richness of the olive tree' (A ω vg pesh). But the difficult reading is not impossible, and should be adopted.

that you stand. There is nothing for you to grow boastful about; you should rather show reverent fear. (21) For if God did not spare those that were branches by nature, no more will he spare you.[1] (22) See then God's kindness and severity; severity for those who have fallen, God's kindness for you, if you continue in his kindness; otherwise you too will be cut away. (23) And they too, if they do not continue in their unbelief, will be grafted in, for God is able to graft them in again. (24) For if you were cut out of that which by nature is a wild olive and—contrary to nature—grafted into the cultivated olive, so much more will they, who belong by nature to the cultivated olive, be grafted into their own olive tree.

The Old Testament quotations at the end of the preceding paragraph (*vv.* 8 ff.) led Paul a little astray from his point. The paragraph as a whole was designed to prove that God had not finally rejected his people, because, as at other critical junctures in Israel's history, there existed an elect remnant, which owed its standing solely to grace yet stood between the people as a whole and complete apostasy. But the final quotations said nothing of a remnant, but spoke only of the blinding of Israel. Since he has thus been diverted from his theme, Paul is compelled to return to the question of *v.* 1, which he now expresses in other terms.

11   **I must repeat my question then: Did they stumble so as to fall altogether?** There is no doubt that the Jews have stumbled (cf. ix. 32 f.) and lost their place; the Gentiles are over-hauling them. But does this mean that they are now out of the race? that they are for ever outside the sphere of salvation? It is probable that some Christians gave a positive answer to this question; there are passages in the gospels which suggest this (e.g. Matt. xxi. 43; xxvii. 25). But this was not Paul's solution of the problem. He answers his own question: **Certainly not.**

---

[1] 'No more will he spare you.' Many MSS. (P⁴⁶ D G ω lat pesh Irenaeus) read 'lest he spare not you', supplying presumably, out of *v.* 20, 'one may well fear . . .'. It has been suggested that this is the correct reading, since it is so well supported, gives characteristically Pauline irony, and is the more difficult reading. But *v.* 20 c (You should show reverent fear) is parenthetical, and it is unlikely that it should be followed up in this way. The variant seems to be a secondary weakening of Paul's warning.

What then of the facts? The defection of the Jews is temporary, and while it lasts serves a definite and important purpose.

What has happened is this. By their stumble (elsewhere this word—παράπτωμα—means 'transgression' but here it must be given its more obvious etymological sense), **salvation has come to the Gentiles, in order to provoke them (the Jews) to envy.** 'Has come' is the simplest but perhaps not the happiest of possible translations here, for Paul does not abandon his usual view, that salvation is a future event (see pp. 27 f., 107); but some such word must be supplied (no verb is expressed in the Greek) in order to make clear that Paul is describing a state of affairs which has actually come about in history. It was the failure of the mission to the Jews that led to the mission to the Gentiles (cf. Acts xiii. 46; xviii. 6; xxviii. 28), who were thereby brought within the scope of salvation and through the Gospel received the assurance that in due time they would possess it (xiii. 11-14).

This was the immediate result of the Jewish apostasy; it had, however, a further purpose. The inclusion of the Gentiles would provoke the Jews to envy. Paul here alludes to the Old Testament passage (Deut. xxxii. 21) which he quoted at x. 19. There was foreshadowed the argument which is to be developed in this paragraph: Israel, seeking righteousness by works, did not believe; the Gospel was accordingly sent to the Gentiles, who accepted righteousness by faith. So far Paul can use past tenses; the next stages must be expressed in terms of purpose and hope. Israel will be provoked to envy by the Gentile attainment of righteousness, and so fly to God's mercy, so that God may in the end bestow righteousness upon her too. The details of this scheme will be unfolded as we proceed.

The point we have reached at present is that by the Jews' stumble the Gentiles have come to be included within the scope of salvation. **But if their stumble has thus come to mean the** 12 **wealth of the world, and the cutting down of their numbers has led to the wealth of the Gentiles, it will mean so much more when their numbers are again brought up to full strength.** For the verse as a whole compare *v.* 15.

The translation of this verse is disputed. The first clause is reasonably clear. Of the Jews' *stumble* we have already heard (v. 11), and seen that through it salvation reached the Gentiles. The only true wealth was thus conferred upon the whole world. In the second clause, it is made explicit that the beneficiaries are Gentiles; but what happens to Israel? Paul uses a word (ἥττημα), which in strict etymology is derived from a verb (ἡττᾶσθαι) meaning 'defeat'. Accordingly some commentators, quoting Isa. xxxi. 8, translate, 'their defeat has led to the wealth of the Gentiles'. But, whatever may be the witness of etymology, Paul is not here speaking of a defeat of Israel, but of a diminution of their numbers by the rejection of all save a remnant, and it is possible that he (wrongly, no doubt) derived his word from a comparative (ἥττων), meaning 'inferior', 'less', 'smaller'.

In the third clause, Paul uses a word (πλήρωμα) which is here taken to mean 'full strength', 'complement'. This seems to yield excellent sense (especially when taken with the interpretation of the second clause advocated above), and is consistent with Paul's usage (e.g. v. 25; Gal. iv. 4); but some, comparing xiii. 10 (love is the *complete fulfilment* of the law), think that it means, 'when they fulfill the will of God'. That is, Israel's sin has conferred a benefit upon mankind; so much more will their obedience.

The details of this verse may thus remain in some obscurity, but its main point is clear. Paul looks beyond the advantages conferred on the Gentiles by the unbelief of Israel to the far greater eschatological bliss which Israel's return will inaugurate. But he is not for the moment addressing himself to

13 Jews and their fortunes. **Now I am speaking to you Gentiles** —and Gentiles might think that a long discussion of the remnant of Israel had little to do with them. **Precisely because I am a Gentile-apostle** (that is, an apostle appointed to

14 preach to Gentiles), **I make much of my office to see if I may provoke to envy my own flesh and blood, and so save some of them.** For Paul's special commission to 'go unto the Gentiles' see especially Gal. ii. 7, 9. The drift of his argument appears to be: I know I am the 'Gentile-apostle', and I know that I am speaking to Gentiles (cf. i. 5, and note). Yet my concern for my fellow-Jews is not derogatory to or inconsistent

with my office; in fact, my work among Gentiles—because it is work among Gentiles—is connected with the Jews. The more I make of my Gentile mission the more jealous will the Jews become, and this will lead in the end to what I desire—their salvation.

Paul's hope here seems surprisingly limited, '. . . and so save *some* of them'. Out of the provocation of Israel as a whole ('my flesh and blood') there may come a few conversions. There is a close parallel in 1 Cor. ix. 22, which illuminates the meaning of 'save', and thus of the verse as a whole. 'Save' here means 'bring to the Christian faith', that is, 'convert'. Evidently, though Paul can hope for the final salvation of all Israel (*v.* 26), he does not hope for it in terms of the actual conversion of all individual Israelites; salvation of them all is a mysterious eschatological event, which is only prefigured in occasional personal conversions.

These conversions, however, few though they may be, truly point to the full return of Israel, which is part of the total hope not of that race only but of the world. **For if their rejection** 15 **has resulted in the reconciliation of the world, what will their acceptance be but life from the dead?** For *reconciliation* in Paul's teaching see v. 10 f., and the notes. Here the idea is perhaps limited (cf. Eph. ii. 16) to the reconciliation of Jew and Gentile in one new people of God. Or it may be that the 'world' means the 'Gentile world'; the meaning would then be that, through the estrangement of Israel the Gentiles had been reconciled to God.

Reconciliation, issuing in peace with God, is in origin an eschatological term, though like other eschatological terms it has been subjected to a Christian revaluation: 'life from the dead' is another such term, and must not be understood in a pietistic sense. Paul means that the final return of Israel (*v.* 26) will be the signal for the resurrection, the last stage of the eschatological process initiated by the death and resurrection of Jesus. The full conversion of Israel therefore stands on the boundary of history.

The next verse forms the transition from *vv.* 11-15 to the elaborate allegory of the olive tree in *vv.* 17-24, though the connexion with the latter is verbal rather than substantial. Paul is arguing for the certainty of the ultimate salvation of Israel, but, as will appear, the exact basis of his argument is not clear.

16 **If the first-fruit** (ἀπαρχή) **is holy, so also is the lump** (φύραμα). The origin of the metaphor is to be found in Num. xv. 20 f.: Of the first (LXX: ἀπαρχήν, the first-fruits) of your dough (LXX: φυράματος, lump) ye shall offer up a cake for an heave offering. . . . Of the first of your dough ye shall give unto the Lord an heave offering throughout your generations. The dedication of the first-fruit loaf released the whole for general consumption; in fact, it would be not inaccurate to say, in terms of primitive religion, that the sanctification of the first-fruit loaf 'de-sanctified' the remainder and so made it available for common use. But Paul's meaning is clear, even though technically open to objection. The pious Israelite might well feel that the bread he ate, though not sacrificial bread, was sanctified by that which had been taken from it for holy purposes.

A second metaphor follows. **If the root is holy, so also are the branches.** The meaning is the same. You cannot divide a living organism, such as a tree; the trunk and branches which grow from holy roots must themselves be holy.

So much for the metaphors. What does Paul intend them to convey? That the 'lump' and the 'branches' signify Israel as a whole is clear. Many commentators, drawing v. 28 into comparison, suppose that 'first-fruit' and 'root' signify the fathers of the Jewish race. This, however, is not the most probable interpretation. Paul is not yet speaking of the relation of Israel to the patriarchs, but of the remnant; as we have just seen (on v. 14) he regards the few Jewish Christians as the pledge of the eventual salvation of all Israel. This is precisely what he brings out metaphorically in this verse, if 'first-fruit' and 'root' refer to the Jewish Christians. This seems the most likely view, though it is not impossible that behind the Jewish Christians Paul sees the figure of Christ himself, whom he actually describes as the 'first-fruit' in 1 Cor. xv. 20. There is Rabbinic precedent for describing Adam as the 'first-fruit loaf',[1] and as Adam was the head of the old humanity so Christ was head of the new (v. 12-21; cf. 1 Cor. xv. 21 ff., 48 f.). If Paul is thinking here of Christ himself as the first-fruits he is only sharpening a thought which

[1] See S.B., iv. 667 f.

is in any case inherent in his argument: the fact that first-fruits and root exist is in itself a mark of God's grace; no claim upon him is established.

It is the root and branch metaphor which suggests to Paul the allegory of the olive tree. This is inserted (cf. *v.* 13) mainly for the benefit of Gentiles. Their own place in the saving process is described, and when Paul speaks also of that of the Jews it is in the first instance for the better understanding, and consequent humility, of the Gentiles. One remark on the allegory as a whole may be made here. Paul knows, and explicitly states, that he is describing a process which is contrary to nature (*v.* 24). The conclusion sometimes drawn that he was a townsman unfamiliar with country life and agricultural practices is therefore absurd. He is speaking not of nature but of grace, and his metaphor takes its origin not in husbandry but in theological and historical fact. Whether, or how far, in this it resembles or differs from the gospel parables is a question which cannot be handled here. Paul at least is not deducing theology from natural processes.

But if some of the branches were broken off, and you, a 17 **wild olive, were grafted in among them and became a partaker in the rich root of the olive tree, do not boast over** 18 **the branches.** The language is technical, even though the process is 'contrary to nature' (*v.* 24). The branches broken off are of course unbelieving Jews; the wild olive branches grafted in are believing (i.e. Christian) Gentiles, who henceforth belong to the main stock of the people of God. As such they enjoy the privileges and benefits described as the 'rich root of the olive tree'. In practice these amount to the supernatural life of the people of God in the last age, alluded to in ch. vi. These privileges, however, give the Gentile Christian no ground for boasting over the unbelieving Jew, for he possesses them by grace, not by right. Moreover, **if you do boast, it is still true that** (these words are inserted to fill a gap in a sentence which, in Greek, is elliptical, and meaningless if translated literally) **it is not you who bear the root, but the root that bears you.** In other words, the Jews really are the people of God, because the Old Testament really is true (cf. iii. 2 f.). Christian Jews are not grafted into paganism, but Christian Gentiles are grafted into Israel. Accordingly, the Gentile who feels disposed to boast (the Greek present tense can bear this meaning) should remember not only that he stands by grace alone but also that the privilege he has acquired is—that of being an Israelite. But he is not yet silenced.

19 **You may say** . . . no doubt Gentile Christians had said this. Again the style recalls that of the diatribe (see p. 43). **'Branches were broken off that I might be grafted in'.** The implication is, 'God prefers me (a Gentile) to the Jews'. To the statement of

20 fact, but not to the implication, Paul replies, **True enough: it was for unbelief that they were broken off, and it is by faith that you stand.** The mission to and inclusion of the Gentiles did not take place because God had grown tired of the Jews and wished for a change. The Jewish 'branches' were broken off because they did not believe (x. 16 f.); the Gentile 'branches' were grafted in not because they were superior in religion or morals (they were not) but because they received the Gospel with faith. **There is nothing** here **for you to grow boastful about; you should rather show reverent fear.**

'To grow boastful' ($\dot{v}\psi\eta\lambda\dot{a}\ \phi\rho o\nu\epsilon\hat{\iota}\nu$): the same expression is used at xii. 16, but in a different sense. What is common to the two is the idea of being 'above oneself'. The proper attitude for the Gentile Christian, as indeed for any Christian, is 'reverent fear', for he must recognize that there is in himself absolutely nothing which can secure his position with God. The moment he begins to grow boastful he ceases to have faith (humble dependence upon God), and therefore himself becomes a candi-

21 date for 'cutting off'. **For if God did not spare those that were branches by nature, no more will he spare you.** The fault of the Jews lay in their boastfulness and self-confidence (ii. 17 f.); if the Gentiles fall into the same ways they will share the same fate. There is no hope, no peace, and no security for man but in faith only.

22 The whole process is a revelation of the nature of God. **See then God's kindness and severity; severity for those who have fallen, God's kindness for you, if you continue in his kindness; otherwise you too will be cut away.** Kindness and severity are equally attributes of God, just as grace and wrath are equally activities of God. Paul does not mean that

God is kind and severe in an arbitrary way (though this is what a superficial reading of his account of God's dealings might suggest). God is always God; his kindness and his severity are correlates of faith and unbelief (*v.* 20), for it was on account of unbelief that some (the rejected Jews) 'fell', and it was on account of faith that believing Gentiles were attributed to Israel. This correlation appears clearly from the fact that both the kindness and the severity are reversible. For 'you', the kindness lasts—as long as you abide in it. The meaning of this is given by ii. 4 f. To abide in God's kindness is to continue in repentance and faith; an unrepentant heart turns kindness to severity. If the Christian Gentile treats his privileges as the Jew formerly treated his, then he too will be cut out of the olive tree.

This process also operates in the reverse direction. **And they** 23 **too, if they do not continue in their unbelief, will be grafted in.** It was unbelief that excluded them; when unbelief is gone, exclusion is at an end. When the unrepentant heart repents and accepts God's judgement whatever it be, severity becomes kindness. This is not to say that man can at any time determine his own acceptance or rejection with God; they will be grafted in because **God is able to graft them in again.** Why should he not? To graft branches once cut from a cultivated olive back into a cultivated olive is a far more natural process than grafting branches of wild olive into a cultivated olive. **For if you were cut out of that which by nature is a** 24 **wild olive and—contrary to nature—grafted into the cultivated olive, so much more will they, who belong by nature to the cultivated olive, be grafted into their own olive tree.** It will be easier—if such things can be compared—to bring back to the holy people a Jew born into the covenants of grace, endowed with the law (which did after all bear witness to the manifestation of God's righteousness by grace through faith—iii. 21), and instructed by the messianic prophecies, than to introduce for the first time a Gentile whose only advantage was the dim vestige of religion which warned him that the world of which he was part was not his but God's (i. 20).

It is at this point that Paul reminds his readers that the process he is describing is an unnatural one. Certainly, in historical terms it is a very strange one. Almighty God chooses a people to be his own: to know and serve him, and to represent him in the world. His relations with them are determined entirely by grace, but they use the law he has given them to pervert these relations; legal relations, they think, will give them greater freedom. Accordingly, when God, in fulfilment of his promise, sends them his Son, they reject and kill him. The message of this gracious act is now taken beyond the chosen people to the Gentiles, some of whom accept it, and take advantage of the universal act of grace performed in the death and resurrection of Jesus to enter into gracious relations with God (that is, to be justified by faith). The chosen people who have now (with few exceptions) lost their position see Gentiles standing in that relation with God which they once enjoyed, are stung to envy and to repentance, and so return not to supplant but to join the Gentiles in the relation of grace. All these events are to be regarded as due to the sovereign freedom and elective purpose of God himself.

When the story is told in this way it is difficult not to conclude that the kindness and severity of God are disposed in arbitrary fashion. But it must be remembered that Paul—inevitably, in view of his belief that the purposes of God would in a very short time be brought to a full close—writes in what must be called a mythological manner; that is, he expresses what he has to say about God and his eternal purposes in historical, or quasi-historical, terms. History did not come to an end when he thought it would do so, and it is consistent with this fact that the reunion of Jew and Gentile within one Church or people has not taken place. History still runs its course, and it is a course which neither Paul nor any other in the first century was able to foresee. But two points are clear. (i) The matters on which Paul commits himself are truths which lie beyond history, because they are truths about God. It will be recalled that, on p. 171, it was pointed out that his doctrine of predestination implies a 'qualitative definition' rather than a 'quantitative limitation' of God's action. God is kind and God is severe; when we view him through Jesus Christ we see his kindness, when we try to approach him in some other way—through, for example, a legalistic religion—we see his severity. (This point is developed in the next paragraph.) (ii) When the meta-historical truths with which Paul is concerned impinge upon history, they do so, in every generation, in the pattern Paul describes. For him, it was an affair of Jew and Gentile; but it was pointed out above (pp. 84, 140) that the true meaning of 'law' is religion. Paul's picture is of the religious and the ir-religious man. The former lives in an atmosphere which should constantly remind him that God is in heaven and he upon earth (Eccles. v. 2); but in this atmosphere he makes himself at home and domesticates his God. The irreligious man stumbles by accident (as he may think) upon the terror and the grace of God, and supplants his brother, because he knows he has no virtue and no piety to offer to his Maker, but trusts the grace he has glimpsed in Christ. And the religious man, or Pharisee, learns with painful inward struggle that he must divest himself of his pride, count his gains loss and his boasts dung, in order to be found in Christ, with a righteousness not of his own fabrication but from God (Phil. iii. 8 f.).

30. xi. 25-32. GOD'S PLAN COMPLETE

(25) For, brethren, I do not wish you not to know this divine secret, lest you be wise—in your own conceit. The secret is that a partial hardening has fallen upon Israel, and will remain until the full number of the Gentiles has come in; (26) when this is done, all Israel will be saved, as it is written, 'Out of Zion shall come a deliverer, and he shall remove from Jacob all his impieties; (27) and this is the covenant I will make with them, when I take away their sins'. (28) As far as the immediate results of the preaching of the Gospel go, they are enemies—for your advantage; when you bear in mind the fact of God's election, they are beloved, on account of the fathers; (29) for God does not go back on his acts of grace and his calling. (30) For as you formerly were disobedient to God, but now (corresponding to their disobedience) have received his mercy, (31) so they also now (corresponding to the mercy you have received) have become disobedient,

in order that they too may now[1] receive God's mercy. (32) For God has shut up all men to disobedience, in order that he may deal with all men in mercy.

The allegory of the olive tree ended, Paul sets out *expressis verbis* the mystery of the divine purpose, and draws to a close the long discussion of chs. ix-xi. Two words are significant for the meaning of the paragraph as a whole: secret and mercy. What Paul describes is not a simple historical process already visible to the human eye. It can be perceived and understood only by divine revelation. In due course it will be worked out on the plane of history, but so far it is a mystery concealed in heaven and disclosed only to the elect (see on *v.* 25). The meaning of the secret is God's mercy. His treatment of the Gentiles (i. 18-32) and of the Jews (ii. 17-24; ix. 32 f.; xi. 7-10), when viewed simply on the historical plane so far as history has yet run its course, may seem to spell anything but mercy— wrath, judgement, vengeance, neglect (cf. iii. 25). But when God is all in all, he will be recognized as—God who has mercy (ix. 16), and already this truth is declared in the Gospel.

This piece of Pauline apocalyptic is not set in motion by the desire to parade 'visions and revelations' (2 Cor. xii. 1), or by mere curiosity about the future and the number of the saved. 25 As is usual with Paul, the motivation is practical. **For** (that is, I have given you this allegory of the olive tree *because*), **brethren, I do not wish you not to know** (cf. i. 13) **this divine secret, lest you be wise—in your own conceit.** Paul is still addressing Gentiles (*v.* 13), who might be inclined to mock at unbelieving Israel, and to congratulate themselves upon their adherence to the Gospel. How much wiser they had been than the Jews, who had rejected it! But the man who thus congratulates himself is wise only in his own estimation (cf. xii. 16; Prov. iii. 7). He fails to recognize (a) that the acceptance of the Gospel implies no merit on his part but is by faith only (*v.* 20); (b) that his faith is itself the result of God's initiative and mercy (ix. 16); and (c) that his faith and inclusion within the people of God are but

---

[1] 'Now', which is found in B א D*, is omitted by P46 A G ω; 33 sah substitute 'subsequently'. 'Now' is a very difficult, but Pauline, reading (see the notes), and the variants must be regarded as secondary 'improvements'.

one stage in the unfolding of God's complete and all-embracing purpose.

From this self-delusion the Gentile may be delivered by the disclosure of God's secret, or mystery. This word is used again at xvi. 25, but in a somewhat different sense; there it refers to the whole plan of salvation in Jesus Christ which was kept secret until the proper moment of revelation. At 2 Thess. ii. 7 it is the 'mystery of iniquity'; at Col. i. 26 f. it recalls Rom. xvi. 25 and the present passage. The most illuminating parallel, however, is 1 Cor. xv. 51, where the mystery is an apocalyptic secret, which the seer is able to make known for the enlightenment of the elect. Here Paul imparts to his readers the secret which makes sense of the otherwise inexplicable course of the last age.

The content of the secret, hinted at in *vv.* 7, 12, and in the allegory, is now stated. **The secret is that a partial harden-ing has fallen upon Israel, and will remain until the full number of the Gentiles has come in; when this is done,** 26 **all Israel will be saved.** 'Partial' renders a phrase which recurs in xv. 15, 24; 2 Cor. i. 14; it may be adjectival (as, apparently, here), or adverbial. The 'hardening' (cf. *v.* 7) was only partial, since there was a remnant that believed. Through this harden-ing arose the Gentile mission (*vv.* 11, 28), and it will continue until its purpose is complete. But what does the 'full number of the Gentiles' mean? From *v.* 12 it appears that it must mean 'totality' or 'complement'; but this might mean either 'all Gentiles that ever were born' or 'all Gentiles intended by God to belong to the elect'. Only the context as a whole can decide between these alternatives, which indeed cannot be taken as strict alternatives, since the 'number intended by God' might be identical with the 'total number'.

When all the Gentiles meet to be included in the people of God have been included, 'all Israel will be saved'. Here we are confronted by a similar problem. In what sense does Paul mean 'all Israel'? 'Israel as a whole' or 'each several Israelite'? There is an interesting parallel to Paul's words in *Sanhedrin*, x. 1: All Israelites have a share in the world to come. This statement certainly does not refer to each several Israelite, for it proceeds to enumerate a long list of exceptions: from 'all Israel' must be subtracted all Sadducees, heretics, magicians, the licentious, and many more. It means that Israel as a whole is destined for eternal life in the Age to Come. This, of course, does not prove that Paul's meaning was the same; but when his two statements, about Gentiles and Jews, are taken together, it seems probable that he is thinking in representative terms (see on the rest of this paragraph, and on xv. 19); first the remnant of Israel, then Gentiles, finally Israel as a whole.

That Israel will be delivered, by the removal of sin, is proved from Scripture: **as it is written, 'Out of Zion shall come a deliverer, and he shall remove from Jacob all his** (these two words are a sense-addition to the Greek) **impieties;** 27 **and this is the covenant I will make with them, when I take away their sins'.** This is a composite quotation, from Isa. lix. 20 and xxvii. 9; compare Ps. xiv. 7; Jer. xxxi. 33. It may be (cf. ix. 33) that Paul drew it from a Testimony Book, or that he himself, subconsciously perhaps, combined the two passages.

The two verses make the same point: God has not done with Israel, but it is preparing a new covenant of salvation in which Israel's sins will be done away. It is because Scripture itself affirms this that Paul can predict that 'all Israel will be saved'.

The paragraph is brought to an end with two balanced sentences, each constructed on the same pattern. Each contains a pair of antithetical clauses explained by a 'for' ($\gamma\acute{a}\rho$) clause. Thus:

$\Big\{$ A—Enemies, for your advantage (*v.* 28)
$\phantom{\Big\{}$ B—Beloved, on account of the fathers (*v.* 28)
$\phantom{\Big\{}$ C—For God does not . . . (*v.* 29)
$\Big\{$ A'—You once . . . but now (*v.* 30)
$\phantom{\Big\{}$ B'—They now . . . but now (*v.* 31)
$\phantom{\Big\{}$ C'—For God has shut up . . . (*v.* 32)

The rhetorical pattern suggests that Paul is writing with care as well as feeling, and his words must be carefully marked.

In relation to God the Jews are at the present time both 28 enemies and beloved. **As far as the immediate results of the preaching of the Gospel go, they are enemies—for your advantage.** This is simply a statement of the facts which have already been described. The Gospel was preached to the Jews, and they rejected it, thereby placing themselves under God's wrath, since the law, which they preferred to the way of faith, produces wrath (iv. 15). Their rejection of the Gospel, however, led to the mission to the Gentiles, and thereby turned out to be to the advantage of the Gentiles. But this is not the whole truth; **when you bear in mind the fact of God's election, they are beloved, on account of the fathers.** 'If some have proved unbelieving, will their unbelief make void the faithfulness of God?' (iii. 3). They are the race whom God elected to be his peculiar people, and their election rests in no way upon their merits or achievements. It is true that when Paul says that they are beloved 'on account of the fathers' his language recalls the Rabbinic doctrine of the merit (*zakuth*) of the fathers, which forms a treasury upon which their sinful descendants can draw; but the resemblance is only superficial, for Paul is not speaking of human merit but of divine election.

For God does not go back on his acts of grace (for this 29 meaning of the word—χάρισμα—see on v. 16) **and his calling.** This is the explanation not simply of God's love for Israel, but also of the paradoxical fact that the same people may be at the same time enemies and beloved. It is at this point also that we may go back to ix. 6-13 and take up Paul's argument about God's freedom in election, and the true Israel. It is often supposed that Paul here contradicts what he has said in ch. ix: here, the Jews are beloved *on account of the fathers*, whereas there it is proved that God is not bound by any human line of descent and is free to call and create his people as he pleases. The underlying truth which connects the two apparently contradictory lines of thought is that, for God, freedom is freedom to act in grace, and that since he is ever the same he never regrets or revokes the acts of grace which he performs, and never annuls the vocation he prepares for men and nations. This is quite the reverse of saying that men by their descent, nationality, or other qualifications, are able to establish a claim upon God and so limit his freedom. If (to put the matter in a paradox) God's freedom is limited at all, it is limited only in the fact of his being God—the gracious God who delights in mercy, and whose wrath (as we shall presently see) exists to serve the ends of his mercy.

The final period (*vv.* 30 ff.) is parallel to the last (*vv.* 28 f.), but goes perhaps deeper. It starts from the same historical cir-

30 cumstances. **For as you formerly were disobedient to God**
—that is, as Gentiles, rebelling against your Creator (i. 18-21,
28)—**but now (corresponding to their disobedience) have
received his mercy**—in accepting the Gospel now pro-
31 claimed to the Gentiles by Paul and his colleagues—, **so they**—
the Jews—**also now (corresponding to the mercy you have
received) have become disobedient**—in rejecting the
Gospel preached first of all (i. 16) to them—**in order that they
too may now receive God's mercy.**

For Jew and Gentile alike, the end of the road is God's mercy;
and for each the road leads through disobedience. The Gentile
story, told in *v.* 30, is straightforward and needs little comment.
The phrase 'corresponding to their disobedience' translates a
Greek dative, which is sometimes taken in a simple instrumental (cf. *v.* 20) and sometimes in a temporal sense.[1] But, both
here and in the next verse ('corresponding to the mercy you
have received'), more is involved then mere instrumentality and
temporality. In each case, behind disobedience and mercy,
stands the same sovereign divine activity (Gaugler, ii. p. 209).
God wills and enacts the one as he wills and enacts the other.

The case of the Jews is less simple. They stumbled (ix. 32 f.)
at the appointed stone of stumbling—Christ, the requirement
of faith, and of nothing other than faith, for justification, and
the extension of the Gospel to the heathen world. The present
age ('now') means for them disobedience, since they have rejected the Messiah God sent them. This we have heard before,
and that Jewish disbelief led to Gentile faith. But now two
further points are added, (a) an 'in order that' (*ἵνα*), and (b) a
'now' (*νῦν*). Apparently, then, the unbelief of the Jews was a
necessary stage on the way to faith—they disbelieved, and disobeyed, *in order that* they might believe; and their return to faith,
and their resumption into the people of God, is to take place
now, in the present age. On the first of these points more will
be said below; it is only the disobedient who can know the mercy
of God. The second introduces what has been described as an
'almost intolerable eschatological tension' (Barth, *op. cit.* p. 417).
Not only the unbelief, but also the return of the Jews is *now*. It
is no doubt true that Paul expected the full eschatological end

[1] See Moule, *Idiom Book*, p. 44.

226

to fall within his own generation (see xiii. 11 f.; 1 Thess. iv. 15; 1 Cor. xv. 51); but it seems in the highest degree unlikely that he actually contemplated a successful operation of rapid missionary work, culminating, in the very near future, in the conversion of every single Jew. He is, rather, speaking of the End, of that which is beyond history and beyond all human understanding, of God all in all, the merciful God. It is the unique, and unenviable, privilege of the men of religion that they are at once believers and disbelievers, and stand at once under the wrath and mercy of God. They live not in the truth but on the edge of it; in the half-light before dawn. When their religion asserts itself and its independent effectiveness, they are lost; when it denies itself, and circumcision of the flesh is seen to point to circumcision of the heart, they are redeemed. And they must share the damnation of the disobedient if they are to be justified in the mercy of God.

For God has shut up all men to disobedience, in order 32 **that he may deal with all men in mercy.** That is, God has brought men into a position which merits nothing but his wrath in order that his relations with them may be marked by nothing but mercy. God's rejections, punishments, and abandonments (i. 24, 26, 28) are rightly understood as the foil of his mercy. Only sinners can be the objects of his mercy, and only those who know that they are sinners can know that they are loved. The righteous 'need no repentance' (Luke xv. 7) and cannot know what it is to be forgiven. Every man must be damned if he is to be justified.

Here at length the full meaning of Paul's 'double predestination' is revealed. God has predestinated *all men* to wrath and he has predestinated *all men* to mercy. If they were not predestinated to the former they could not be predestinated to the latter. It is true that the stress here does not lie on the 'all men' but on the 'disobedience' and the 'mercy'; Paul does not intend to make a definite pronouncement about the ultimate destiny of each individual man. But the hope of mankind is more, not less, secure because it is rooted in the truth about God, rather than in a truth about man himself.

Paul expresses almost the same truth in similar words in Gal. iii. 22: The Scripture hath shut up all things under sin, that the

promise by faith in Jesus Christ might be given to them that
believe. For faith is man's assent to the mercy which came to
action in Jesus Christ, and the opposite of the disobedience
which refuses God's mercy by seeking to deserve his favour.

31. xi. 33-6. THE PRAISE OF GOD

**(33) O the depth of God's wealth and wisdom and know-
ledge! How unsearchable are his judgements! How his
ways baffle our attempts to track them down! (34) For
'Who has known the mind of the Lord? Who has been
his counsellor?' (35) 'Who first gave to him, that recompense might be made him?' (36) For of him and through
him and unto him are all things. To him be the glory
for ever. Amen.**

Precisely because Paul sees that the tangled problems of
existence and history find their solution not in man but in God,
the chapter ends with an ascription of praise to God.

33 **O the depth of God's wealth and wisdom and knowledge!** It is possible to make 'wisdom' and 'knowledge' dependent upon 'wealth': '. . . the depth of God's wealth both of
wisdom and of knowledge'; but it seems better to treat all these
words as independent. For God's wealth compare ii. 4; ix. 23;
Col. i. 27. God is of infinite resource, and his plans rest upon
infinite wisdom and knowledge.

**How unsearchable are his judgements! How his ways
baffle our attempts to track them down!** Who would have
thought of the means just described by which his mercy is
brought to bear on all men? But he whom men cannot find
when they seek him has freely and graciously revealed himself
and his purposes in Christ.

34 Two Old Testament quotations follow. **For 'Who has
known the mind of the Lord? Who has been his counsellor?'** (Isa. xl. 13 (LXX)). This quotation emphasizes the
profundity and inscrutability of God's counsels.

The second quotation takes up a different point: God acts in

grace, and it is therefore impossible to build up a store of merit
with him by reason of which one may claim a reward; whatever
he gives he gives freely. With God, man never earns a recompense; he can only be loved and treated with mercy. **'Who** 35
first gave to him, that recompense might be made him?'
(Job xli. 11 (not LXX)).

God is the source of all wisdom and of all love: **For of him** 36
and through him and unto him are all things.

It is sometimes maintained that in this verse Paul employs a
formula drawn from Hellenistic mysticism and theology.[1] Stated
in this form, the hypothesis is unnecessary. Paul's propositions,
that all things are from, through, and unto God, are axioms of
biblical theology, and he himself has emphasized them, especially
in chs. ix-xi, as strongly as any biblical writer. The whole process of salvation, including its negative aspects of disobedience
and wrath, is due to God's initiative. He remains in control of
the process from beginning to end, putting his eternal purposes
into effect through the acts of the Son and the Spirit. And all
things find their end in him, for he has 'shut up all men to disobedience, in order that he may deal with all men in mercy',
while the 'creation itself also shall be liberated from the corrupting bondage in which it lies' (viii. 21), and 'all things co-
operate for good to those who love God' (viii. 28). It remains,
however, a true and valid observation that there are close
verbal parallels to Paul's words in Stoic writers,[2] and it is quite
likely that Paul chose to express his biblical faith in Stoic words,
which originally bore a quite different meaning. The connecting
link is no doubt to be found in Hellenistic Judaism.[3]

The God in whose mercy all things originate, and in whose
mercy all things end, is the only proper object of worship and
praise: **To him be the glory for ever.** The *sola gratia* and *sola*

[1] In addition to the commentaries see especially E. Norden, *Agnostos
Theos* (1913), 240-50.

[2] E.g. M. Aurelius, iv. 23: 'All that is in tune with thee, O Universe
(κόσμος), is in tune with me! Nothing that is in due time for thee is too
early or too late for me! All that thy seasons bring, O Nature (φύσις), is fruit for
me! From thee are all things, in thee are all things, unto thee are all things.'

[3] There are several examples in Philo, e.g. *The Special Laws*, i. 208: 'The
division of the animal into its limbs [Philo is allegorizing sacrificial regulations]
indicates either that all things are one or that they come from one and return
to one'.

fide of these eleven chapters can issue only in this *soli Deo gloria*. What it means to give glory to God, and how far removed this is from mere pious ejaculations, will appear in chs. xii-xvi.

32. xii. 1, 2. THE GROUND OF CHRISTIAN ETHICS

(1) I exhort you, therefore, brethren, by God's mercies, to offer your bodies as a living sacrifice, holy and well-pleasing to God; this is the spiritual worship you owe him. (2) And do not be conformed to this age, but be transformed by the renewing of your mind, that you may try and approve what is the will of God, what (that is) is holy and acceptable and perfect.

It is pointed out in most commentaries that a major division of the epistle falls between chs. xi and xii; chs. i-xi form the dogmatic part of the epistle, chs. xii and xiii (or xii-xv) the ethical. There is, of course, a measure of truth in this observation; but it is a serious mistake to treat the two parts of the epistle as distinct from each other. Paul's dogmatic teaching is misunderstood if it is not seen to require ethical action, and his ethical teaching cannot be grasped if it is not recognized that it rests at every point upon the dogmatics. So far from its being a contradiction of the doctrine of justification by faith (good works returning, as it were, by a back door after their formal expulsion), it is best understood as an exposition of the obedience which is an essential element in faith (i. 5), and of the gratitude which redeemed and justified man is bound to feel towards the merciful God.

This connexion between Paul's dogmatics and his ethics is emphasized by the opening words: **I beseech you, therefore, brethren** (i. 13), **by God's mercies.** The word 'therefore' (οὖν) can be, and sometimes is, treated as no more than a transition-particle, but since it is supported by the appeal to the mercies of God it seems best to give it its normal meaning. For 'the mercies of God' forms a not inadequate summary of what is contained in chs. i-xi, and especially in chs. ix-xi; and, in

Paul's view, the proper response to the kind of argument conducted there is not to speculate upon the eternal decrees, or one's own place in the scheme of salvation, but to be obedient. Obedience well summarizes the following words, in which Paul exhorts his readers **to offer your bodies as a living sacrifice, holy and well-pleasing to God.**

The language throughout this clause is sacrificial; not only the word 'sacrifice' itself, but also 'offer', 'holy', and 'well-pleasing' are technical terms. By 'body' Paul means the whole human person, including its means of expressing itself in common life (cf. vi. 6, 12). The 'mercies of God' on the one hand move men to offer him what is essentially a sacrifice of thanksgiving; on the other, it is through these mercies, and not through any merit of their own, that men are able to bring a sacrifice to God.

It is not quite certain how the last words of the verse are to be constructed. It is possible to take them (as here) in apposition to 'sacrifice': **this is the spiritual worship you owe him.** It is also possible, though perhaps less likely, that they are in apposition to the whole sentence: I beseech you . . . to offer your bodies . . . in such a way that this is the spiritual worship you owe. The difference is not great.

It is hardly possible to find a satisfactory rendering of the words here translated 'spiritual worship' (λογικὴ λατρεία); compare 1 Pet. ii. 2, 5. Etymologically, the adjective means, 'pertaining to the logos, or reason', and was therefore naturally applied, especially by the Stoics, to that which related man to God. Thus, in a famous passage, Epictetus declared, 'If I were a nightingale I would do what is proper to a nightingale . . .; but in fact I am a rational (λογικός) creature, so I must praise God' (*Discourses*, I, xvi. 20 f.). In the *Corpus Hermeticum* a hymn of praise to God is called a rational or spiritual sacrifice (λογικὴ θυσία; xiii. 19, 21). Paul means, a worship consisting not in outward rites but in the movement of man's inward being. This is better described as 'spiritual worship' than as 'rational', for Paul is not thinking of what is meant in modern English by 'rational'.

The Hellenistic parallels do not prove that Paul's thought was based on Stoic material. The Old Testament itself knows inward as well as material sacrifice (e.g. Ps. li. 17). This was not forgotten in later Judaism. For example, Deut. xi. 13 (. . . to serve him with (the Hebrew might be translated *in*) your heart . . .) was interpreted to mean that as there was a service of the altar (cf. ix. 4), so there was also a service of the heart (S.B. iii. 26); and after the destruction of the Temple in A.D. 70 it was said that, though other sacrifices had ceased, the sacrifice of praise and thanksgiving remained. It was probably with examples such as these in mind that Paul wrote of the Christian's spiritual worship; but his phrase (especially the adjective) looks back to Stoic language, mediated through the Hellenistic synagogue.[1]

All men owe obedience to God, though the Christian, with a clearer perception of God's mercies, is under a special obligation. Paul now proceeds to an exhortation based upon a unique Christian conviction. It is expressed in eschatological form; in fact, all the exhortation of chs. xii, xiii is contained within an eschatological framework, for xii. 2 bids Christians not to be conformed to this age, and xiii. 11-14 points to the new day which is at hand.

2 **Do not be conformed to this age, but be transformed by the renewing of your mind.** The 'mercies of God' are the ground of the Christian's self-sacrifice to God; but they are also the record of the way (traced out in chs. i-xi) in which God has brought his eternal purposes to their fulfilment in Christ. Paul never goes so far as to say that the Age to Come has come; for him, 'this age' is still, as in Jewish apocalyptic, the existing framework of human and demonic society. But, since the life, death, and resurrection of Jesus, 'this age' can no longer be the regulative principle of life for those who have died and been raised with Jesus (vi. 3 ff.). *In Christ* they have entered the new age; already they have received the first-fruits of the Spirit (viii. 23), and are under obligation not to the flesh but to the Spirit (viii. 12). In the present verse Paul expresses this truth in new terms.

An attempt is sometimes made to distinguish between 'conformed' (συσχηματίζεσθαι) and 'transformed' (μεταμορφοῦσθαι). The former is said to refer to outward form only, the latter to inward being. The attempt is probably baseless: (a) conformity

---

[1] Philo, for example, writes: 'The soul . . . ought to honour God not irrationally (ἀλόγως) nor ignorantly, but with knowledge and reason (λόγῳ)' (*Special Laws*, i. 209).

to this age is no superficial matter; (b) Pauline usage does not support a difference between the two verbs (cf. 2 Cor. iii. 18 with Phil. iii. 21).

Being conformed to this age results in an 'unfit mind' (i. 28). To recognize and share the act of redemption accomplished in the death and resurrection of Jesus means the renewing of the mind. Paul's use of this word (νοῦς), notwithstanding a superficial resemblance, differs radically from that of the Greek writers. The mind is not necessarily good; it must be renewed. 'Renewal' is used at Titus iii. 5 for that which is wrought in baptism; the cognate verb is used at 2 Cor. iv. 16; Col. iii. 10. These passages are instructive. Paul is able to speak of a radical renewal of human nature because the old age is disappearing and the new age is at hand; the renewal which is begun in conversion and baptism and advanced with every Christian decision taken ends in the glory of God.

In this world, renewal is most clearly shown in moral life. Its aim is **that you may try and approve what is the will of God, what (that is) is holy and acceptable and perfect.** For 'try and approve' see pp. 56, 104; more than testing is implied. The Christian finds out the will of God not to contemplate it but to do it. It goes without saying that what is known to be God's will is—perfect. Paul knows no other moral criterion than this. For the mind's recognition of the will (or law) of God, compare vii. 25; it is the renewed mind (not mind as such) that is capable of this recognition. And even the renewed mind needs a good deal of instruction: hence the detailed advice and exhortation of the following paragraphs.

33. xii. 3-21. THE CHRISTIAN OFFERING

(3) For, through the grace God gave me, I tell you, every one, not to think more highly of yourselves than you ought to think, but to be sober-minded about yourselves, as God has given to each of you a measure of faith. (4) For as we have many members in one body, and all the members do not have the same function, (5) so we, who are many,

are one body in Christ, and severally members of one another. (6) Since then we have gifts of grace differing according to the grace God has given us, if the gift be prophecy, let us exercise it according to the proportion of faith; (7) if it be ministry, let us attend to our ministry; if one be a teacher, let him attend to his teaching; (8) if an exhorter, to his exhortation; the man who practises charity, let him do it whole-heartedly, let the president act with zeal, let the man who does acts of mercy do them with cheerfulness. (9) Let your love be free from dissimulation. Abhor that which is evil; cleave to that which is good. (10) With the love that befits a brotherhood be affectionate to one another; give each to other the higher rank in honour; (11) do not allow your Christian zeal to slacken; be fervent in the Spirit, serve the Lord;[1] (12) rejoice in hope, show endurance in affliction, persevere in prayer. (13) Minister to the needs[2] of the saints, practise hospitality with enthusiasm. (14) Bless those who persecute you, bless and do not curse them. (15) Rejoice with those who rejoice, weep with those who weep. (16) Have a common mind; do not set your mind on exalted things, but keep company with the humble; 'do not be wise in your own estimation'. (17) Return no one evil for evil; plan to lead an honest life before all men. (18) If it be possible—that is, as far as it rests with you—live at peace with all men. (19) Do not avenge yourselves, beloved, but leave room to God's wrath; for it is written, 'Vengeance is mine, I will recompense, saith the Lord'. (20) Rather, 'if your enemy is hungry, feed him; if he is thirsty, give him drink; for by doing this you will heap up burning coals upon his head'. (21) Do not be overcome by evil, but overcome evil with good.

[1] The Western text (D* G it Ambrosiaster) has 'serve the time' (καιρῷ). This is probably no more than a mechanical blunder for 'Lord' (κυρίῳ). A reasonable meaning can be got out of it, but 'serving the Lord' is much more suitable to the context.

[2] Again the Western text (D* G it) diverges, and instead of 'needs' (χρείαις) has 'remembrances' (μνείαις)—that is, the remembering of the saints and their needs in prayer. This is not impossible, but the reference to hospitality which follows makes it more likely that Paul wrote 'needs' and that the variant arose through a mechanical slip in copying.

33. xii. 3-21. THE CHRISTIAN OFFERING

This paragraph illustrates the principles laid down in *vv.* 1 f. It is not a complete account of Christian ethics, and it is not a Christian casuistry, for it is in no sense legalistic; yet it covers a wide field, and touches the order and conduct of church life in addition to more evidently moral questions.

The first sentence is closely linked with *vv.* 1 f. by means of a 'for'; Paul is about to give an authoritative exposition of his ethical first principles, and states the ground of his authority for doing so. **For, through the** (apostolic—cf. xv. 15; also *v.* 6) **3 grace** (cf. i. 5) **God gave me, I tell you, every one.** As an apostle, Paul has a special gift of grace for the building up of the churches (2 Cor. xiii. 10). He has in mind the possibility that one group of Christians may think themselves superior to others —as, for example, Gentile to Jewish Christians (cf. xi. 18 ff.)— and therefore charges them **not to think more highly of yourselves than you ought to think, but to be sober-minded about yourselves.** An injunction of this kind probably implies that there were Christians in Rome who did think too highly of themselves. They may have been Gentiles, or, possibly, Christians who possessed special and showy 'gifts of grace' (*v.* 6) and despised others (cf. 1 Corinthians *passim*). Such pride belongs to 'this age', after which Christians must not fashion themselves (*v.* 2). Sober-mindedness is one of the Greek virtues, mentioned by Aristotle (*Nicomachean Ethics*, 1117 b 13) next after courage; it means soundness of mind, prudence, discretion; moderation, especially with regard to things of sense. Paul (as the context shows) uses the word differently, and establishes it not in general ethics but in the words, **as God has given to each of you a measure of faith.** Compare *v.* 6 and Eph. iv. 7. 'Faith' is used here in a sense somewhat different from that which it has in the rest of the epistle, and more akin to that of 1 Cor. xiii, where faith is a power given by God to do certain things (for example, to remove mountains). Men's opinions of themselves should be in proportion not to their natural capacities but to God's gifts; if this is so they will never (even though God calls them to be apostles) be boastful, for they will remember that they have nothing they have not received (1 Cor. iv. 7). The man who is humble before God is unlikely to be arrogant before his fellow-creatures.

The reason why Christians should be not arrogant but humble and loving to one another is now expressed in a new 4 way. **For as we have many members in one body, and all** 5 **the members do not have the same function, so we, who are many, are one body in Christ, and severally members of one another.** The metaphor of the body, used to describe a group of men who have common interests and activities, was not infrequent in antiquity. An example often quoted is the speech put by Livy (ii. 32) into the mouth of Menenius Agrippa on the occasion of the secession of the Roman *plebs*. Senate and people, Agrippa argued, could no more dispense with each other than stomach and limbs; they formed a unity within one body. One aspect of Pauline usage cannot easily be paralleled; this is the description of the Church as the body *of Christ*. This phrase, however, does not occur in Romans, where (as the 'as . . . so' shows) we have no more than simile or analogy. It is implied by *v.* 4 that Christians have diverse functions which nevertheless are all necessary to the proper working of the body of which all are parts; there is no room, therefore, for any to think too highly of himself or to despise another (1 Cor. xii. 12-31). The phrase 'one body in Christ' is, however, a stage on the way to 'the body of Christ', and it is important to note the origin of the latter term. Evidently it is closely related to the Pauline 'in Christ' (see p. 127 f.), and its setting is accordingly not so much sacramental (Dodd, pp. 194 f.) as eschatological. It was the body of Christ which died in the messianic affliction and rose to life in the Age to Come; those who are to share in this process must enter into and become part of the 'body of Christ' (understood now in a new, extended sense). There is, of course, a very close relation between this and the Pauline doctrines of baptism (vi. 3-11; Gal. iii. 27) and of the eucharist (1 Cor. x. 16 f.); but the relation, if it may be set out in a diagram, is not

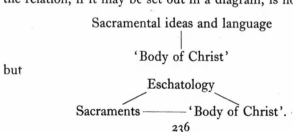

Sacramental ideas and language

|

'Body of Christ'

but

Eschatology

Sacraments ———— 'Body of Christ'.

236

These considerations, which show the background of Paul's use of the term *body*, make clearly visible the importance of unity and the dreadful consequences of the lack of it. To fall out of unity, out of the one body, is to fall back into the old world of sin and death.

The various members of the Church have therefore, not in themselves but in the grace of God, a variety of functions which are to be exercised in unity. **Since then we have gifts of grace 6 differing according to the grace God has given us** (cf. *v.* 3) ... The word 'gift of grace' (χάρισμα) has occurred several times in different senses (i. 11; v. 15 f.; vi. 23; xi. 29); here it means an actualization, a practical expression, of the grace (χάρις) of God under which the Church stands. In this sense the whole life of the Church, not its ministry only, is 'charismatic'; but the total effect of this passage (cf. 1 Cor. xii-xiv) shows that this supernatural conception of the Church's life does not exclude the notions of discipline and authority.

The construction of this passage is obscure. *V.* 6 begins with a participle, and up to the full stop which must be placed at the end of *v.* 8 there is no finite verb. It is possible to construct the participle (having, ἔχοντες) with *v.* 5: We are one body in Christ, having gifts. ... But it is better to take it as the introduction of a new sentence, and to supply imperatives (as the new form of clause beginning with 'if one be ...' requires): Having (that is, since we have) gifts, let us ... God's gifts are not given for the self-congratulation of those who receive them, but for employment in the building up of the body.

There follows a series of gifts, some of which suggest, more or less clearly, ministerial office (for detailed discussion see below). These are prophecy, ministry (διακονία), teaching, and exhortation; we may add the reference to 'the president'. It is, however, quite impossible to regard this as a list of ministers; there was no special order of those who practised charity, or of those who did acts of mercy. The present list should be compared with that of 1 Cor. xii. 8 ff., rather than that of 1 Cor. xii. 28. To Paul, the Spirit suggests primarily function and activity, rather than office.

If the gift be prophecy, let us exercise it according to the proportion of faith. For New Testament prophecy, see especially 1 Cor. xii and xiv, where it is distinguished from glossolalia, not mentioned here. It was expressed in inspired but intelligible speech, and sometimes though not always included prediction of future events (e.g. Acts xi. 27 f.). Like Old Testament prophecy it was primarily an immediate communication of God's word to his people, through human lips. Paul urges prophets to do their work according to the proportion of faith (it is possible to translate, 'of *the* faith', 'faith' representing 'the Christian religion'; but this is unlikely). The word 'proportion' is difficult, but probably means much the same as 'measure' in *v.* 3. Like other Christians, the prophet must be sober-minded about his own activities and his own importance. God has equipped him with faith for his task; he must employ it to the full but not seek to go beyond it.

7 **If it be ministry, let us attend to our ministry.** The word 'ministry' (διακονία) means simply 'service' (xv. 31), but it is already on the way to becoming a technical term. It is impossible to find a precise rendering for it here, but probably service to the needy is meant (cf. 'he who practises charity', 'he who does acts of mercy'). For the word 'minister' (deacon, διάκονος) in the New Testament see especially xvi. 1; 1 Cor. iii. 5; 2 Cor. iii. 6; vi. 4; xi. 23; Eph. iii. 7; vi. 21; Phil. i. 1; Col. i. 7, 23, 25; iv. 7; 1 Tim. iii. 8, 12; iv. 6.

If one be a teacher (the construction changes, showing that Paul is now giving injunctions to various groups), **let him**
8 **attend to his teaching; if an exhorter, to his exhortation.** Exhortation, especially when placed beside teaching, suggests the work of the preacher; but it would be wrong to deduce an absolute distinction between teaching and preaching, just as it would be wrong to distinguish between practising charity and doing acts of mercy. Each means a communication, effected in different ways, of the truth of the Gospel to the hearer; in the one it is explained, in the other applied. Yet it could never be explained without application or applied without explanation.

The man who practises charity (that is, imparts what he has to others), **let him do it whole-heartedly.** Paul several times (especially 2 Cor. viii. 2; ix. 11, 13) uses, in connexion with giving, the word here translated 'whole-heartedly' (and its cognates). The meaning is probably not 'with liberality' but 'being without *arrière-pensée* in one's gifts'.

Let the president act with zeal. It is uncertain whether this clause refers to an office. 'The president' translates a participle. The verb in question is used in quite untechnical fashion at Titus iii. 8, 14; in 1 Tim. iii. 4, 5, 12 it is used in a transitional sense—Church officers must be able to *preside* satisfactorily over their own households; in 1 Thess. v. 12; 1 Tim. v. 17 it is used of those who preside over churches. It is certain that in Romans (and 1 Thessalonians) it does not describe any office with precision; it rather refers to a function which may have been exercised by several persons, perhaps jointly or in turn. There is no indication whether the 'president' presided at a service (like the Synagogue service) of preaching and teaching, at the eucharist, or in a church meeting convened for deliberative or disciplinary purposes.

Let the man who does acts of mercy do them with cheerfulness. Paul's phrase recalls the 'deeds of love' often emphasized in Rabbinic writings (e.g. *Aboth*, i. 2, quoted on p. 178). 'Cheerfulness' points in the same direction (cf., e.g., *Leviticus Rabba*, xxxiv. 9: When a man gives alms he should do it with a joyful heart). To a Christian, kindness is a delight, not a duty. Paul adds, **Let your love be free from dissimulation.** 9 Of course, if love is not spontaneous it cannot be cheerfully expressed.

There now follows (*vv.* 9-13) a series of clauses containing only participles, with no finite verb. It is evident and undisputed that these participles must be understood as imperatives —'Abhor', 'cleave', etc. But why should participles be used in this way? It has been argued[1] that in Hellenistic Greek a usage had grown up in which the participle could stand for the imperative. Satisfactory evidence for this belief, however, has not been adduced, and a much more probable explanation can be found.[2] In Rabbinic Hebrew participles are used to express, not direct commands, but rules and codes. The participles in Romans (and in 1 Pet. ii. 18; iii. 1, 7 ff.; iv. 7-10) occur in

[1] Moulton, *Prolegomena*, p. 182.
[2] See D. Daube, Appended Note, 'Participle and Imperative in 1 Peter', in E. G. Selwyn, *The First Epistle of St. Peter* (1946).

similar codes, and it seems quite probable that they represent original Hebrew participles. If this be a correct linguistic explanation it will follow that the material in *vv.* 9-13 goes back to a Semitic source originating in very primitive Christian circles. These verses present a very interesting picture of early Christian life, but call for little explanation; they illustrate various aspects of the general command of love (xiii. 8 ff.).

Abhor that which is evil; cleave to that which is good.
10 **With the love that befits a brotherhood** (this word—φιλαδελφία—seems not to have been used metaphorically before the time of the New Testament) **be affectionate to one another; give each to other the higher rank in honour**
11 (cf. Phil. ii. 3); **do not allow your Christian** (it seems necessary to add this explanatory adjective) **zeal to slacken; be fervent in the Spirit, serve the Lord.** Apollos, who subsequently was further instructed though not rebaptized was, according to Acts xviii. 25, 'fervent in Spirit'. Whatever the meaning in Acts, the parallel with 'the Lord' shows that here 'Spirit' means not
12 the human spirit but the Holy Spirit. **Rejoice in hope, show endurance in affliction, persevere in prayer.** For hope, see p. 103; for endurance, see p. 46; for affliction, see p. 103. Christian life, for all its fervent zeal, can never be so busy a 'doing' that it fails to look beyond all human activity. Christian rejoicing, which endures through affliction, is rooted in the Christian hope of what God will do, and at all times the Christian looks beyond his immediate environment to God in prayer.

13 **Minister to the needs of the saints.** 'Minister to' is literally 'share in', 'partake of'. The verb is one which Paul regularly uses in the context of Christian charity (xv. 27; Gal. vi. 6; Phil. iv. 15). The cognate noun is used more generally, but compare xv. 26. For 'the saints' see on i. 7; it is unlikely that there is here a special reference to the Jerusalem church (see xv. 25 f., 31).

Practise hospitality with enthusiasm. This was evidently a very important Christian duty in the early Church; compare Heb. xiii. 2; 1 Clement i. 2; x. 7; xi. 1; xii. 1; Hermas, *Mandate*, viii. 10. For the adjective 'hospitable' see, for example, 1 Tim. iii. 2; Titus i. 8.

With the next verse the construction changes abruptly, and
the imperatival participles disappear. This corresponds to the
fact that Paul appears to draw on a new source—the gospel
tradition. **Bless those who persecute you, bless and do not** 14
curse them. These words recall a saying from the Sermon on
the Mount (Plain).

Matt. v. 44: Love your enemies, and pray for them that
persecute you.

Luke vi. 28: Bless them that curse you, pray for them that
despitefully use you.

Certainly, Paul quotes neither of these verses, but it is probable
that he has behind him the tradition of the Lord's words. Why
then does he not quote them, referring to his authority, as he
does at 1 Cor. vii. 10; 1 Thess. iv. 15? The same question will
arise at vv. 17-20; xiii. 9 f. The answer is probably that Paul,
unlike some of his contemporaries, did not regard the sayings of
Jesus as constituting a new legalism. For him the importance of
Jesus was not legislative but historical and theological; accordingly he used material that came to him from the historical
tradition, but because it was intrinsically suitable, rather than
to establish doctrine.

Rejoice with those who rejoice, weep with those who 15
weep. Here infinitives are used for imperatives; but this sub-
stitution has a respectable history in the Greek language. Those
who, because they have faith, are no longer self-centred, can
show true sympathy with others, since they can rank their
neighbours and their affairs above themselves.

Have a common mind (cf. Phil. ii. 2—this is a mark of 16
love); **do not set your mind on exalted things, but keep
company with the humble.** Here the imperatival participles
return, and continue as far as v. 19. It would be possible to
translate: Condescend to lowly things (taking ταπεινοῖς as
neuter). This is suggested by the neuter 'exalted things'
(ὑψηλά); but in the New Testament the adjective (ταπεινός) is
never used of things but always of persons. Usage of the verb
(Gal. ii. 13; 2 Pet. iii. 17), however, is not decisive, and it is
impossible to feel confident that either translation is correct to
the exclusion of the other. It is well to remember that Greek

occasionally allows an ambiguity impossible in English; Paul may have been aware, and may have approved, of both ways of taking his words. Both are supported by the Old Testament quotation that follows. **'Do not be wise in your own estimation.'** See Prov. iii. 7, already alluded to in xi. 25, where it has a particular application to a situation in which Gentile Christians might be inclined to think themselves superior to their Jewish brethren. Here the application is general.

17 **Return no one evil for evil.** Compare Matt. v. 38-42; Luke vi. 29; and see on *v.* 14. **Plan to lead an honest life before all men.** Paul seems to depend on Prov. iii. 4 (LXX). Christians as such lead a public life, and it is important that they should not behave in such a way as to bring discredit upon the faith. The word Paul uses is perhaps stronger than 'honest'; it refers to a life that an honest Greek would recognize as right and good. The next command is similar (note the recurrence of 'all men'):

18 **If it be possible—that is, as far as it rests with you—live at peace with all men.** Compare Matt. v. 9. There is no Christian virtue in provoking strife, whether inside or outside the Church; limits may, however, be imposed on peaceable relations by the attitude of others. But even when peace is broken

19 by another, the Christian is not to seek revenge. **Do not avenge yourselves, beloved, but leave room to God's wrath.** Paul himself writes only 'the wrath', and, were it not for the quotation that follows, which makes it clear that he is speaking of God, it would be possible to translate, 'Avoid wrath'. **For it is written, 'Vengeance is mine, I will recompense, saith the Lord'.** There are occasions when God's wrath is rightly put into effect by human agency (xiii. 4), but this is always by special divine appointment (xiii. 1); no private person is at liberty to assume that his own vengeful feelings will carry out the divine sentence. Here Paul's quotation (Deut. xxxii. 35) rests upon the Hebrew text; contrast *v.* 17.

Scripture not merely reserves vengeance to God alone; it

20 points out a more excellent way. **Rather, 'if your enemy is hungry, feed him; if he is thirsty, give him drink; for by doing this you will heap up burning coals upon his head'.** Again Paul turns to the LXX (of Prov. xxv. 21 f.). In view of *v.* 21, it can scarcely be doubted that the 'burning coals' are the

fire of remorse. If an enemy is treated in this way he may well be overcome in the best possible fashion—he may become a friend. **Do not be overcome by evil, but overcome evil with good.** 21 This is not merely prudential; it is the way God himself has proceeded against his enemies (cf. v. 8). The mercy of God (to which Paul appealed at the beginning of this chapter, *v.* 1) will triumph over the rebellion and disobedience of men (xi. 32); the mercy of those on whom God has had mercy may similarly prove victorious.

34. xiii. 1-7. AUTHORITIES

(1) Let every one be in subjection to the supreme authorities: for there is no authority that is not ordained by God, and the authorities which in fact exist have been appointed by God. (2) It follows that he who sets himself against the authority resists God's ordinance, and those who resist will be responsible for their own condemnation. (3) For the rulers are no terror to the man who does good works, but only to the man who does evil. If you wish not to be afraid of the authority, do what is good, and you will have praise from it. (4) For he is God's servant, appointed to promote what is good. But if you do what is evil, you may well fear; it is not for nothing that he bears a sword, for he is God's servant, an instrument of vengeance to carry out God's wrath[1] against the man who practises evil. (5) It is necessary therefore to be in subjection, not only through fear of God's wrath, but also for conscience sake. (6) Moreover, this is why you pay taxes, for these men are God's public servants, attending upon the purpose I have described. (7) Render to all men what is due to them. Pay the tax to him to whom the tax

[1] There is some variation in the order of words here, and the Western text (D* G it) omits altogether the reference to God's wrath ('he is God's avenging servant against . . .'). But the reference to wrath was probably found stylistically awkward, given different positions in the sentence, and even omitted for this reason. It represents, however, an essential element in Paul's thought.

is due, the levy to him to whom the levy is due; pay reverence to him to whom reverence is due, honour to him to whom honour is due.

The new paragraph, a self-contained treatment of a special theme, appears at first to be introduced somewhat abruptly. In fact it has been prepared for by the exhortations to humility, to live an honest life in the eyes of all the world, to live at peace, and to give place to God's wrath, of ch. xii. Obedience to magistrates forms an excellent practical example of all these Christian virtues; and there may well have been good reasons, unknown to us (though the disturbances *impulsore Chresto* (see Introduction, p. 6) come to mind), why this example should have been chosen.

1   **Let every one be in subjection to the supreme authorities.** So far it has been assumed that the authorities Paul has in mind are human authorities, in particular the governing authority of the Roman Empire under which Paul and his readers lived. This is the view of many commentators, but it has been challenged by Dr. O. Cullmann,[1] who argues that the word 'authorities' (ἐξουσίαι) refers not to the state itself, but to the 'invisible angelic powers that stand behind the State government' (*op. cit.* p. 195). This may appear a small distinction; in fact the difference is very great, as appears if two questions are asked (a) Must Christians be in subjection to the magistrates, or to angelic powers? (b) Are the angels or the magistrates of divine appointment?

The matter cannot be decided on purely linguistic grounds. Paul does elsewhere use the same word with the meaning of 'angelic authorities' (e.g. Col. i. 16); but it is also used of magisterial authority (e.g. Luke xii. 11). The latter meaning is attested in Greek contemporary with the New Testament; for example, Josephus, *Jewish War*, ii. 350 (The powers (ἐξουσίαι— the Roman procurators of Judaea) should be conciliated by flattery, not irritated). There is thus (at the least) no difficulty in supposing that Paul is here referring to the state, or its administration. There is, of course, no question that he does so in *vv.* 3-7; and the tone of his references elsewhere (e.g. Col. ii. 15)

[1] *Christ and Time* (English Translation, 1951), pp. 191-210.

to spiritual-angelic (or perhaps better, demonic) authorities, suggests that it is very unlikely that he would bid his readers be in subjection to them. We may therefore for the moment assume that Paul is speaking of the relation of Christians to the state, though the full justification of this view may for the moment be reserved.

The 'every one' of the translation conceals a Semitic expression (*every soul*); and in what follows Paul expresses what is a characteristically Jewish point of view. All should obey the authorities, **for there is no authority that is not ordained by God, and the authorities which in fact exist have been appointed by God.** Many parallels can be cited from Jewish authors, for example, Wisdom vi. 3; Josephus, *Jewish War*, ii. 140 (No ruler attains his office save by the will of God). From the time of Pompey this attitude was given practical effect by the offering of daily sacrifice on behalf of the Roman authorities. Its roots lie in the Old Testament conviction that God is the ruler of all nations and of all history, and it may be described as an aspect of the doctrine of providence, arrived at by taking seriously the fact of God's lordship. In order to protect his creatures from the consequences of unbridled sin he provides them with civil rulers, just as he provides them with sun and rain. The state thus has its appointed place in the providential order which God has established for the good of mankind. To say this does not confuse the state with the Church, or civil law with the Gospel, any more than it confuses the universe itself, and natural law, with Church and Gospel. The authorities are provisions of the merciful God.

It follows that he who sets himself against the authority 2 **resists God's ordinance** (a word etymologically connected with 'appointed' in *v.* 1), **and those who resist will be responsible for their own condemnation.** The first part of this sentence draws an immediate inference from *v.* 1; the second asserts that the resistance to God's ordinance which is implied by resistance to authority does not escape judgement. This is true of resistance to any divine ordinance, but when resistance is offered to the state divine judgement comes into operation at once by means of the state's own judicial procedures. **For the** 3 **rulers are no terror to the man who does good works**

(literally, to the good work), **but only to the man who does evil** (literally, to the evil work). 'The rulers' are the same as 'the authorities', though with a more directly personal reference. The word itself (ἄρχοντες) is capable of the same ambiguity. It is used of spiritual powers (e.g. Eph. ii. 2), and of earthly rulers (e.g. Acts iii. 17). Magistrates may well strike a guilty fear into the heart of the evil-doer, but not into the good. The man whose conscience is clear has nothing to dread. This simple observation points the practical way to an untroubled life. **If you wish** (Paul's construction is a colloquial form of conditional sentence; see B.D. p. 217) **not to be afraid of the authority, do what is good, and** (Paul passes over to a positive account of the office of the authority) **you will have praise from it** (Paul uses the pronoun appropriate to 'authority', which is feminine in Greek; 'him' would be more natural in English). What Paul means by 'what is good' is not explicit. Abstention from evil is certainly included; it cannot be certainly deduced that the doing of what is socially good is positively intended, but there is no reason why 'good' should be understood in a purely negative and individualist sense. Praise (in the form of statues or inscriptions) was sometimes publicly bestowed upon those who made notable contributions to the welfare of the state. By encouraging such benefactions, the state could

4 make a positive contribution to the common life; **for he is God's servant, appointed to promote what is good.** The word servant (διάκονος) was in process of becoming a technical Christian term (see xii. 7; xvi. 1); it cannot bear any such sense here, but it is not for that reason without theological significance. Behind the more technical use of the word and its cognates lies, not the idea of service in general, but that of a ministry performed in the first instance by Jesus himself and then by him through the Church, which furthers God's eschatological purpose. In this purpose the state and its representatives have a part to play, alongside that of the apostles and their helpers.

The negative service of the state is as real as the positive. **If you do what is evil, you may well fear; it is not for nothing that he bears a sword, for he is God's servant** (as above, διάκονος), **an instrument of vengeance to carry out**

God's wrath against the man who practises evil. God's wrath, which belongs properly to the last day (ii. 5), is capable of being brought forward into the present (i. 18); one means by which this future wrath is anticipated is the magistrate's sword. This last expression recalls the technical term *ius gladii*, by which was meant the authority (possessed by all higher magistrates) of inflicting sentence of death (cf. Tacitus, *Histories*, iii. 68). We saw above that the action of the state was to be regarded as an aspect of God's providence; in this his wrath finds a place, for it represents his resistance to evil. Accordingly the state takes its place as avenger, bringing the wrath of God himself to bear upon evil-doers. It is thus, paradoxically, an instrument of God's long-suffering (ii. 4), for through this partial manifestation of his wrath the power of evil is restrained and its final judgement and defeat deferred; compare 2 Thess. ii. 6 f.

Paul resumes and explains the instruction he first gave in *v.* 1. **It is necessary therefore to be in subjection, not only 5 through fear of God's wrath, but also for conscience sake.** Two facts direct the Christian to give obedience to the authorities. One is that if he fails to do so God's wrath will be visited upon him, by means of the magistrate's sword; the other, that he is bound as a Christian to recognize the divine authority of the state as God's servant, so that his conscience (ii. 15; ix. 1) itself will impel him to render obedience. A particular example follows: **Moreover, this is why you pay taxes.** The state 6 requires not merely the good will but the active support of the citizen. **For these men are God's public servants, attending upon the purpose I have described** (that is, of promoting good, and of restraining evil). The word Paul uses here to describe the state authorities (λειτουργοί) was in common use for public officials, and especially for those who carried out public works in the service of the state. The word in itself (although Paul uses it to describe his own office—xv. 16) is not a theological term, but derives theological significance from the genitive, 'of God'. The Roman magistrates, little though they knew it, were public servants not of Rome but of God; it was his work they did. In this fact lay their true authority, and their right to receive their 'dues': **Render to all men what is due 7 to them. Pay the tax** (or tribute, direct taxation) **to him to**

whom the tax is due, the levy (indirect taxation, such as customs dues) **to him to whom the levy is due; pay reverence to him to whom reverence is due, honour to him to whom honour is due.** For the teaching of this verse, compare Mark xii. 17 (and parallels); 1 Pet. ii. 17. Honour and respect are due to earthly rulers not because they are powerful and influential *men*, but because they have been appointed by God. It follows that to treat them with less than their due of honour is to dishonour God; and honour without its practical corollary of the due payment of taxes for the maintenance of the authority would be a mockery.

Paul's attitude to the state, that is, to the Roman Empire, under whose authority he lived, was that of many, though not all Jews, and was on the whole that of the primitive Church. It may also be described as that of the *petit bourgeois* under the Empire. It must not be forgotten that Nero, though known to us from such ill-disposed writers as the senatorial historian Tacitus and the Christian Tertullian, was a popular Emperor, especially with the provincials, whose affairs were not badly conducted during his principate. The relief and gratitude which had greeted the re-establishment of a reliable and benevolent state under Augustus had not yet been dissipated. But to view Paul's attitude as a mere expression of lower-class provincial loyalty is quite inadequate. Paul's motive is primarily theological, not sociological, and to be understood it must be placed in the eschatological context of his thought as a whole. For him, as for most ancient thinkers, the world was much less secure, and much nearer to the brink of disaster, than it has appeared in modern times (until, perhaps, very recently). The stable order of society was constantly threatened by demonic powers, and the catastrophes preceding the End could not be far away. To Christians, it was highly desirable (though by no means certain) that the world should continue until the return of Christ, when death would be swallowed up in victory. The imperial government acted as a restraining power (2 Thess. ii. 6 f.; see *Expository Times*, lxv (1954), 371 f.) which afforded Christians a peaceful existence and the opportunity of preaching the Gospel. Accordingly it was their duty to maintain the machinery of the state, and to recognize in it God's own appointed means of preserving the stability and moral order of the world, and of putting his wrath into operation before the 'day of wrath'.

If this view of Paul's use of 'authority' is adopted, it is possible to recognize that the New Testament is consistent in its attitude to the state, for when (as in Revelation) the state appears to be the enemy of Christians the fact is that demonic powers have usurped the state's authority. These are the true enemy, and their victory over the state, shown by the rise of persecution, is interpreted as a sign that the end is at hand (Mark xiii. 9-13; Revelation *passim*). Thus Dr. Cullmann's interpretation of 'authority' in Rom. xiii (see p. 244) turns out to be almost the exact opposite of the truth: the 'authorities' are the state, appointed by God as a bulwark against demonic powers.

35. xiii. 8-10. THE LAW OF LOVE

(8) Owe no man anything—but remember the debt of love you owe one another; for he who loves someone other than himself has fulfilled the law. (9) For 'Thou shalt not commit adultery', 'Thou shalt do no murder', 'Thou shalt not steal', 'Thou shalt not covet', and any other commandment there be, are all summed up in this one saying: 'Thou shalt love thy neighbour as thyself'. (10) Love works no harm to the neighbour; that is why love is the complete fulfilment of the law.

Having dealt with the relation of the Christian to the state, Paul concludes (for the present) his treatment of Christian ethics by returning to the all-inclusive command of love. From the precept 'Render to all men what is due to them' he passes to its negative corollary: **Owe no man anything**—that is, do not 8 leave your obligations to them unfulfilled. It is not clear how the following words should be translated. They are introduced by an expression (εἰ μή) which in Paul's writings usually means 'except' (e.g. 1 Cor. i. 14). If this interpretation is accepted, Paul means that the only debt Christians ought to incur is that which they are bound to incur and can never completely discharge—the debt of mutual love. We might render: 'Let your only indebtedness be the mutual love you are bound to owe as Christians'. This would imply a special reference to Christian love within the Church (cf. xii. 10), over against universal love for non-Christians. Of course, Paul does not mean that Christians should love only Christians (xii. 14, 17, 19 ff.); yet there is a unique mutuality of love within the Christian fellowship which has a special significance because it is the unifying force within the Body of Christ (cf. John xiii. 34 f.). It is, however, possible that Paul's conjunction (εἰ μή) should be translated 'but'. If this is done the word translated 'owe' in the opening clause must be considered to take its alternative meaning 'ought' when it is applied to the second clause: 'Owe no man anything—but you ought to love . . .'. The change involved in passing from the notion of 'rendering every man his due' to the positive and sacrificial quality of Christian love seems to justify the choice of the latter alternative, and (in order that the sense of *debt* may not be lost) we may proceed, **But remember the debt of love you owe one another.**

The debt, or obligation, is not constituted by a natural relationship; it is created by the command of God. **For he who loves someone other than himself has fulfilled the law.** What Paul means by 'the law', and the fulfilment of it, must be discussed below (on *v.* 10). In this verse he does not use the word 'neighbour' (*vv.* 9 f.), and his choice of a different word is significant. Just as Christian faith means that a man is prepared to worship and obey God rather than himself, so Christian love means that his attention is directed away from himself and towards those who are essentially—other than himself (cf. Phil. ii. 4). Love for the *neighbour* can too easily be misinterpreted as 'love for the like-minded man who is congenial to me'; love is not Christian love if it cannot include love for the man who differs from me in every way.

What Paul means by the fulfilling of the law begins to appear
9 in the next verse. **For 'Thou shalt not commit adultery'** (Ex. xx. 14; Deut. v. 18), **'Thou shalt do no murder'** (Ex. xx. 13; Deut. v. 17), **'Thou shalt not steal'** (Ex. xx. 15; Deut. v. 19), **'Thou shalt not covet'** (Ex. xx. 17; Deut. v. 21; as at vii. 7 Paul provides no object for the verb 'to covet'), **and any other**

commandment there be, are all summed up in this one saying: 'Thou shalt love thy neighbour as thyself' (Lev. xix. 18). Paul quotes the LXX accurately. The meaning so far is clear: if you love your neighbour (Paul now uses this word because he is quoting; it must be assumed that he puts into it the meaning indicated by *v.* 8) you will treat him as the law requires—that is, you will not offend against him in respect of such matters as adultery, murder, theft, and coveting. That the law could be summed up in some such single precept was not unknown in Judaism. The same use of Lev. xix. 18 is found in Mark xii. 31 (and parallels). Paul gives no indication here that he was aware of Jesus' use of the same Old Testament passage. For the problem raised by his silence, see on xii. 14.

Love works no harm to the neighbour—does not (for 10 example) wish to murder him. This is of course an understatement (for a more positive evaluation of love—which nevertheless still contains many negatives—see 1 Cor. xiii); but it is regarded by Paul as the ground for the claim of *v.* 8, for he continues, **That is why love is the complete fulfilment of the law.** The meaning of 'complete fulfilment' ($\pi\lambda\acute{\eta}\rho\omega\mu\alpha$) is disputed, but it must be decided in the light of the use of the cognate verb in *v.* 8. The man who loves has fulfilled the law, that is, he has done what the law requires; the love, therefore, which he exercises constitutes the fulfilment of the law's requirement. Thus love is not the *completion* but the *performance* of the law. *V.* 9 shows that by the law Paul means the Old Testament law in its preceptual character. Love fulfils all negative and positive commandments inclusively, from Lev. xix. 18 downwards. When Paul says this, however, he is not instituting a new, though simplified, legalism. He does not say that man is justified by fulfilling the law through love; rather he is pointing out the ethical expression of the true meaning of the law, which, when rightly understood, itself points to the way of faith (see p. 59), which expresses itself in love (Gal. v. 6). The new Christian obligation, the 'law of love', or 'law of Christ', is more fully discussed by Paul in 1 Cor. ix. 21; Gal. v. 14; vi. 2. It is not a means of salvation, but the ethical channel through which the new life in Christ flows.

36. xiii. 11-14. THE URGENCY OF THE TIME

(11) All these things you must do the more zealously because you know the time in which we live. You know that it is already the hour for you[1] to awake out of sleep, for salvation is nearer to us now than when we first believed. (12) The night is advanced, the day is near; let us put off therefore the works of darkness, and let us put on the armour of light. (13) Let us, as if the day were already here, walk honourably, not in carousing and drunkenness, not in lasciviousness and uncleanness, not in strife and envy; (14) rather put on the Lord Jesus Christ, and take no thought in advance for the flesh, with a view to fulfilling its desires.

It was pointed out above (p. 232) that the whole exhortation of chs. xii, xiii is enclosed within an eschatological framework. In xii. 1 f. the reader is urged to dissociate himself from the present age; this requirement inevitably becomes more pressing when it is seen that the present age is hastening to its close, and that the Age to Come is near at hand. It is in this vein that this section of the epistle is concluded.

11   **All these things** (not only the command to love but the substance of chs. xii, xiii in general) **you must do the more zealously because you know the time in which we live.** 'The time' (καιρός) is a common eschatological term, fairly frequent in Paul's writings; for example, iii. 26; 1 Cor. iv. 5; vii. 29. The 'time in which we live' is that of the unique manifestation of God's righteousness preceding the judgement. It is further defined in the following words: **You know that it is already the hour for you to awake out of sleep.** Like 'time', 'hour' is an eschatological term, though it is not characteristic of Paul (e.g. 1 John ii. 18). 'Sleep' too is a metaphor which often occurs in eschatological admonitions (e.g. 1 Thess. v. 6-10). Men who live on the edge of the Age to Come cannot

---

[1] Instead of 'you', 'us' has very strong support (P46 D G ω lat pesh), but is probably due to assimilation to the first person plural in the next clause.

afford to relax their vigilance; **for salvation is nearer to us now than when we first believed.** The position of the pronoun in this sentence is such that it would be equally possible to translate (with AV), 'Now is our salvation nearer than . . .'; but Paul is not thinking of salvation in a pietistic way as something that happens to *us* in *our* experience, but as a universal eschatological event. The lapse of time between the conversion of Paul and of his readers and the moment of writing is a significant proportion of the total interval between the resurrection of Jesus and his *parousia* at the last day. The consummation of God's final redemptive act is near.

This truth is next expressed in metaphor. **The night is advanced, the day is near.** That 'the day' is not simply the day of judgement (ii. 5) is shown by the corresponding 'night'. Paul means that this age has almost run its course, and that accordingly the Age to Come must very soon dawn. It is vitally important to draw the appropriate practical inference.

Let us put off therefore . . . and let us put on . . . According to Dr. E. G. Selwyn[1] these words introduce fresh sections in that common catechetical code which he believes to lie behind many of the New Testament epistles. For the former word see I Pet. ii. 1 f.; James i. 21; Col. iii. 8; Eph. iv. 22, 25; Heb. xii. 1; and for the latter (1 Pet. iv. 1); Col. iii. 10, 12; Eph. iv. 24; 1 Thess. v. 8; Gal. iii. 27. It is certain that the metaphors are widespread in early Christian literature, and it is quite possible that some standardization of catechumen-instruction took place. Yet it must not be forgotten that the metaphor is a very simple one, which might easily have occurred independently to many different minds. In the present passage, for example, the reference to night and day could have suggested the metaphor of putting off night clothes and putting on day clothes.

They are not, however, clothes which are put on and put off. Paul's readers are urged to put off the **works of darkness** and to put on the **armour of light:** activities proper to the 'night', that is, to the old age before the coming of the Messiah, must be abandoned (cf. Col. iii. 5); for them, a new life of positive effort ('armour' includes offensive weapons) must be substituted. For the latter metaphor, compare 2 Cor. vi. 7; also 1 Thess. v. 8;

[1] *The First Epistle of St. Peter* (1946).

Eph. vi. 13-18. When a man embarks upon the Christian life he enters a career of conflict.

13 The image of night and day has not been lost sight of ('armour of light'), and Paul returns to it. **Let us, as if the day were already here** (it is implied that it is not yet here; cf. *v.* 12, the day is *near*), **walk honourably.** It would be equally possible to translate his words, Let us walk honourably as it is proper to walk in the day (which is in fact here). But the interpretation adopted in the translation is more appropriate to the context. Paul requires that Christians should live as if the Age to Come (this, rather than the day of judgement, is in mind) were actually here—as in some sense it is. For this sort of command, which is fundamental to Paul's conception of Christian ethics, compare vi. 11 f. 'Honourably' is very nearly, 'with nothing to be ashamed of'.

Negative examples follow. **Not in carousing and drunkenness** (cf. Gal. v. 21; 1 Pet. iv. 3): the nouns are difficult to distinguish. Paul perhaps uses them more or less as synonyms, reinforcing each other; the former, however, may suggest the revelling, the latter, the actual drunkenness which results from it. Both nouns are in the plural, suggesting frequent indulgence. **Not in lasciviousness** (the Greek word is used in a different sense at ix. 10) **and uncleanness** (again the two nouns are plural), **not in strife** (cf. i. 29; 1 Cor. i. 11; iii. 3; 2 Cor. xii. 20; Gal. v. 20; Phil. i. 15) **and envy** (cf. 1 Cor. iii. 3; 2 Cor. xii. 20; Gal. v. 20). The last pair evidently is a Pauline formula. All these practices constitute a failure in love, which 'works no harm to the neighbour' (*v.* 10).

14 Instead of indulging in these immoral practices, **rather put on the Lord Jesus Christ.** Compare Gal. iii. 27, where Paul uses a past (aorist) tense; in baptism, Christians have already put on Christ, entering into him by incorporation into his crucifixion. But the relation thus sacramentally begun must be morally renewed (cf. vi. 11 f.). Those who have put on Christ in baptism must put on Christ by living in conformity with his mind (cf. Phil. ii. 5). This must be their sole object; it accordingly follows that they must **take no thought in advance for the flesh** (see pp. 137, 146) **with a view to fulfilling its desires** (see on vii. 7). They cannot serve God and mammon. The flesh

will present its claims powerfully enough; there is no need to go half-way to meet it. That to which men should look forward and for which they should prepare is the Age to Come and the judgement; this they will do by cultivating love and expressing it in the ways indicated in chs. xii, xiii.

37. xiv. 1-12. THE STRONG AND THE WEAK

(1) **Welcome a man who is weak in faith, and do not take him in simply for discussions of his scruples. (2) One man has faith so strong that he can and does eat all things; but the weak man eats[1] vegetables only. (3) Let not the man who eats despise the man who does not eat, and let not the abstainer judge the man who does eat, for God has welcomed him. (4) Who are you to judge another man's servant? It is to his own master that he stands or falls; yes, and he shall stand, for his master is able to make him stand. (5) Again,[2] one man distinguishes day from day, while another counts all days alike. Let each one be fully convinced in his own mind. (6) He who is concerned about the day, is concerned to the Lord. And he who eats, eats to the Lord, for over his meal he gives thanks to God; and he who abstains, abstains to the Lord, and over his meal he gives thanks to God. (7) For none of us lives to himself and none of us dies to himself; (8) for if we live, we live to the Lord, and if we die, we die to the Lord. Whether then we live or die we are the Lord's. (9) For Christ died and came to life for this very purpose, namely, that he might reign as Lord over both the dead and the living. (10) Well then, you—why do you judge your brother? Or you—why do you despise your brother? For we shall all stand before God's judgement seat. (11)**

---

[1] An important group of MSS. (P46 D* G lat) reads, 'But let the weak man eat . . .'. The text makes a statement; the variant gives a precept, which is in accord with v. 23. It is not impossible that the variant is original, but on the whole it seems more probable (especially in view of the construction in v. 2) that Paul is here stating the facts of the situation rather than recommending a course of action. [2] Omitting 'for' (γάρ) with P46 B D G ω pesh.

For it is written, 'As I live, saith the Lord, every knee shall bow to me, and every tongue shall render praise to God'. (12) Every one of us therefore shall give account of himself to God.[1]

In xi. 13-24, Paul urged Gentile Christians not to think too highly of themselves over against their Jewish brethren. In xii. 3, 16 f., he gave a more general warning to the same effect. In the long section xiv. 1–xv. 13 he returns to a similar theme, apparently with special reference to a problem which exists among his readers. Exactly what this problem was must remain uncertain. Two groups emerge, the 'strong' and the 'weak', and their theological importance and their relative duties in mutual forbearance are made clear; but what their views were, and what were the origin and ground of their divergence, is obscure. It is natural to suppose that we have here in active form the mutual disparagement of Jew and Gentile, envisaged in ch. xi as a possibility to be avoided. The distinguishing of one day from others (*v.* 5) is easily explained on this view, and so is the abstinence from meat (*vv.* 2, 21), for though Judaism is not a vegetarian religion a Jew would abstain from meat unless he was certain that it had been correctly slaughtered. Two points, however, must be noted on the other side. (1) There was a large Jewish colony in Rome (see Introduction, p. 6), and it must be regarded as certain that suitable meat could be obtained by anyone who wished to do so; (2) abstinence from wine also is involved (*vv.* 17, 21), and this is not a Jewish practice.

1 **Welcome** (cf. *v.* 3) **a man who is weak in faith:** receive him into the Christian family. For 'weak' Christians, see xiv. 1–xv. 13 *passim*; also 1 Cor. viii. 7-11; ix. 22. Their 'weakness' is expressed in a number of abstentions which will be noted in detail below; it attests a failure to grasp the fundamental principle, which page after page of this epistle emphasizes, that men are justified and reconciled to God not by vegetarianism, sabbatarianism, or teetotalism, but by faith alone—or, better, by God's own free electing grace, faith being man's recognition

---

[1] The words 'to God' are omitted by B G it, perhaps rightly. The short text is intelligible, but the tendency to add to it would be very strong. 'To God', if an addition to Paul's text, is undoubtedly correct interpretation.

that all is dependent not upon himself but God. So strong is this emphasis that it comes as a surprise to find that Paul recognizes that both strong and weak have a place in the Church, and that both can stand before God and be accepted by him. How this can be will appear in the following pages.

The remaining words of *v.* 1 are very difficult to translate. They might be literally rendered, 'not for disputes of doubts'. It is almost certainly wrong to take the genitive 'of doubts' as a genitive of definition, describing 'disputes' (AV, 'not to doubtful disputations'). The doubts are the doubts of the weak Christian, and Paul's advice to his readers is, **do not take him in simply for discussions of his scruples.** He is to be welcomed not as an opportunity for theological debate on the part of his superiors, but as one 'for whom Christ died' (1 Cor. viii. 11); that is, he must be accepted in love.

In the next verse, Paul sets out, in their simplest form, the facts of the case. **One man has faith so strong that he can** 2 **and does eat all things;** that is, he is completely uninhibited by relics of a pagan or Jewish past, expressing itself in religious scrupulosities. Like Paul himself (who undoubtedly is one of the 'strong'), he knows that the 'kingdom of God is not eating and drinking' (*v.* 17). **But the weak man eats vegetables only;** that is, he believes that foods have a religious value, and that his relation with God demands that he avoid the use of meat. Who is this 'weak man'? Paul allows us to learn three things about him: (1) He eats vegetables and no meat (*vv.* 2, 21); (2) he regards some days as having special importance (*vv.* 5 f.); (3) he does not drink wine (*vv.* 17, 21). It is impossible to pick out from the many examples of religious scrupulosity to be found in antiquity any single group of persons corresponding exactly with those described here by Paul. They were not orthodox Jews (p. 625). Their scruples recall those of the Pythagorean Apollonius of Tyana, who avoided meat and wine.[1] The closest parallel, perhaps, is to be found in the heretics of Colossae. These men gave special veneration to certain days (Col. ii. 16), and practised various kinds of abstinence (Col. ii. 16, 21 f.); it is probable that they arose out of some kind of fusion between Judaism and gnosticism. It may be that some

[1] Philostratus, *Life of Apollonius*, i. 8.

such fusion had occurred in Rome, though the 'weak' in Rome were much more Christian (and much less gnostic) than the heretics of Colossae. It is of course possible, and has been maintained, that Paul was speaking of the scrupulous in general, without reference to particular persons; it seems, however, more probable that he is addressing a real than a hypothetical situation.

3   There must be no ill-feeling between the two groups. **Let not the man who eats despise the man who does not eat.** This he may be tempted to do, for the strong inevitably tend to despise those who are weaker—in mind and conscience as in other matters—than themselves. **And let not the abstainer judge the man who does eat.** The peculiar danger of the weak is censoriousness; for the weak Christian is apt to suppose that his fellow-Christian, who does something he (the weak man) regards as sinful, must be sinning against his conscience, although in fact his conscience is more enlightened, and does not condemn the course of action in question. But the weak man, who abstains, must not judge his brother in this way, **for God has welcomed** (cf. *v.* 1) **him.** If God himself is willing to receive the meat-eater into his household, the weak Christian has no reason to take offence.

This verse is not only an exhortation to charity; it implies an acute analysis of the situation, in which it appears that both strong and weak are exposed to the same danger. The weak is exposed to the danger of externalizing God's righteousness, and supposing that his outward acts and abstentions *are* the righteousness of God, and that vegetarianism and the like constitute in themselves a sufficient standing for man before God. This is evidently false. But as soon as the strong despises the weak he falls into the same error, for he is treating his actions, or his 'faith' ('faith...to eat'!—*v.* 2), as a visible sign of his superiority. For this reason, neither is in a position to condemn the other.

4   Paul proceeds to develop his point in a different way. **Who are you to judge another man's servant?** It is the weak man who is addressed; see *v.* 3. That is, Paul is here taking the part of the strong Christian. **It is to his own master that he stands or falls**—his master, not his fellow-Christian, determines the acceptability of his service. **Yes, and he shall stand, for his master is able to make him stand.** God alone is the judge

of his servants; and before his judgement the achievements of strong and weak alike are dissolved; but it is he also who establishes their works (Ps. xc. 17), whether the free action of the strong or the observances of the weak. These alike are incomplete and lack significance in themselves (cf. ii. 7); but God has the power to complete them and fill them with meaning.

Paul turns to another example of the different beliefs and practices of weak and strong. **Again, one man distinguishes** 5 **day from day, while another counts all days alike.** This verse is most easily explained on the view that the weak, whether full Jews or not, keep the Sabbath. Compare Gal. iv. 10; Col. ii. 16. Whether this be true or not, we are confronted here with a significant difference in Christian practice. Paul does not pronounce upon it, but comments, **Let each one be fully convinced in his own mind.** See the note on iv. 21; compare Col. iv. 12. It is probable that 'own' (ἴδιος) has at least some of its proper force, though it is true that in Hellenistic Greek the word has sometimes an 'exhausted' sense. Each man should be convinced in his *own* mind, not affected by the contentions of others; and he should act in accordance with his own convictions. Only when he does so act is the statement of the next verse true.

He who is concerned about the day, is concerned to the 6 **Lord. And he who eats, eats to the Lord, for over his meal he gives thanks to God; and he who abstains, abstains to the Lord, and over his meal** (of vegetables) **he gives thanks to God.** The sabbatarian observes the seventh day rest not because he values the institution as an invention of his own, but because he believes that he is obeying a divine command: he keeps it with reference to the Lord who commanded it. Again, both the meat-eater and the vegetarian observe the (originally Jewish) custom of saying a blessing (that is, a thanksgiving to God) over their meals. Their meals, therefore, whatever they may consist of, are eaten with reference to the Lord; they are not secular functions. Here it appears that strong and weak, whom we have already seen (p. 258) to be exposed to the same danger, share equally in the same positive virtue. In what he does, each gives thanks to God, that is, each recognizes his lordship. We may contrast i. 21: the heathen 'did not glorify him as God or give thanks to him'; they did not recognize his lordship.

Strong and weak are both servants, belonging to and dependent on the same Lord. The strong is not independent, and the weak is not abandoned to his own resources.

7 **For none of us lives to himself and none of us dies to himself.** Paul does not mean (as is sometimes supposed) that our actions affect our fellow-men, but that we live in relation to

8 God. **For if we live, we live to the Lord, and if we die, we die to the Lord. Whether then we live or die we are the Lord's.** Paul is speaking of Christians, and what he says is scarcely more than a definition. The faith and obedience of a Christian mean that he belongs not to himself but to God. Further, they are not confined to this life only. Having already 'risen with Christ' (Col. iii. 1), the Christian belongs to him even in death.

It might have been supposed that in *vv.* 7 f. Paul was speaking of a relation with God enjoyed by all men in virtue of their

9 creation. That this is not so is shown by *v.* 9: **For Christ died and came to life for this very purpose, namely, that he might reign as Lord over both the dead and the living.** The slave-lord relationship between the Christian and Christ rests entirely upon the death and resurrection of Jesus, which led to his exaltation and heavenly reign. It has been suggested that the verse should be analysed into two parallel statements:

Christ died that he might reign as Lord over the dead;
Christ came to life that he might reign as Lord over the living.

This, however, is not probable (cf. iv. 25 and note); the death and resurrection together formed one complex event which ushered in the period of Christ's reign. It is, nevertheless, probable that Paul intended the rhetorical balance of the sentence: die—dead, come to life—living.

Paul returns to the main theme and addresses at once both the weak (who is prone to judge) and the strong (who is prone

10 to despise). **Well then** (in view of what has been said), **you— why do you judge your brother? Or you—why do you despise your brother?** Compare *vv.* 3 f. A further argument is now added: **For we shall all stand before** (not each other's but) **God's judgement seat.** In the end everyone must

recognize that God, and not his own wisdom, or folly, or even conscience (1 Cor. iv. 4), is the arbiter. Freedom and scrupulosity alike (as human practices) fail to touch the cardinal point of justification. This is reinforced by Old Testament references. **For it is written, 'As I live, saith the Lord** (cf. Isa. xlix. 18), 11 **every knee shall bow to me, and every tongue shall render praise to God'** (cf. Isa. xlv. 23). **Every one of us** 12 **therefore shall give account of himself to God.** He is not accountable to his fellow-men, but he *is* accountable to God. This should lead him to avoid judging, and at the same time to examine the bases of his action. If he supposes that either his abstinence or his intelligent and well-instructed 'faith' will justify him, he would do well to think again, and to consider what it means to stand before God's judgement seat. Only God's creative verdict, heard in anticipation by humble and obedient faith, can justify the most religious or the most irreligious of men. The strong, then, is right; but if he boasts of his superiority he instantly becomes as wrong as the man he despises. The weak is mistaken, yet accepted; and he must not put himself in God's place, and judge the strong.

38. xiv. 13-23. WALKING IN LOVE

(13) Let us therefore no longer judge one another; but come rather to this decision, that you will not put a stumbling-block or an offence in your brother's way. (14) I know, I am quite confident in the Lord Jesus, that nothing is unclean in itself; only to a man who reckons anything to be unclean, to him it is unclean. (15) This fact must govern our attitude. For if your brother is grieved on account of food which you eat, then you are no longer walking in love. Do not by your food destroy him for whom Christ died. (16) And do not let this good thing of yours become a source of reproach. (17) For the kingdom of God is not eating and drinking, but righteousness and peace and joy in the Holy Spirit. (18) For he who serves Christ in this way is pleasing to God and irreproachable

with men. (19) Let us therefore ardently pursue the things that make for peace and the things that make for mutual building up. (20) Do not for the sake of food destroy the work of God. All things are clean, but they work harm to the man who eats them so as to cause offence. (21) It is well not to eat flesh nor to drink wine, nor to do any other thing by which your brother may be made to stumble. (22) Keep to yourself before God the faith which you have.[1] Blessed is he who does not waver in respect of what his conscience affirms; (23) but if the waverer eats, he is condemned, because what he does is not of faith; and everything that is not of faith is sin.[2]

The point of the previous paragraph is assumed and summarized: **Let us therefore no longer** (the tense of the verb
13 supports the view that Paul is addressing a real, not a hypothetical, situation) **judge one another.** Neither strong nor weak is in a position to adopt the superior attitude of the judge. Paul now presses on to a further point, using the word 'judge' (κρίνειν) in a verbal play impossible to reproduce in English. The word changes its sense (though it retains the fundamental meaning of 'come to a decision'), and also its tense, for whereas the reader has been told to stop judging, he is now urged to come, once for all, to a specific judgement. **Come rather to this decision, that you will not put a stumbling-block or an offence in your brother's way.** Paul has already laid it down (xiii. 8 ff.; xii. 9 f.) that the supreme command is that of love. This must therefore be applied to the present problem, and its application will mean that each man will seek not to express his own convictions but to serve the interests of his brother Christian. This he will do by taking care not to place in his way anything that might cause him to fall from his Christian faith and practice. His actions must not be governed by self-interest. This principle Paul proceeds to apply.

[1] The relative ('which'—ἥν) is omitted by D G ω lat pesh. This seems to be an attempt to ease a difficult construction. If the short reading is accepted, we may translate either 'Have you faith? Keep it to yourself before God' or 'You have faith. Keep it . . .'. The former alternative is preferable.

[2] The textual problems of the last chapters of the epistle begin at this point. See Introduction, pp. 10-13.

I know, I am quite confident in the Lord Jesus, that 14
nothing is unclean in itself. Paul underlines emphatically this
deduction from his theological principles. When the whole of
life lies equally under the judgement and under the grace of God
it is idle to mark out certain areas as in a special sense 'unclean'.
The word (κοινόν) means properly 'common'; hence 'profane',
and, in the religious sense, 'unclean'. This derived use of the
word is almost exclusively Jewish. Paul's attitude is to be found
in the gospels (cf. Mark vii. 14-23), but it is incompatible with
orthodox Judaism, even though Paul himself seems to have
believed that he could at will revert, when occasion demanded
it, to Jewish practice (1 Cor. ix. 19-23). 'Uncleanness' cannot
affect those relationships (sin, acquittal, peace, and the like)
which Paul grasped as central. This is his own view, and that of
the strong; yet there is something to set over against it.

Only to a man who reckons anything to be unclean, to
him it is unclean. Paul has stated his own view uncompromis-
ingly; but he acknowledges at once that there are others who
take a different view. Many a man can be found who regards a
certain food as unclean; if he were to eat it, he would be defiled,
not because the food is in itself unclean, or offensive to God, but
because his action is an offence against his conscience, and sinful
(v. 23). To him, 'it is unclean'; the language is not rigorously
logical, but clear enough. The doubtful eater cannot 'give God
thanks' (v. 6); he is acting disobediently. **This fact must** 15
govern our attitude (these words are an insertion, required to
make sense of the 'for' which follows). **For if your brother is**
grieved on account of food which you eat (these last three
words also are an addition, which brings out the sense—the
'brother' is grieved not by food in general but by the food which
his fellow-Christian eats), **then you are no longer walking in**
love. How is the 'brother' grieved? (i) The mere sight of a
Christian doing what he (however wrongly) regards as sinful
will give pain to his sensitive conscience. (ii) He may nevertheless be emboldened by his fellow's example to do that which he
regards as sinful; but he will do it with a bad conscience, as a
waverer, who is condemned by his doubts (v. 23). Thus the
attitude of the strong Christian, unless carefully regulated, is
almost certain to result in injury to the weak Christian. To allow

this to happen is not to walk in love. Therefore, **Do not by your food destroy him for whom Christ died,** that is, your weak Christian brother. It is possible to do what is itself right in such a way, and in such circumstances, as to undo the effects of the death of Christ. The same truth is now expressed more generally.

16 **Do not let this good thing of yours become a source of reproach.** 'This good thing of yours' is probably 'your Christian freedom'. This in itself is good; but wrongly used, used, that is, in defiance of love, it can serve only to bring disgrace upon the Church.

To insist upon one's freedom without regard to the scruples of others is not only to fail in the primary Christian virtue of love but to misunderstand the real basis of the Christian faith.

17 **For the kingdom of God is not eating and drinking, but righteousness and peace and joy in the Holy Spirit.** Faith is not 'faith to eat all things' (*v.* 2); Christian privilege is not the privilege of being able to eat and drink what one likes.

The phrase 'kingdom of God' is not frequent in Paul's writings: 1 Cor. iv. 20; vi. 9 f.; xv. 50; Col. iv. 11; 1 Thess. ii. 12; 2 Thess. i. 5; compare Col. i. 13; 1 Cor. xv. 24; Eph. v. 5. It often refers to the future, occasionally (as here) to the present. The infrequent usage is against the view (Denney) that the phrase could here almost be translated 'the Christian religion'. (i) Reference to the kingdom emphasizes that the life of faith, though it is truly a life of freedom, is nevertheless life under the rule of God. Christian freedom is gained by presenting one's members as slaves to God (vi. 13). (ii) It was recognized by at least some Jews (e.g. in *Berakoth*, 17 a) that 'in the Age to Come there is neither eating nor drinking . . .'. If this was true of the Age to Come, conditions in the kingdom of God as anticipated in the present age could not be radically different. It follows from both considerations that to set too much store by the Christian's privilege of eating what he likes without religious scruple, is to fall into error as serious as that of reverting to Jewish food laws. Compare Gal. vi. 15, which also throws light on the reference to the Holy Spirit, by whom the anticipation of the kingdom of God in the present is effected (viii. 23).

Righteousness, peace, and joy might be described as the fruit of the Spirit (Gal. v. 22). It is true that in Romans, and elsewhere in Paul's writings, righteousness and peace usually describe an objective relation with God; but in this verse joy is certainly subjective, and probably determines the sense of the other two words. Righteousness therefore will be righteous action (which, of course, is bound to spring out of the objective relation of righteousness); peace will be a peaceful state of mind (which again arises inevitably out of the relation of peace with God).

The next verse follows immediately. **For he who serves** 18 **Christ in this way** (that is, by recognizing that food and drink are secondary matters) **is pleasing to God** (cf. xii. 1 f.) **and irreproachable** (tried and approved; cf. pp. 56, 104) **with men.** In this way, the whole Christian fellowship will be built up, and Christian life will not become a 'source of reproach' (v. 16).

Let us therefore ardently pursue the things that make 19 **for peace and the things that make for mutual building up.** The Church is one body in Christ (xii. 5). It cannot make for the unity of this one body if the several members are more concerned to practise their private convictions than to live in love. What they should seek is the peace of the community, and its edification. 'Edification' is for Paul not individualistic but corporate. The Church is God's building (cf. 1 Cor. iii. 9), and 'building up' means the building up of the Church. This observation determines the sense of the next sentence. **Do not for** 20 **the sake of food** (which you would like—and feel free—to eat) **destroy the work of God,** that is, not the individual Christian (as in v. 15 b), but the Church, the outcome of God's work in Jesus Christ. Inconsiderate behaviour may lead to the destruction of that which God himself has wrought.

Paul now returns to a point even further back in the argument; v. 20 b recalls v. 14. **All things are clean;** compare Mark vii. 19. **But they work harm to the man who eats them so as to cause offence.** This translation involves a certain amount of interpretation of Paul's Greek, which is elliptic and obscure. The first words are, literally, 'But evil to the man who . . .'. They may mean simply 'Evil *happens* to the man who . . .', but in the context it seems more probable that 'all things' continues to form (in thought, if not grammatically) the subject. 'All things are clean, but *they cause* evil to the man who . . .'. The closing words, 'so as to cause offence', are 'through offence', 'through a stumbling-block'. The preposition (διά) is evidently used to describe 'attendant circumstances', but even so its bearing is not clear, for we cannot be certain who is the eater. *V.* 21 suggests that he is the strong Christian, who by his eating causes offence and lays a stumbling-block before his weaker brother, who may be tempted to do that of which his conscience disapproves (*v.* 23). It is not, however, impossible that the eater is the weak Christian who eats *because* he has been tripped up and made to stumble by the strong man's action, and thus suffers injury because he is acting against conscience. It may be, perhaps, that the vagueness and obscurity of Paul's sentence is due to the fact that he is thinking of both possibilities, and expresses himself so as to allow for both.

If this be so, Paul turns at once to give specific advice to the
21 strong. **It is well not to eat flesh nor to drink wine** (this shows that the weak abstained from wine as well as meat). **nor to do any other thing by which your brother may be made to stumble.** It is far more important to preserve unharmed the conscience of your fellow-Christian and the unity of the Church than to exercise your undoubted right as an instructed Christian to eat flesh and to drink wine. This does not mean that all Christians should take vows of abstinence. The infinitives 'to eat' and 'to drink' are aorists, and the meaning seems to be that if on any particular occasion it seems likely that to eat flesh or to drink wine will cause a brother to stumble, it is right on that occasion to abstain (so B.D. p. 150). Eating and drinking are not wrong in themselves, and on other occasions the danger may not arise.

22 **Keep to yourself before God the faith which you have.** For this use of *faith*, cf. *vv.* 1 f. True faith is an invisible relation between man and God, a confidence in God so complete that the man who has it knows that no religious scrupulosity can add to the security of his relation with God. But the moment 'faith' begins to parade itself as a visible thing which can be demonstrated by such acts as eating flesh and drinking wine, it ceases to be faith and becomes weakness. This is not to say that the position of the strong is wrong. **Blessed is he who does not waver in respect of what his conscience affirms.** This sentence cannot be translated with confidence. The subject is,

literally, 'he who does not judge himself'; but this man clearly corresponds to the waverer of *v.* 23, and it seems well to bring out the correspondence which is suggested by the Greek forms (ὁ μὴ κρίνων ἑαυτόν—ὁ διακρινόμενος). 'Judge' is used in the sense of 'condemn'. The sphere in which judgement does or does not take place is 'what he tries and approves'; the sense of testing is represented in the translation by the introduction of the word conscience. Once this man's faith and reason have affirmed a course of action he does not waver: happy is he in that he does not.

There are others, however, who do waver. They are not fully convinced that as Christians they stand under grace and not under law. These men must be warned. **If the waverer eats,** 23 **he is condemned, because what he does is not of faith; and everything that is not of faith is sin.** If, for example, the waverer eats meat, it will not be because he has 'faith so strong that he can and does eat all things' (*v.* 2), but because he would like to do so; because he fears the scorn of his stronger brother; because it is inconvenient or irksome to observe the rules he believes to have divine authority; or for some such reason. To act on such terms is not to 'give God thanks' and recognize his lordship (*v.* 6), but rather to make one's own convenience or pleasure the standard of one's actions, and thus to fall back into the worst kind of idolatry, in which the idol is—self. To eat, therefore, *in these circumstances*, is sin. There is only one proper relation between God and man, that which is described on man's side as faith; every other relation is a false, negative relation—in fact, sin. It is this sin which the strong Christian may, by unguarded behaviour, trip his brother into committing; nevertheless, the weak Christian is responsible, and is condemned, for his own act.

39. xv. 1-13. UNITY IN LOVE

(1) We who are strong ought to bear the weaknesses of those who are not, and not to please ourselves. (2) Let each one of us please his neighbour with some good

purpose, so as to effect building up. (3) For even Christ did not please himself; on the contrary, as it is written, 'The reproaches of those who reproached thee fell on me'. (4) (For all the things that were written beforehand in Scripture were written for our instruction, that we, through our endurance and through the exhortation that comes from Scripture, might have hope. (5) And may the God from whom all endurance and exhortation spring grant to you that you may have a common mind according to Christ Jesus, (6) that with one accord, with one mouth, you may glorify the God and Father of our Lord Jesus Christ.)

(7) So welcome one another, as Christ also welcomed you,[1] to the glory of God. (8) For I tell you that Christ has become[2] a servant of the 'circumcision', for the vindication of God's truth, so as to confirm the promises made to the fathers, (9) and that the Gentiles may glorify God for his mercy, as it is written, 'For this cause I will praise thee among the Gentiles, and I will sing praise to thy name'; (10) and again he says, 'Rejoice, ye Gentiles, with his people'; (11) and again, 'Praise the Lord, all ye Gentiles, and let all the peoples praise him'. (12) And again, Isaiah says, 'There shall be the root of Jesse, and he who rises up to rule the Gentiles; in him shall the Gentiles hope'. (13) May the God who is thus the ground of hope fill you with all joy and peace in your faith, that you may abound in hope, in the power of the Holy Spirit.

In this paragraph, addressing primarily the strong (v. 1) but also turning to the whole Church (v. 7), Paul shows how the

[1] Instead of 'you', B D* sah read 'us'. There would be a natural inclination to change 'us' into 'you' in harmony with the second person plural of the verb 'welcome'; this observation is in favour of 'us'. But Paul had used the first person in v. 1, whence it might be introduced into the present verse by readers who failed to note that whereas in v. 1 Paul was addressing the strong, and counting himself with them, in this verse he was addressing the whole body. 'You' is the more probable reading.

[2] Instead of 'has become' (γεγενῆσθαι), B C* D G read 'became' (γενέσθαι). The perfect implies that Christ continued to be what he became, the simple past tense that he did not. The former is the more difficult, and more probable reading.

attitude of love which he has advocated might work in practice, and also supplies a further reason for adopting it.

We who are strong (Paul is one of the strong—none knows   1
better than he that man does not stand or fall by his abstinences)
ought to bear the weaknesses of those who are not. Their
weaknesses are their special practices, their abstinences from
meat, wine, and the like, erroneous in themselves and troublesome to their fellow-Christians. 'Bear' is in Greek (βαστάζειν)
as ambiguous as it is in English. Here it probably means 'endure' (as at Matt. xx. 12; Acts xv. 10), as the following clause
suggests. It is less probable that it means 'carry' (as at Gal. vi.
2); though it is possible that Paul means to make use of the
ambiguity of the word and to play upon both meanings. Strong
Christians must endure the vagaries of their weak brethren, and
help them in their difficulties.

Further, we who are strong ought **not to please ourselves.**
See the note on viii. 8; compare Phil. ii. 4. We must not consult
our own interests but those of others; especially of those weaker
than ourselves. Paul continues: **Let each one of us please his**   2
neighbour with some good purpose (as vague in Greek as in
English, but probably explained by the following words), **so as**
to effect building up. For 'building up' see on xiv. 19.

Paul now produces a further argument for the course of
action he commends: he appeals to the example of Christ. **For**   3
even Christ did not please himself. The verb sums up the
work and character of Christ throughout his earthly life. Paul
adduces none of the incidents known to us in the gospel tradition (cf. p. 241); yet it must be admitted that in one word
he gives an admirable summary of the impression conveyed by
the gospels. Instead of appealing to narrative he appeals to
prophecy: **on the contrary, as it is written, 'The reproaches**
of those who reproached thee fell on me' (Ps. lxix. 9). The
use of Scripture at this point is significant. It means that the
example of Christ is more than an example; it belongs to the
pattern of revelation. To this point Paul returns in *v*. 7; for the
present his quotation leads him to a parenthesis on the use of
Scripture.

For (the conjunction justifies the application of the passage   4
just quoted to the problem in hand) **all the things that were**

written beforehand in Scripture were written for our instruction; compare 1 Cor. ix. 9 f. The special use of Scripture is to foster hope. It was written **that we, through our endurance** (cf. ii. 7; v. 3 f.) **and through the exhortation that comes from Scripture, might have hope.** This is not perfectly clear. The word translated 'exhortation' (παράκλησις) sometimes means 'comfort', but, followed as it is by a genitive, is most naturally taken as in the translation; but this does not explain why exhortation should be coupled with endurance as the ground of hope. We may conjecture that Paul's real meaning is: Scripture exhorts us to endure in hope, and gives us good ground for doing so. But it must be admitted that this is not what he says. It may be best to paraphrase his words thus: In a situation marked by reproaches (*v.* 3) we have hope (a) because we practise that endurance which looks to God for the meaning of its present lot, and (b) because Scripture, by foretelling our situation, encourages us to pass through it in hope.

5   Paul turns back to the main theme. **And may the God from whom all endurance and exhortation spring grant to you that you may have a common mind according to Christ**
6 **Jesus** (cf. Phil. ii. 5), **that, with one accord, with one mouth, you may glorify the God and Father of our Lord Jesus Christ.** It is possible, though incapable of proof, that Paul is drawing upon a liturgical doxology. In any case, the emphasis lies not upon the form of words used but upon the unanimity with which it is uttered.

    In *v.* 7 Paul returns to his main theme, and gathers up what he has written since he began to deal with it in xiv. 1 (cf. xiv. 3).
7 **So welcome one another, as Christ also welcomed you, to the glory of God.** The last five words form an adverbial phrase (suggested perhaps by *v.* 6), but it is not evident to which verb they apply. On the whole it is more likely that they should be taken with 'welcomed'; this is suggested by *vv.* 8 f. But it is probably not wrong to take them with both verbs. Christ's act in welcoming men is directed to the glory of God; but so is the unity of Christian men in love. When the strong receive the weak, and the weak the strong, they are in the most significant way glorifying God.

    A new thought is now introduced, but unfortunately the

language is so obscure that it is difficult to be sure of its bearing on the argument. **For** (evidently the new material is intended to 8 add further justification for the precept 'Welcome one another') **I tell you that Christ has become a servant of the 'circumcision'.** In the present translation the use of inverted commas is intended to make it plain that *circumcision* is taken as a collective, equivalent to 'the Jews'. Christ became (and—as the perfect tense shows—remains) a servant of the Jews, who, especially when described as the 'circumcision', may be regarded as the most awkward and irritating of scrupulous persons. He thus provides an example for all strong Christians (cf. *v.* 3). This seems to be the best interpretation. Other suggestions are (i) Christ became a minister of circumcision in that he carried out the promises implied in the covenant the seal of which was circumcision, and (ii) he has become a minister of circumcision even to Gentiles, because he has admitted them to all the privileges promised to the Jewish Church, of which circumcision is the symbol.

Why did Christ become a servant of the 'circumcision'? **For the vindication of God's truth, so as to confirm the promises made to the fathers, and that the Gentiles may 9 glorify God for his mercy.** The fathers of the Jewish race had been promised a Messiah, and if the Messiah had not been sent into the realm of circumcision God's truth, or faithfulness, would have been impugned. The construction of the sentence now becomes very difficult. There are two main possibilities. (i) The whole sentence is dependent on the 'I tell you' at the beginning of *v.* 8; the two main verbs (infinitives in Greek) are 'has become' and 'may glorify', 'so as to confirm' being parenthetical. In outline the sentence runs: I tell you that Christ has become . . . (so as to confirm . . .), and that the Gentiles are to glorify . . . (ii) The governing sentence is 'Christ has become', and on this the two other verbs ('to confirm' and 'that they may glorify'—both infinitives in Greek) are dependent. In outline the sentence runs: Christ has become . . . so as to confirm . . . and that the Gentiles . . . Each of these constructions is harsh because each involves a change of subject; but it seems evident from the connexion of thought that the statement about Christ controls the sentence, and accordingly alternative (ii) should be chosen (as in the present translation). The coming of Christ may be viewed in two ways. On the one hand he came to vindicate God's faithfulness by fulfilling the promises which had been made within Judaism. On the other hand he came that the Gentiles might be included with Israel among the people of God. As the Jews glorify God for his faithfulness, so the Gentiles will glorify him for his mercy.

The inclusion of the Gentiles is not to be regarded as a happy afterthought; it was foretold in Scripture. This Paul proceeds once more (cf. ix. 25 f.; x. 19 f.) to document. **As it is written, 'For this cause I will praise thee among the Gentiles, and I will sing praise to thy name'.** The quotation is from Ps. xviii. 49 (= 2 Sam. xxii. 50); the point (as in the quotations that follow) lies in the reference to Gentiles, and, secondarily, in

10 the offering of praise for God's faithfulness and mercy. **And again he says, 'Rejoice, ye Gentiles, with his people'**

11 (Deut. xxxii. 43); **and again, 'Praise the Lord, all ye Gentiles, and let all the peoples praise him'** (Ps. cxvii. 1).

12 **And again, Isaiah says, 'There shall be the root of Jesse, and he who rises up to rule the Gentiles; in him shall the Gentiles hope'** (Isa. xi. 10; cf. xi. 1). In all these passages, Paul sees a reference to 'Gentiles'; in most, or all, of them, the original meaning was 'nations'. Paul in general shows no interest in the Davidic descent of Jesus (see on i. 3), and offers no exposition of it here.

This discussion of the relations between strong and weak in the Church comes to an end with a brief prayer for the readers.

13 **May the God who is thus** (that is, in the light of the passages just quoted) **the ground of hope fill you with all joy and peace in your faith, that you may abound in hope, in the power of the Holy Spirit.** The true content and goal of faith is not the right to eat and drink, but joy and peace in the Holy Spirit (cf. xiv. 17). Hope also occupies a prominent place in this prayer; compare *v.* 4. The quotations of *vv.* 9-12 have led Paul back again to the great theme of the union of Jew and Gentile in Christ, an event significant in itself, but still more significant in that its completion marks the full end of God's purposes (xi. 12, 15). It seems unlikely that the introduction of this theme is here merely ornamental (Lietzmann). It may be

that the division existing at Rome was simply that between Jew and Gentile (see p. 256); or that Paul is arguing *a majori ad minus*—if God can unite these he can unite anyone; or that *v.* 6 concludes the argument, and that *vv.* 7-13 are a summary which looks back to chs. ix-xi as well as to ch. xiv.

40. xv. 14-33. PAUL'S PLANS AND GOD'S PURPOSE

(14) But I am confident, my brethren, yes, I myself am confident about you, that you yourselves are full of goodness, replete with all knowledge, and able also to admonish one another. (15) But I have written to you somewhat boldly, partly with the intention of reminding you of what you already know, because of the grace that was given me from God (16) that I might be a minister of Christ Jesus to the Gentiles, acting as a priest for the Gospel of God, in order that the offering of the Gentiles might be acceptable, sanctified in the Holy Spirit. (17) Here then is the glorying I have in Christ Jesus, in things relating to God; (18) for I will not dare to say anything of the things which Christ did not carry out through me for the obedience of the Gentiles—in word and deed, (19) in the power[1] of signs and portents, in the power of the Spirit; so that from Jerusalem and round about as far as Illyricum I have completed the Gospel of Christ,[2] (20) being in this way ambitious to preach the Gospel not where Christ had been named, lest I should build upon someone else's foundation. (21) I acted rather so as to fulfil the Scripture, 'They shall see, to whom it was not told about him; and they shall understand, who have not heard.'

(22) So these many times I have been hindered from coming to you; (23) but now, since I have no more scope

---

[1] P⁴⁶ D G it have 'in his power', an unusual expression which may be original. *God's* power, expressed in signs and portents is, of course, intended.

[2] The Western text (D G it) has: 'So that from Jerusalem as far as Illyricum and round about the Gospel has been completed'. This is evidently a weakening of Paul's words.

in these parts, and for some[1] years have had a desire to come to you (24) when I am on my way to Spain . . .; for I hope to see you on my way, and to be helped thither on my way by you, if I may first have my fill of your company—in part; (25) but now I am travelling to Jerusalem, engaged in ministering to the saints. (26) For Macedonia and Achaea have decided to make a contribution to the poor among the saints who are in Jerusalem. (27) They have decided, yes, and they are under obligation to them; for if they shared their spiritual things with the Gentiles, the Gentiles ought to minister to them in the things of flesh and blood too. (28) So when I have completed this matter, and sealed them this fruit, I shall be off to Spain, through you; (29) and I know that when I come to you I shall come to bring and to find a full measure of the blessing of Christ.

(30) I beg you, brethren, through our Lord Jesus Christ and through the love created by the Spirit, to join me in earnest prayers to God on my behalf, (31) that I may be delivered from the disobedient in Judaea, and that my ministry to Jerusalem[2] may prove acceptable to the saints, (32) that by the will of God I may come to you with joy, and that we may find mutual refreshment.[3] (33) The God of peace be with you all. Amen.[4]

The main theological argument of the epistle is at an end (though there are in this paragraph remarks which have important theological implications). Paul turns to consider his own plans. These were not merely personal, but bound up with the divine plan (cf. chs. ix-xi) for the short period before the *parousia*. He begins with a *captatio benevolentiae* (cf. i. 12). He has written strong words, and does not wish by tactlessness to ruin his relations with the church in Rome before setting

---

[1] The majority of mss. (including P[46] A D G) have 'many years'. This is a more usual expression, and to be rejected.

[2] B D* G have 'my gift (or, offering—δωροφορία) in Jerusalem'.

[3] There is much textual confusion at this point. P[46] and B omit altogether 'and that we may find mutual refreshment'. This may be not unconnected with the fact that P[46] continues immediately with the Doxology (xvi. 25 ff.).

[4] For the reading of P[46] at this point, and the problem of the text of the last chapters of the epistle, see Introduction, pp. 10-13.

foot in the city. Of course this does not mean that he is insincere in what he says.

But I am confident, my brethren (see on i. 13), **yes, I** 14
myself am confident about you, that you yourselves (notwithstanding my rebukes and admonitions) **are full of goodness, replete with all knowledge, and able also to admonish one another.** These words do not suggest that the Roman church had been founded by an apostle.

Why then had Paul written? **I have written to you some-** 15
what boldly, partly (we do not learn the other part of Paul's intentions) **with the intention of reminding you of what you already know** (this is more than tact; the believer who has accepted the Gospel knows the essence of the truth, but he may—and generally does—need many reminders), **because of the grace that was given me from God** (cf. i. 5; xii. 3, 6) **that I might be a minister of Christ Jesus to the Gentiles.** 16
For the word 'minister' see on xiii. 6; in itself it means no more than 'public servant' in the most general sense, but here the context points to priestly service. Paul's activity is directed specifically to the Gentiles; compare xi. 13, and especially Gal. ii. 9. Paul serves by **acting as a priest for the Gospel of God** (i. 1), **in order that the offering of the Gentiles might be acceptable, sanctified in the Holy Spirit.** Paul acts as a priest in presenting to God an offering which consists of ('of the Gentiles' is appositional) the Gentile Christians who have been converted in his missions. This living sacrifice (cf. xii. 1) is acceptable not in virtue of its own intrinsic merit, but because it has been set apart for divine use by the Holy Spirit, given to the converts in their conversion and baptism. It is noteworthy that it is at this point that Paul uses the language of priesthood to describe his office; noteworthy also that (by accident, as it were) a Trinitarian formulation is introduced (. . . of Christ Jesus . . . of God . . . in the Holy Spirit).

The authority of the epistle thus rests upon Paul's vocation to act as a special minister of Christ in relation to the Gentiles. This vocation, and its evident fulfilment in his activity hitherto, are the sole source of his confidence. **Here then is the glorying** 17
(v. 2) **I have in Christ Jesus, in things relating to God.** As a priest, he acts *coram Deo*. Things that were gain to him by human

reckoning he had already counted loss for Christ (Phil. iii. 7).
18 **For I will not dare to say anything of the things which Christ did not carry out through me for the obedience** (i. 5) **of the Gentiles.** The sentence is confused because Paul is trying to say two things at once. These are (i) I would not dare to speak of this if it were not Christ's work (rather than mine); (ii) I would not dare to speak of this if it were not Christ's work through me (rather than anyone else). The conversion of the Gentiles has been the work of Christ, through Paul. This double fact is that in which he can glory. It implies that he himself as an apostle holds a special place in the unfolding of the events of the last days (see on i. 1, apostle).

The apostolic work is further described: **in word and deed,**
19 **in the power of signs and portents, in the power of the Spirit** (for the work of the Spirit as the accompaniment of the apostolic preaching cf. 1 Cor. ii. 4). The Gospel is the power of God working toward salvation (i. 16), and though salvation in its fullness lies in the future its effects are felt in the present also. Thus **from Jerusalem and round about** (*either* round about Jerusalem, *or* in circuit from Jerusalem to Illyricum) **as far as Illyricum I have completed the Gospel of Christ.** For Paul's preaching in Jerusalem see Acts ix. 29. He had not been active in Judaea (Gal. i. 22). His missionary journeys had begun in Antioch and taken him round the eastern end of the Mediterranean and through several of the provinces of Asia Minor. Thence he had crossed the Aegean to Macedonia, and visited Greece (Athens, Corinth). Acts gives no account of work in Illyricum, though from Macedonia the *Via Egnatia* struck across the Balkans to the eastern coast of the Adriatic, and it is not impossible that Paul or his associates had made tentative excursions in this direction as far as Illyricum. It is evident therefore that when Paul says that in this region he has completed the Gospel of Christ, he does not mean that he (or anyone else) has preached the Gospel to every person in it, but that it has been covered in a representative way. The Gospel has been heard; more could not be expected before the *parousia*. Thus Paul is free, or, rather, is impelled to break new ground in the fulfilment of the eschatological programme entrusted to him as an apostle (*v.* 23). In doing so he would only be continu-

ing to follow the principle which had always guided his activity: **Being in this way ambitious to preach the Gospel not** 20 **where Christ had been named** (the position of the negative invites the supplement, 'but where he had never been heard of'), **lest I should build upon someone else's foundation.** Paul's motive is not simply to avoid possible rivalry but to cover as wide an area as possible. The metaphor of building (cf. 1 Cor. iii. 10 ff.) is not chosen at random; the Church as a whole is the new temple, or new Jerusalem, of the last age. For his missionary method Paul is able to cite scriptural support: **I acted** 21 **rather so as to fulfil the Scripture, 'They shall see, to whom it was not told about him; and they shall understand, who have not heard'** (Isa. lii. 15).

These considerations have an evident bearing upon Paul's plan to visit Rome, for this church was not of his founding. It is possibly the delicacy of the situation that leads to the obscurity of Paul's words here, and the actual breaking off of the sentence in *v.* 24 (cf. i. 11 f.). **So these many times I have been** 22 **hindered from coming to you; but now, since I have no** 23 **more scope in these parts** (as is explained in *v.* 20), **and for some years have had a desire to come to you** (cf. i. 13) **when I am on my way to Spain. . . .** The connexion of the 24 opening particle (διό) is not clear. The meaning suggested by the context is, 'I have been prevented by the fact that up to now I have been fully occupied in the East'; but 1 Thess. ii. 18 suggests that a different kind of hindrance may be meant.

Since the eastern end of the Mediterranean had been dealt with and Paul had 'no more scope in these parts' there remained for missionary work the north coast of Africa (from Alexandria to the province of Africa), Gaul, and Spain. Strangely, Paul never alludes to African territory; but he expresses the intention of making a missionary journey to Spain (quite possibly intending to take Gaul (Narbonensis) on the way). His immediate task, however, was a visit to Jerusalem (*v.* 25), the outcome of which is told in Acts xxi-xxviii. Paul reached Rome, but as a prisoner. Was he ever able to carry out his plan of visiting Spain? There is no certain evidence. There is no further reference to Spain in the New Testament, and most later writers are evidently reduced to conjectures based on no more evidence than we ourselves possess. A release from prison, and a Spanish journey, are not impossible. More than this cannot be said with certainty.

The sentence breaks off, and Paul repeats himself in order to make the essential point clear: he wishes to visit Rome, but this visit will not contravene his principle of avoiding mission fields already worked, because he will take Rome on the way as he passes to fresh work. **For I hope to see you on my way, and to be helped thither** (to Spain) **on my way by you, if I may first have my fill of your company—in part;** for Paul will never really have his fill of Christian fellowship with the Roman Christians. In what way he hoped for help from them does not appear.

Before the journey to Spain intervenes a more immediate

25 task. **But now I am travelling to Jerusalem** (Acts xx. 3, 16, etc.), **engaged in ministering to the saints.** 'Ministering' (like 'ministry' in *v.* 31) is one of Paul's terms for his collection on behalf of the Jerusalem church. For the verb, see 2 Cor. viii. 19 f.; for the noun, *v.* 31; 1 Cor. xvi. 15; 2 Cor. (vi. 3); viii. 4; ix. 1, 12 f. (cf. Acts xi. 29; xii. 25). 'The saints' also has (in addition to its use as a term describing Christians in general—see i. 7) an almost technical sense. It denotes the Christians of Jerusalem here and at *vv.* 26, 31; 1 Cor. xvi. 1, 15; 2 Cor. viii. 4; ix. 1, 12. See below on 'the poor' (*v.* 26). Paul's collection occupied a good deal of his time and attention. It must have been a politic expedient, designed to foster unity between the Jewish and Gentile wings of the Church; but it was far more than this, for, as the context shows, it was intended to play a vital part among the events of the last days.

26 Paul proceeds to give further details. **For Macedonia and Achaea have decided to make a contribution** (literally, 'a fellowship', or 'a sharing'—another of Paul's quasi-technical terms: 2 Cor. viii. 4; ix. 13; cf. *v.* 27; Gal. vi. 6; Phil. iv. 15) **to the poor among the saints who are in Jerusalem.** Paul's use of 'poor' recalls the righteous and trustful poor of the Psalms (e.g. Ps. ix. 18); in Hebrew, *'ebyonim*. Whether the successors of the poor saints in Jerusalem are to be found among the Jewish Christians later called Ebionites cannot be discussed here. It must not be forgotten that Paul may use the word

278

'poor' in its literal sense. It was because these saints had little money that a collection was made for them. **They have decided,** 27 **yes, and they are under obligation to them** (cf. i. 14; viii. 12; also xiii. 8); **for if they** (the Jewish Christians) **shared their spiritual things** (not 'spiritual gifts', for these came direct from the Spirit; but the original tradition which, interpreted by the Spirit, was the basis of the Gospel) **with the Gentiles, the Gentiles** (the subject is not expressed, but there can be no doubt what should be supplied) **ought to minister to them in the things of flesh and blood** (the Greek mentions flesh only, but this is liable to misunderstanding) **too.** This is only fair.

Paul winds up this statement of his plans. **So when I have** 28 **completed this matter, and sealed them this fruit** (the metaphor is commercial, but Paul curiously omits to say that having sealed his produce he means also to deliver it), **I shall be off to Spain, through you** (v. 24); **and I know that when I** 29 **come to you I shall come to bring and to find a full measure of the blessing of Christ.** Literally rendered, the last words run, 'in the fullness of the blessing of Christ'. By this somewhat vague language Paul probably means to suggest that both sides, he and his hosts, will share in the blessing; compare i. 11 f.

The execution of the plans will not be without risk. **I beg** 30 **you, brethren, through our Lord Jesus Christ and through the love created by the Spirit** (literally, the love of the Spirit; the genitive cannot be objective, and the clue is given by v. 5), **to join me in earnest prayers to God** (another 'unintended' Trinitarian formulation; cf. v. 16) **on my behalf.** 'Earnest prayers' conceals a metaphor drawn from the games, of a kind of which Paul was evidently fond; compare Phil. i. 27; iv. 3; and especially Col. iv. 12. All should pray **that I may be** 31 **delivered from the disobedient** (or, perhaps, unbelieving; cf. ii. 8; non-Christian Jews are meant) **in Judaea** (no doubt Paul had reason to fear what they might do), **and that my ministry** (cf. v. 25) **to Jerusalem may prove acceptable to the saints** (probably he had reason to regard this also as uncertain; his relations with the Jerusalem church were not assured), **that by the will of God** (cf. i. 10) **I may come to you** 32

with joy, and that we may find mutual refreshment. For
the last clause compare 1 Cor. xvi. 18; 2 Cor. vii. 13; Philem.
7, 20; for the mutuality, compare *v.* 29.

The present section of the epistle closes with a brief prayer,
33 probably already reflecting liturgical use: **The God of peace**
(cf. xvi. 20; 2 Cor. xiii. 11; Phil. iv. 9; 1 Thess. v. 23; 2 Thess.
iii. 16; also Test. Dan v. 2, but it does not appear to have been a
regular Jewish expression) **be with you all. Amen.** For Paul's
use of 'peace' see pp. 101 f.

41. xvi. 1-23. PERSONAL GREETINGS

**(1) I commend to you our sister Phoebe, who is deaconess
in the church in Cenchreae, (2) that you may receive her
in the Lord in a way worthy of the saints, and help her in
any matter in which she may have need of you; for she
herself has been a protectress of many, and of me myself.
(3) Greet Prisca and Aquila, my fellow-workers in Christ
Jesus, (4) who risked their lives for mine, to whom not I
only but also all the churches of the Gentiles are grateful.
(5) And greet the church which meets in their house.
Greet Epaenetus my beloved, who is the first-fruits of
Asia unto Christ. (6) Greet Mary, who toiled much for
your benefit. (7) Greet Andronicus and Junias, my kinsmen and my fellow-prisoners, who are notable in the
ranks of the apostles, and were Christians before me. (8)
Greet Ampliatus my beloved in the Lord. (9) Greet
Urbanus our fellow-worker in Christ, and Stachys my
beloved. (10) Greet Apelles, that genuine Christian. Greet
the slaves of the household of Aristobulus. (11) Greet
Herodian my kinsman. Greet those slaves of the household of Narcissus who are in the Lord. (12) Greet Tryphaena and Tryphosa, who toil in the Lord. Greet Persis,
my beloved, who toiled hard in the Lord. (13) Greet
Rufus, that outstanding Christian, and his mother—who
is also mine. (14) Greet Asyncritus, Phlegon, Hermes,
Patrobas, Hermas, and the brethren who are with them.**

(15) Greet Philologus and Julias, Nereus and his sister, and Olympas, and all the saints who are with them. (16) Greet one another with a holy kiss. All the churches of Christ greet you.

(17) I beg you, brethren, to give attention to those who cause divisions and offences, contrary to the teaching you learned. Keep away from them. (18) For such men do not serve our Lord Christ but their own belly, and through their gentle and fair speech deceive the hearts of the innocent. (19) Avoid them, for the report of your obedience has reached all men. That is why I rejoice over you, and I wish you to be wise over what is good, uncontaminated with evil. (20) But the God of peace will soon crush Satan under your feet. The grace of our Lord Jesus Christ be with you.[1]

(21) Timothy my fellow-worker greets you, and so do Lucius and Jason and Sosipater my kinsmen. (22) I Tertius, who wrote the epistle in the Lord, greet you. (23) Gaius, who is my host, and the host of the whole church, greets you. Erastus the city treasurer greets you, and so does brother Quartus.

This paragraph consists mainly of personal greetings, together with a short section (*vv.* 17-20) of admonition and encouragement. For an account of the textual phenomena of the last chapter of the epistle, see Introduction, pp. 10-13. The view has often been maintained (on grounds partly textual) that xvi. 1-23 was not addressed to the church of Rome. It is said (a) that Paul is unlikely to have known so many members of the Roman church, which he had never visited; and (b) that some of the names mentioned point rather to Ephesus (which Paul knew well) than to Rome. Neither these nor the textual arguments are convincing. (a) In writing to a strange church Paul might very naturally include as many personal greetings as he could in order to establish as close contact as possible. (b) The possibility of movement on the part of members of the Pauline churches

---

[1] The words 'The grace of our Lord Jesus be with you' are omitted here by the Western text (D G it), which has an almost identical formula in *v.* 24. The majority, including P⁴⁶ B א, do not contain *v.* 24.

must be reckoned with. See below on Prisca and Aquila; for the migration from Asia Minor to Tusculum of a household of 500 persons (including slaves), who formed a 'house-church' of initiates of Dionysus, see Lietzmann pp. 129 f. (c) Arguments based upon names are worth little in view of the fact that men of all races met in Rome. Literary and other evidence for the occurrence of the names in this chapter will be found in Lietzmann and Michel.

The first two verses are devoted to Phoebe, a Christian travelling to Rome (or Ephesus, if xvi. 1-23 be addressed there).

1 **I commend to you our sister Phoebe, who is deaconess in the church of Cenchreae** (the eastern port of Corinth). 'Commendatory letters' were well known in the ancient world, certainly to Paul himself (2 Cor. iii. 1). Phoebe is described as a 'sister', that is, a Christian. For the masculine title see on i. 13; the feminine appears at 1 Cor. vii. 15; ix. 5 (*not* Rom. xvi. 15). Phoebe is further described in this translation as a *deaconess*; but it cannot be regarded as certainly correct to use this technical term. The word itself (διάκονος) does appear to have been on the way to technical use by the time this epistle was written (xii. 7), but whether it was so used of women is not certain. 1 Tim. iii. 11 may describe female deacons, or possibly the wives of deacons. Deaconesses are mentioned in the *Apostolic Constitutions* (ii. 26, 57; iii. 7, 15), and earlier (*c*. A.D. 112) Pliny (*Epistles*, X. xcvi. 8) speaks of *ancillis quae ministrae dicebantur*. In the New Testament period the line between the 'part-time helper' and the minister set apart to the service of the Church was not as sharply drawn as it is today, and it may therefore be that the question whether Phoebe was a 'deaconess' or a valued church worker is wrongly put.

Whatever her precise status, Phoebe had as a Christian a claim upon the hospitality and help of the Roman church. Paul 2 commends her, **that you may receive her** (it would be possible to place a full stop after *v*. 1, and to begin *v*. 2, Receive her) **in the Lord in a way worthy of the saints, and help her in any matter in which she may have need of you.** To receive her 'in the Lord' is to receive her as a Christian, and to receive her 'in a way worthy of the saints' is to do so as Christians who practise the law of love should—*Christiano more* (Bengel).

Phoebe deserves such treatment, **for she herself has been a protectress of many, and of me myself.** The Greek noun here (προστάτις) is often equivalent to the Latin *patrona*, but Phoebe cannot have stood in this relation to Paul (since he was born free, Acts xxii. 28), and the word must therefore have the more general sense given in the translation.

Having transacted this business, Paul sends greetings to his friends. **Greet Prisca and Aquila, my fellow-workers in** 3 **Christ Jesus, who risked their lives for mine, to whom not** 4 **I only but also all the churches of the Gentiles are grateful.** These two are no doubt the Aquila and Priscilla of Acts (ch. xviii. *passim*); compare 1 Cor. xvi. 19. They had been expelled from Rome (see Introduction, p. 6), made their way to Corinth, and thence to Ephesus. There is no reason why they should not have returned to Rome, especially if Romans was written after the death of Claudius (13 October 54). That 'all the churches' had reason to be grateful to them confirms that they had numerous contacts over a wide area. How, or on what occasion, they risked their lives on Paul's account, is completely unknown to us. Paul adds, **And greet the church which** 5 **meets in their house.** The first Christian meeting-places were no doubt the private houses of those Christians who were fortunate enough to have them.

Greet Epaenetus my beloved, who is the first-fruits of Asia unto Christ, that is, the first convert in Asia. Compare 1 Cor. xvi. 15.

Greet Mary, who toiled much for your benefit. For 6 'toiled' compare *v.* 12. The present verse suggests the meaning, 'to take part in Christian work', and this is confirmed by Paul's usage in general, for example, 1 Cor. xv. 10.

Greet Andronicus and Junias, my kinsmen (that is, 7 probably, fellow-Jews; cf. *vv.* 11, 21—it is a fair inference that others not so described may be Gentiles, though this does not apply to Prisca and Aquila, and perhaps not to Rufus) **and my fellow-prisoners** (we do not know when they were imprisoned with Paul, but there is no reason why the word should be taken metaphorically), **who are notable in the ranks of the apostles** (a much more probable rendering than 'well known to the apostles'), **and were Christians before me.**

Andronicus and Junias were, it appears, apostles, and senior in standing to Paul himself. For Paul's use of the word *apostle* see on i. 1. In the New Testament the word is sometimes used of the twelve disciples specially appointed by Jesus, but also in a wider sense, as here.

9 **Greet Urbanus our fellow-worker** (cf. *vv.* 3, 21) **in**
10 **Christ . . . Greet Apelles, that genuine Christian.** The adjective is the opposite of that used in i. 28; the pair are used, for
11 example, of genuine and counterfeit coins. **Greet Herodian**
12 **my kinsman** (see on *v.* 7) . . . **Greet Tryphaena and Tryphosa, who toil in the Lord.** 'To toil in the Lord' means 'to work as a Christian' but not necessarily 'to do Christian (that is,
13 church) work'. But see on *v.* 6. **Greet Rufus, that outstanding Christian** (the adjective is literally 'elect', which can be used of all Christians, as at viii. 33; there would be no point, however, in using it in this sense here), **and his mother—who is also mine.** A Rufus is mentioned in Mark xv. 21 as one of the sons of Simon of Cyrene. It has often been remarked that he plays no part in Mark's story and must have been named only for identification. This means that he must have been known in the church (probably Rome) for which the second gospel was written. For what it is worth, this confirms the view that this chapter was addressed to Rome, not Ephesus.

15 **Greet Philologus and Julias, Nereus** (possibly a name borne by a freedman of Nero's) **and his sister, and Olympas,**
16 **and all the saints who are with them. Greet one another with a holy kiss.** Compare 1 Cor. xvi. 20; 2 Cor. xiii. 12; also 1 Thess. v. 26; 1 Pet. v. 14. Later (e.g. Justin, 1 *Apology*, 65) the kiss became a part of the liturgy; it may be that this was so earlier, and that the apostolic letters were read in the course of the Church's worship, being taken at this point in it.

All the churches of Christ (represented by Paul, who speaks from the base of oriental Christianity to Rome, whence he himself means to go to the West) **greet you.**

Here the greetings break off, and we have four verses in quite different vein. It is not necessary to regard them as an interpolation; such parenthetical remarks are in Paul's style. They may reflect additional information brought to him before the letter was completed. The circumstances which evoked this vigorous admonition can only be conjectured.

I beg you, brethren, to give attention to (for the word cf. 17 Phil. iii. 17, where it has the opposite motive) **those who cause divisions** (Gal. v. 20) **and offences** (as, e.g., at xiv. 13; possibly the division between weak and strong is still in mind), **contrary to the teaching you learned**—the teaching of the all-sufficiency of faith and the all-importance of love. **Keep away from them. For such men do not serve our Lord Christ** 18 **but their own belly** (cf. Phil. iii. 19; not by gluttony but by their preoccupation with food laws), **and through their gentle and fair speech deceive the hearts of the innocent. Avoid them** (a supplement to explain the 'for' (γάρ) which 19 follows), **for the report of your obedience** (the Greek has 'for your obedience') **has reached all men.** The Christians of Rome must not spoil the report of them which is in general circulation. **That is why I rejoice over you** (because you are known to be obedient), **and I wish you to be wise over what is good** (that is, with a view to doing it), **uncontaminated with evil** (that is, so that you do not do it).

Paul concludes this parenthetical section with a renewed assertion of his confidence. **The God of peace** (xv. 33) **will soon** 20 **crush Satan under your feet.** There may be an allusion here to Gen. iii. 15, though if so Paul must be referring to the Hebrew text, for the LXX translates differently. In any case, Paul is looking forward to the final defeat of the prince of evil, and believes that this defeat will take place soon (cf. xiii. 11).

Paul adds, **The grace of our Lord Jesus be with you.** He uses this or similar expressions at 1 Cor. xvi. 23; Gal. vi. 18; Phil. iv. 23; Col. iv. 18; 1 Thess. v. 28; 2 Thess. iii. 18. At 2 Cor. xiii. 14 it is expanded into a Trinitarian formula. Compare the opening greeting (i. 7).

The greetings, broken off in *vv.* 17-20, are now resumed, but the names now mentioned are those of Christians in Paul's company who send their salutations with his. **Timothy my** 21 **fellow-worker greets you, and so do Lucian and Jason and Sosipater my kinsmen** (for this word see on *v.* 7). For Timothy see especially Acts xvi. 1 etc.; and many Pauline epistles; for Jason, Acts xvii. 5-9; for Sosipater, Acts xx. 4

22 (Sopater). **I Tertius, who wrote the epistle in the Lord, greet you.** For Paul's custom of dictating his letters compare 1 Cor. xvi. 21; Gal. vi. 11; Col. iv. 18; 2 Thess. iii. 17; (Philem.

23 19). **Gaius** (cf. Acts xix. 29; xx. 4; 1 Cor. i. 14; 3 John 1), **who is my host, and the host of the whole church** (which met in his house (cf. *v.* 5); or possibly Gaius entertained travelling Christians), **greets you. Erastus** (cf. Acts xix. 22; 2 Tim. iv. 20) **the city treasurer greets you, and so does brother Quartus.**

For *v.* 24, which is added in some MSS. (The grace of our Lord Jesus Christ be with you all. Amen) see on *v.* 20, the proper place of these words.

42. xvi. 25-7. THE DOXOLOGY

(25) Now to him who is able to establish you, according to my Gospel and the preaching of Jesus Christ, according to the revelation of the mystery, which through eternal ages has been kept in silence (26) but has now been manifested through the prophetic writings, made known according to the decree of the eternal God, so as to produce the obedience of faith for all the Gentiles, (27) to the only wise God, through Jesus Christ, to whom[1] be glory for ever and ever.[2] Amen.

For the textual problems connected with this last paragraph of the epistle see Introduction, pp. 10-13. Apart from the textual evidence, its contents themselves raise doubts regarding the Pauline authorship. The language recalls that of the Pastoral Epistles, not least in its not very convincing imitation of Paul's style. The substance is not distinctively Pauline. For the whole, compare Eph. iii. 20 f.; 1 Tim. i. 17; Jude 24 f.

25 **Now to him who is able to establish you** (cf. i. 11), **according to my Gospel** (cf. ii. 16) **and the preaching of**

---

[1] 'To whom' is omitted by B pesh. The result is to produce a straightforward ascription of praise to God, whereas the text translated is (like the translation) ungrammatical. The more difficult text should be accepted.

[2] 'And ever' is omitted by P⁴⁶ B C L—perhaps rightly.

Jesus Christ (elsewhere in Paul (1 Cor. i. 21; ii. 4; xv. 14; cf.
2 Tim. iv. 17; Titus i. 3) 'preaching' (κήρυγμα) never has a
genitive of content, as here), **according to the revelation of the
mystery** (1 Cor. ii. 7-10; Eph. iii. 3-6; 2 Tim. i. 10; Titus i. 2 f.),
which through eternal ages (2 Tim. i. 9; Titus i. 2) **has been
kept in silence** (Paul uses this word only in 1 Cor. xiv. 28, 30,
34—of women and others keeping silence in church; but cf.
Ignatius, *Ephesians*, xix. 1) **but has now been manifested** 26
through the prophetic writings (a statement which, in the
combination of 'now' and 'prophetic writings' is curious in
itself, and naturally gave rise to the addition, known to Origen
and Jerome, of 'and the appearing of our Lord Jesus Christ'; it
may be an attempt to counteract the generally Marcionite
character of the Doxology—see Introduction, pp. 11 f.), **made
known according to the decree** (cf. 1 Tim. i. 1; Titus i. 3—
1 Cor. vii. 6; 2 Cor. viii. 8 are not parallel) **of the eternal God**
(this expression does not occur elsewhere in the New Testament; cf. 1 Tim. i. 17), **so as to produce the obedience of
faith for all the Gentiles** (cf. i. 5), **to the only** (cf. 1 Tim. i. 27
17; Jude 25) **wise** (there is no parallel in the original text of
1 Tim. i. 17, and no other in the New Testament) **God, through
Jesus Christ, to whom** (the doxology up to this point has prepared us for an ascription of glory to God the Father; the
author now forgets the datives he has already set down, and
ascribes glory to Christ) **be glory for ever and ever. Amen.**

The defective construction may serve to remind the reader
that glory should be ascribed at once to God the Father, the
Creator (i. 20), in whose unfathomable wisdom and mercy (xi.
33-6) the work of salvation was planned, and to Jesus Christ his
Son, through whom and in whom redemption was effected (iii.
26; v. 8).

INDEX OF NAMES AND SUBJECTS

INDEX OF NAMES AND SUBJECTS

INDEX OF GREEK WORDS AND PHRASES DISCUSSED